D1002502

Recovery from Alcoholism

LIBRARY OF SUBSTANCE ABUSE AND ADDICTION TREATMENT

A Series of Books Edited By
Jerome David Levin, Ph.D.

Substance abuse and addiction are the third most common cause of mortality in the United States. They are among the most prevalent mental illnesses, not only in the United States, but throughout the world. They are also notoriously difficult to treat. Mental health professionals see few patients whose lives or illnesses have not been profoundly affected by their own use or that of their families or peers. Addiction is not peripheral but central to the human condition and research into it is illuminating our understanding of self.

The *Library of Substance Abuse and Addiction Treatment* is dedicated to providing mental health professionals with the tools they need to treat these scourges—tools ranging from scientific knowledge to clinical technique. Non-ideological, it is equally open to behavioral, cognitive, disease model, psychodynamic, and least harm perspectives. An overdetermined disorder affecting millions of people requires multiple viewpoints if it is to be successfully treated. The *Library* provides those multiple perspectives for clinicians, students, and laypeople as articulated by the most insightful workers in the field. Practical, utilitarian, scholarly, and state-of-the-art, these books are addressed to all who wish to deepen their understanding of and increase their clinical efficacy in treating addiction.

RECOVERY FROM ALCOHOLISM

Beyond Your Wildest Dreams

Jerome D. Levin, Ph.D.

JASON ARONSON INC.
Northvale, New Jersey
London

Copyright © 1991 by Jerome David Levin

First softcover edition 1994

All rights reserved. No part of this book may be used or reproduced in any manner what-
soever without written permission from Jason Aronson Inc. except in the case of brief quo-
tations in reviews for inclusion in a magazine, newspaper, or broadcast.

ISBN 1-56821-186-4
Library of Congress Catalog Card Number 93-74242

Printed in the United States of America on acid-free paper. For information and catalog
write to Jason Aronson Inc., 230 Livingston Street, Northvale, New Jersey 07647-1726. Or
visit our website: http://www.aronson.com

In memory of
David Wilson

ABOUT THE AUTHOR

Jerome Levin, Ph.D., is a faculty member of the Humanities Department at the New School for Social Research as well as Director of the New School's Alcoholism and Substance Abuse Counselor Training Program. He is also Adjunct Associate Professor of Social Science at New York University. Dr. Levin is the author of *Treatment of Alcoholism and Other Addictions: A Self-Psychology Approach, Introduction to Alcoholism Counseling: A Bio-Psycho-Social Approach, Slings and Arrows: Narcissistic Injury and Its Treatment, Theories of the Self,* and the forthcoming *Couple and Family Therapy of Addiction.* He is co-editor, with Ronna H. Weiss, of *The Dynamics and Treatment of Alcoholism: Essential Papers.* He conducts a private practice in psychodynamic psychotherapy in New York City and Long Island.

Contents

Introduction

This book is about drinking and about sobriety. It is about drinking too much and what to do about it. It is a book that will help in evaluating drinking. It is a book that inspires hope.

There is an AA slogan that says that the fruits of sobriety are "beyond your wildest dreams." It is a slogan few, if any, drinkers find believable, yet it is true. We in America drink a great deal and consider drinking a prerogative of adulthood. "God's good creature," as our puritan ancestors called alcohol, accompanies us through life. "Tying one on" for the first time is the closest thing we have to a rite of passage from childhood to adulthood. We drink at ceremonial occasions of all sorts: birth, marriage, and death are all marked by drinking. Men have always drunk to feel more manly; the ability to hold his liquor being the mark of a real man. Nowadays most women drink, too—to belong, to socialize, to feel more feminine. Alcohol: accentuator of joy, assuager of grief—who would want to be without it?

Incredibly, vast numbers, in fact millions, of people choose to live without alcohol and they do very well, thank you. Some of these people avoid alcohol out of fear. They grew up in alcoholic households and have seen all too much of "demon rum." Others abstain for religious reasons, and still others simply don't enjoy it. However, the nondrinkers who probably interest you the most are those who have found that the costs of drinking — to their physical health, their psychological well-being, their relationships, and their bank accounts — outweigh the benefits. You may be one of them or perhaps you suspect that you would be happier as one of them. You wonder if you are drinking too much. Yet you don't want to quit, there is too much you enjoy about drinking. Besides, the mere idea of stopping frightens you. What would life be like without a drink now and then? You may be confused — you want to be able to drink without paying too high a price, but you're not sure you can. Should you change your drinking habits rather than stop?

This book speaks to all who are in conflict about drinking. It will help you understand what alcohol does to you and what it is about its effect that is so pleasurable. It will help you understand more about yourself and your environment, and how your personality, the people you grew up with, and the people now in your life influence your drinking style. It will help you clarify your confusion, resolve your conflicts about drinking, and decide what is the best course to take.

I have been working with problem drinkers, alcoholics, and their families for many years. By training, I am a rehabilitation counselor. I wrote my doctoral dissertation on personality change in members of Alcoholics Anonymous. It was during my research for that degree that I first realized the phenomenal potential for growth and joy that people suffering from alcohol dependency possess. In the years since I wrote that dissertation, it has been my good fortune to share in many a journey from despair to hope, from suffering to satisfaction, from pain to joy. It is a privilege to do the work I do and I am grateful that I have the opportunity to do it.

I am also a psychoanalyst. Psychoanalysis is one of the great attempts of the human mind to understand itself. Its theories are tentative, provisional, and constantly being revised. I find psycho-analysis incredibly stimulating and exciting. It is limited in the direct help it can give to people while they are hooked, but it does help people understand themselves and it can enrich their sobriety. I believe that insight and self-understanding are intrinsically valuable and that they heal. But insight is not enough, we need to act on our insights.

In addition to working directly with patients, I teach and supervise students learning to be alcoholism counselors and students learning to be psychotherapists. I am director of the Alcoholism Counselor and Substance Abuse Counselor Training Programs at the New School for Social Research in New York's Greenwich Village. In response to the needs of my students I have written two books, *Treatment of Alcoholism and Other Addictions* and *Alcoholism: A BioPsychoSocial Approach,* which are addressed to students and mental health professionals. One of these books applies the principles of psychotherapy to the problems of alcoholism and addiction. The other is a basic college text. They are rather technical books.

Teaching students and writing for professionals is fine, but it is rather indirect. So I decided to skip the middlemen and speak directly to the people who drink and who sometimes worry about their drinking—to speak to you. That's why I wrote this book. I enjoyed writing it. I hope that you enjoy reading it, but I hope far more that you find it useful and helpful. If you are a mental health professional, you can also benefit from reading this book. Most probably you drink, and the people you treat drink, so it makes sense for you to learn more about drinking.

I love what I do. Teaching and doing therapy are a real joy for me—at least most of the time. Let me share my enthusiasm with you. You will learn much and get a good deal of therapeutic help along the way. You and I can have some fun as well. Our topic is surely a serious one, but we need not be overly solemn in our discussion of it. You can think of me as Dr. Levin, the professor and therapist, or you can think of me as Jerry, a fellow human being who has known and struggled with the full gamut of human emotions. I am both: an expert on alcoholism and problem drinking *and* a guy who has been around the block a time or two. Both Professor Levin and Jerry can be useful to you. Most of my patients start out calling me Dr. Levin and wind up calling me Jerry. If you wish to, you may do the same. I have also been called lots of other things. There may be times as you read this book that you will call me some of those other names. That's fine too.

Of course the focus isn't going to be on me, it is going to be on you and that is as it should be. It is hard to admit that somebody knows more about you than you do about you. When it comes to your drinking that may be the case, and in a sense I do know more than you do about your drinking. But I am going to share my knowledge with you so that you can become your own expert.

Perhaps you are concerned not about your drinking but a loved one's. Here, too, are confusion, conflict, and pain. The seeming irrationality of what you are witnessing vastly compounds your misery. Are you overreacting or is your loved one in trouble? Is it his or her problem or yours? Fortunately, knowledge and understanding diminish anxiety and fear. This book will help you to such an understanding of your husband's or wife's, daughter's or son's, mother's or father's, alcohol use and misuse. It will help you help them and help yourself.

If you think you or somebody you love is having a problem with alcohol, don't be afraid, don't be ashamed. Read on, learn, and feel comforted. After all, we are talking about one of the most common problems in America. Help is available and you or your loved one can benefit from it.

As they say in AA, "First things first." The place to begin is to learn more about "God's good creature," demon rum, and why people like you drink it.

CHAPTER 1

The Reasons Behind Drinking

People drink to feel the mild disinhibition that accompanies the depressant effect of alcohol on the brain. They like the up that goes with this, along with that kick-up-your-heels feeling so many people get from a few drinks. Anxiety disappears, relaxation replaces it, and a warm and joyful feeling overtakes the drinker. People also drink because they enjoy the atmosphere, the ritual, and the company that goes with it. Alcohol breaks down barriers. It lets us feel closer to other people. It can serve as a social cement. We feel less self-conscious and more a part of our crowd, our fraternity, our drinking companions.

Warmth, closeness, joy, euphoria, disinhibition, freedom from care, relief from anxiety, and expressiveness are all mediated by the effect of a few drinks on the nervous system. It is no mystery why people drink.

People drink in many different ways. Some folks are *social drinkers*—people who enjoy a drink or two at a party or a glass of wine with dinner. They can take it or leave it—alcohol isn't very important to them. Others are what I call *life-style drinkers* — people who drink regularly, sometimes a little and sometimes a lot, and for whom drinking is important. It is built into the fabric of their lives. Life-style drinkers may relish the cocktail hour, they may stop for a few beers after work, or they may regard dinner without wine unthinkable — a form of barbarism. Some people consider life-style drinking unwise or unhealthy. That's a value judgment with which you probably don't agree. Life-style drinkers believe that drinking enhances their lives and don't associate drinking with adverse consequences — with causing them problems. For the most part that's true. Not so for *problem drinkers* — by definition, people who are having problems because of their drinking. They may or may not be aware of the connection between their drinking and their difficulties in life. Finally, there are *alcoholic drinkers* — those who drink because they have a disease.

People drink too much for complex reasons. Researchers disagree on the causes of drinking too much. One says that the cause of excessive drinking lies in the drinker's genes, another that it lies in the drinker's personality, and yet another that it lies in the drinker's environment. I believe that all of these contribute to drinking too much as do the pharmacological properties of alcohol itself. I am going to distinguish three types of drinking too much: getting drunk, problem drinking, and addictive drinking. Addictive drinking is also called alcoholism.

GETTING DRUNK

There are many reasons people get drunk. The most obvious is by choice. People sometimes simply decide to get drunk. "Tonight I'm really going to tie one on." At sometime or another you've probably done exactly that. In addictive drinking the element of choice disappears. Drinking too much because you feel like it is a far freer act than taking a drink to stop the shakes. Addiction to alcohol is unmitigated slavery.

Perhaps you wonder why people choose to tie one on. Frustration is the most common reason. "To hell with it! Tonight I'm going to forget all my troubles and if anybody doesn't like it they can go hang themselves." Angry? Yes. Immature? Yes. Alcoholism? No. You may be surprised by the idea that getting drunk can be an angry act. Drinking to deal with frustration is more easily understood. Frustration, however, usually leads to anger — anger at being frustrated. They are two sides of the same coin. Angry drinking both expresses the anger — "they can all go hang themselves" — and quells the anger by anesthetizing it as alcohol does all feelings. Getting drunk, or at least fairly high, by choice may be a reaction to any intense feeling. Drunkenness may be used as a way of assuaging anxiety, depression, rage, or any negative emotion. The aim of getting buzzed is not oblivion. The drinker is usually looking for a high, but overreaches it.

This brings us back to the basic reasons why people drink too much. On the pharmacological side, alcohol affects judgment and a frequent reason that people drink too much is miscalculation. The booze hits them harder than they anticipated. The first two drinks impair their judgment so they drink a third, which does the job. This has happened to just about everybody. "If I had only stopped after the third I wouldn't have this miserable headache." People also drink too much because of the occasion, the setting, the crowd. It's expected. This certainly is the case with a lot of teenage heavy drinking, but is not restricted to the kids. A college reunion, for example, may be an occasion on which heavy drinking is virtually required. One's crowd has a lot to do with it too. In some social settings getting blotto is virtually obligatory. At least that's what you thought when you matched the Joneses drink for drink at their pool party last night. Peer pressure plays a major role here as it does in a great deal of drinking behavior. Finally, people get drunk because they don't know the correct way to drink. It takes experience to learn to know when to stop and how to hold your liquor. Just like everything else you have to learn *how* to drink.

Getting drunk for any of the above reasons doesn't mean too much if it is a rare occurrence. It does not predict problem drinking nor does it predict alcoholism. It is, however, an experience you don't want to have very often. If you do, your drinking too much is starting to mean something else. Of the reasons for getting blotto — poor judgment, loosened control induced by alcohol, inexperience, the occasion, the crowd, the setting, and "just feeling like it," it is "just feeling like it" that is most dangerous. Drinking heavily to handle feelings — painful or joyful — is not a good thing to do with any frequency. It should be far down on your list of coping mechanisms.

PROBLEM DRINKING

The second meaning of drinking too much is getting in trouble because of drinking. Statistical surveys show that a huge number of Americans either are or have been problem drinkers. Problems include quarrels, strained family relations, impaired health, arrests for driving while intoxicated (DWI), or for drunkenness, fights, difficulties on the job, and financial troubles. The same surveys show that some problem drinkers return to social drinking and some do not.

There are many reasons that people become problem drinkers. Problem drinking is certainly related to alcohol's pharmacological properties. Getting in accidents, driving while impaired, being too hung over to get to work, fighting with your spouse — all are direct consequences of alcohol's effects on the central nervous system. Alcohol abuse builds tolerance — you have to drink more to get the same effect. Problem drinkers sometimes have trouble because they become hooked. Not totally hooked — just hooked enough so that they need more alcohol to get high. Drinking more to get the same effect doesn't work. You drink more to get the same old good feeling but instead of feeling good you get into a fight. That doesn't make any sense to you, but it is easily explained. Alcohol in high doses (it's a drug) does more than make you high — it impairs your judgment.

Alcohol not only builds tolerance, it also induces psychological dependence. Before you know it, you need that drink to socialize, to give a speech, to make love, to relax, to end the day. I have heard at least three people say "I'm so nervous that I need a drink to get behind the wheel." They weren't trying to be funny. Drinking too much sneaks up on you. Suddenly you need or think you need alcohol to do — whatever. This may or may not get you into trouble. Even if it doesn't, it is not a good way to be — it's not free.

How about heredity? Do our genes contribute to the problem-drinking variety of drinking too much? Well there are two types of problem drinkers: situational and prealcoholic. Situational problem drinkers are reacting to a current stress or their alcohol consumption has snuck up on them to the point that it affects them adversely. Heredity isn't a big factor here. It doesn't cause this type of problem drinking. Prealcoholic problem drinkers are on their way to alcoholism. Some prealcoholic problem drinkers drink that way because they have a genetic predisposition to do so, but for the most part heredity isn't the main reason people drink so much that it causes them trouble. There are interesting exceptions — the kind of people who get into serious trouble with the first drink. The first time they picked up a drink they broke up the bar and punched a cop. It hasn't gotten any better since. That's called pathological intoxication. The experts believe that such people react to and metabolize alcohol differently from the way the rest of us do. Most people who suffer pathological intoxication become alcoholics, but not all. If you react to alcohol in such a way, the only solution is not to drink at all. You can't change your neurochemistry or your liver enzymes.

How about environment? Yep! It's a real big factor. If you run with the heavy hitters, you are far more likely to become a problem drinker. Social circles where drinking is a way of life are conducive to trouble with alcohol. Most people in such circles don't injure themselves in obvious ways. Rather they may be subtly damaging their health, blunting their emotions, and impoverishing their relationships. If you run with such a crowd, be aware that tolerance, increased intake, psychological dependence, and real, even if subliminal, problems are very much risks of this life-style. If you change your milieu, your drinking may no longer be socially acceptable, and that may get you into trouble.

Finally, personality has something to do with problem drinking. Drinking too much seems to be connected with a variety of personality traits: obstinacy — "I'll drink as much as I please"; defiance — "Nobody can tell me what to drink"; impulsivity — "Give me another one"; difficulty tolerating emotional pain; and unresolved emotional conflict. Self-medicating painful feelings such as depression often leads to problem drinking.

ALCOHOLISM

The worst kind of drinking too much is called alcoholism. The World Health Organization defines alcoholism as drinking in excess of community standards in such a way that the drinker's well-being — vocational, financial, interpersonal, emotional, or physical — suffers. In other words, if you are drinking more than the norm in your environment *and* your drinking is seriously hurting you, then you are alcoholic. Alcoholics Anonymous has several interesting things to say about alcoholism. On one hand it says, "It is the disease that tells you that you don't have it," a reference to alcoholic denial. On the other hand, AA calls alcoholism a "self-diagnosed disease." What this means is that underneath their denial alcoholics know what havoc they have been wreaking on themselves and that recovery depends on making this knowledge fully conscious. The American Psychiatric Association considers alcoholism a disease. So do the American Medical Association and the American Psychological Association.

The distinction between problem drinking and alcoholism is not always easy to make. It is not difficult to figure out that a woman who has had seven hospitalizations for detoxification from alcohol, who has lost her job, her mate, and her children because of her drinking, and who continues to drink in spite of liver disease, is alcoholic. But what about the eye surgeon who drinks four martinis each evening without any visible ill effects, who occasionally takes a tranquilizer to steady her nerves before operating, and who gets high Saturday nights? Is she alcoholic? Maybe, but it's not so clear cut.

Quantity, self-diagnosis, violation of community standards, impairment of a major life area, psychological dependence, problem drinking with a lot of problems, and physical dependence have all been used to define alcoholism. Physicians and researchers stumble over the definition of alcoholism. They can't quite agree. Although there is a continuum ranging from occasional drinking to social drinking to life-style drinking to problem drinking to alcoholism, there seems to be something different about addictive drinking—about alcoholism. AA speaks of an invisible line between problem drinking and alcoholism that people cross. Once across there is no return. I agree.

How do you know you have crossed the invisible line? The key issues are *progression* and *loss of control*. Some problem drinkers can return to problem-free drinking. Alcoholics cannot. No matter what alcoholics do to improve their drinking, sooner or later it gets worse. That's called progression. As one of my patients put it, "Whenever I drink everything turns to shit." The other essential point is loss of control, the inability to predict what will happen when you drink. This does not mean that alcoholics get blind drunk every time they drink, but it does mean that anything can happen. A social drinker may occasionally choose to get drunk; this is not alcoholism. The alcoholic chooses not to get drunk, yet wakes up three days later in a hotel room not knowing how he got there. This is alcoholism.

Alcoholism is a disease. Problem drinking is not a disease. A behavioral disorder perhaps, a social malady, but not a disease in the medical sense. Dorland's *Medical Dictionary* (1965) defines disease as "a definite morbid process having a characteristic train of symptoms." Alcoholism is a disease in this medical sense. Benjamin Rush, surgeon general of the American Revolutionary army, was the first to recognize alcoholism as a disease. Some of his remedies, such as severe whipping, were a little extreme, but there are those who would still advocate them. Thomas Trotter, an early nineteenth-century British navy doctor, also considered alcoholism a disease and cited both heredity and "premature weaning" as causes. These men were exceptions. Until recently alcoholism has been regarded as depravity, as sin, and as a moral weakness.

The disease concept of alcoholism was rediscovered by Alcoholics Anonymous. Bill Wilson, one of AA's founders, was a frequent patient in Knickerbocker Hospital, an expensive drying-out tank. The medical director of Knickerbocker, Dr. Silkworth, taught that alcoholism was "an allergy of the body and an obsession of the mind." Wilson later took this over and incorporated it into AA literature. From there it gradually won acceptance. In 1960 one of the great scholars of alcoholism, Emil Jellinek, wrote a book entitled *The Disease Concept of Alcoholism.* Shortly thereafter the World Health Organization accepted the disease concept, followed by the American Medical Association, the American Psychiatric Association, and the American Psychological Association. Although many people, including alcoholics themselves, still believe that alcoholics are sinners and alcoholism depravity, all of our official bodies now regard it as a disease.

Alcoholic drinkers drink too much because they have an illness. They are sick. What causes this illness? Alcohol itself is one cause. Alcoholics drink too much because they drink, paradoxical as that sounds. They build tolerance needing more to get the same effect *and* they become psychologically dependent on alcohol. Sometimes people, and not only alcoholics, drink too much to prevent withdrawal symptoms. This is surprisingly common. Taking some "hair of the dog that bit you" the next morning is quite popular. This is drinking to prevent withdrawal. Prolonged heavy drinking compromises the nervous system in such a way that judgment is impaired, impulse control diminished, and emotional pain intensified. All of this can cause you to drink too much because you are drinking. Alcoholism is a progressive, potentially fatal disease. After a certain point, people drink too much simply because their alcoholism is progressing. In these ways, alcohol causes alcoholism; drinking causes drinking too much. Don't underestimate the power of alcohol itself to induce emotional regression, distort thinking, and cripple your capacity to anticipate consequences in precisely a way that leads to the next drink. When people stop drinking, they are truly amazed to discover how much of their desire to drink was caused by drinking.

Some experts on alcoholism think that personality factors are an important reason why people drink too much in an alcoholic way. Others do not. I believe that personality has a lot to do with drinking. People who drink alcoholically have certain characteristics in common. They are impulsive, self-centered, grandiose, depressed, have low frustration tolerance, and suffer abysmally low self-esteem. These traits constitute the "clinical alcoholic personality." What the experts argue over is the existence of a prealcoholic personality. Alcohol certainly affects personality; how much personality causes alcoholism is up for grabs. AA takes no stand on this issue, as it takes no stand on scientific questions in general, but it does enjoin its members to work on their character defects. AA calls alcoholism a "disease of attitudes." These diseased attitudes are the personality components of alcoholic drinking.

One of the oldest theories about personality and alcoholic drinking is called the "dependency conflict hypothesis." Simply stated, it says that people, particularly men, who can't accept their natural human need for support and love from others, covertly meet this need by drinking. The prototype is the two-fisted, tough saloon drinker who rides into the sunset alone except for his horse. Totally self-sufficient, right? Wrong. He needs his horse and his bottle, not necessarily in that order. What we are talking about is his pseudo self-sufficiency. Drinking alcohol isn't considered dependent behavior so our loner cowboy's need for emotional support can be met without him or anybody else knowing it. Given some variations this scene can be played out in New York City just as well as in Silver City. Many people who come for treatment for alcoholic drinking turn out to have tried to resolve a dependency conflict in precisely this way.

There is evidence that hyperactive children and overly aggressive, defiant adolescents are more prone eventually to drink alcoholically. In general, freewheeling, to-hell-with-the-consequences attitudes predispose a person to alcoholism. Yet the opposite type, the shy and inhibited who drink to be able to be freewheeling, can also develop alcoholism.

Low self-esteem also disposes a person to alcoholism. In fact, the "who needs you or anybody else" attitude is just a front covering lack of self-esteem and hunger for love and approval. Difficulties in dealing with anxiety and self-medication of depression also play a role in many people's alcoholic drinking.

People with any type of personality can become alcoholic, but insecurity, low self-esteem, difficulty in handling frustration, hyperactivity in childhood, and overly aggressive, defiant attitudes all predispose one to alcoholism. However, personality factors alone do not cause people to drink alcoholically. It also takes an environment that sanctions heavy drinking. Biological susceptibility also plays a role.

There is strong evidence that there is a genetic factor in some forms of alcoholism. There are many types of alcoholism, ranging from alcoholism that develops from drinking to relieve intolerable emotional pain to the type where an inborn genetic defect is the most important factor causing the alcoholic drinking. What is inherited is unknown. Probably it has something to do with the way alcohol affects the brain and the way it is metabolized.

The kind of drinking too much that is most affected by genetic factors is called early-onset alcoholism. It is the kind of alcoholism that develops very early, sometimes with the first drink, and is severe. It is found mostly in men. If you have this type of alcoholism—every time you drink disaster ensues—you are probably not reading this book. If you are, you need help now.

Genetic factors also play a role in the slower, more insidious type of alcoholism that affects both men and women. Some people enjoy alcohol much more than others. It relaxes them more and is a highly effective tension reducer. These are inborn differences that predispose them to alcoholism. It is possible to breed strains of rats who have an appetite for alcohol, which is not a normal rodent predilection.

If there is alcoholism in your family, you are at considerably higher risk of drinking alcoholically than the general population. The more alcoholism and the closer it is to you the greater the risk. Children of alcoholics are well advised to drink with caution, if at all.

How do alcohologists know that heredity plays a role in alcoholism? Several ways. Family studies show that alcoholism runs in families, but this could be environmental. Twin studies compare identical and fraternal twins. If one identical twin is alcoholic, it is far more likely that the other will also be alcoholic than it is if they are fraternal. The trouble with this is that identical twins are treated more alike. Adoption studies in which children of alcoholics adopted in the first weeks of life by nonalcoholics are followed for thirty or more years are the most convincing. Children of alcoholics raised by nonalcoholics develop alcoholism at a substantially greater rate than the general population and this is the strongest evidence for a genetic factor in some forms of alcoholic drinking.

If you are male, 40, Irish, Catholic, not religious, went to college, make good bucks, live in a big city in the Northeast, and spend a lot of time with heavy hitters, your chances of being alcoholic are much better than average. Gender, age, ethnic background, religious affiliation, secular versus religious orientation, education, socioeconomic status, and the degree of approval of drinking by your family and friends, especially of heavy drinking or drinking to deal with problems, are all implicated in drinking alcoholically. Researchers say they can predict alcoholism. Statistically, environmental and sociological factors correlate—i.e., go with—alcoholism in pretty definite ways. That does not mean that all alcoholic drinkers are urban, red-nosed, Irish college graduates. Far from it. What it does mean is that background, current environment, and attitudes toward drinking have a lot to do with why people drink alcoholically.

Men become alcoholic more often than women; the middle-aged than the young or old; Irish, English, Northern Europeans, and people from the Caribbean than Southern Europeans. Catholics and mainstream Protestants are more likely to become alcoholic than Jews and fundamentalist Protestants; the secular more than the religious; the well educated and the affluent or the very poor more often than the working class; the urban more than the rural; Northerners more than Southerners; and most important, those who live in environments that permit or encourage heavy drinking and drinking as a way of solving problems more than those who do not. These factors are potent, but not determining. Sooner or later you will meet an elderly, poor, orthodox Jewish woman from rural Arkansas, who doesn't know a soul who likes to drink, who is alcoholic.

People drink alcoholically for all of the reasons I discussed. The proportion of pharmacology, personality, genetic predisposition and environmental factors varies from case to case, from the "primary alcoholic," who is prewired to self-destruct if he drinks; to the highly functional, well-adjusted salesman who gets hooked after spending forty years entertaining; to the depressed, poorly adjusted introvert who drinks alcoholically in a futile attempt to maintain self-esteem. The first is alcoholic mostly because of his genes; the second is alcoholic mostly because of alcohol; the third is alcoholic mostly because of personality conflicts; and the alcoholism of all three was retarded or accelerated by their environments.

CHAPTER 2

Drinking Too Much

In this chapter I am going to ask you to listen to the musings of a series of drinkers as they ruminate about their drinking. Each and every one of them is worried about his or her drinking and suspects that he or she drinks too much. They all know, yet don't want to know, and don't quite allow themselves to know fully, that their drinking is causing them grief. Each of these drinkers' monologues is a bit exaggerated — enlarged, so to speak — so you can see yourself writ large. You won't relate to all of them and some of them won't be at all like you, but at least one will be like you.

AA members are advised, "Identify, don't compare." At most AA meetings there is a speaker, who tells the story of his or her relationship with alcohol. Members are enjoined to focus on ways they are like the speaker, rather than the ways in which they are different. It is the commonalities, not the distinctions, that they are to attend to. Those attending the meeting are specifically urged to identify with the speaker's *feelings*. Comparison increases distance; identification lessens it. Focusing on how much of what the speaker drank and where she drank it, rather than on how her drinking made her feel, is a way of creating distance. "She drank wine, I drink beer. She lost her job, I never did that. She had liver trouble, I never got sick from drinking," are all ways of seeing one's drinking as different from the speaker's. It is a way of denying or minimizing one's own difficulties with alcohol. Identification with the speaker, or in our case, with the muser, especially identification with his or her feelings, does the opposite. Comparison with the speaker's life circumstances, vocational status, social background, or preferred beverage rather than identification with his or her feelings serves to establish how different the listener is from the speaker, a difference that can easily be used in the service of denial — denial by the listener of his or her difficulties with alcohol. For instance, "I drink bourbon, she drank daiquiris, so my drinking isn't like hers and certainly not as bad," is a pretty good example of such "disidentification."

The injunction "Identify, don't compare" undercuts the issue of disidentification to defend one's drinking. I am going to ask you to try to identify with the ruminations of Andy, which you are about to read, and with the interior monologues of a number of other drinkers. Unlike AA speakers, none of these folks has admitted that there is anything wrong with his or her drinking, much less that he or she might be alcoholic, but all of them worry about their drinking. As you read their thoughts, ask yourself if there is anything about your drinking that resembles theirs, including their concern about their drinking. Although not all of them are alcoholic, all of them drink too much. Perhaps you do too. As you read, concentrate on the consequences of their drinking. Try to identify with the speakers' feelings — their concerns, their denials, their anxieties, their sadnesses, their desperations, and their anger. Ask yourself if your drinking is at all like theirs and if alcohol is causing you any of the same problems. As you do this remind yourself that "alcoholism is the disease that tells you that you don't have it," and that stressing the differences between your drinking and the speakers' may be a way of protecting your own drinking.

Not all problem drinking is alcoholism, but people have a

tendency to put unpleasant awarenesses, such as trouble with alcohol, out of mind, so problem drinking gets minimized or denied in much the same way as does alcoholism. The drinking folks who are going to let us share their thoughts about drinking are very different in personality from one another and in their relationship to alcohol. It is not likely that you will strongly identify with all of them, but you will be able to identify with one or more of them if you allow yourself to do so. Some of their thoughts and behaviors may seem extreme—don't let that get in your way. Adjust the intensity up or down and try to see if there is anything in any of their patterns that strikes home.

You can evaluate your drinking in two complementary ways. One is through identification and introspection. That is the way I have been telling you about. Seeing yourself in another is powerful and compelling, so is insight. But potent emotional forces can interfere with identification, so it is helpful to have another, more objective, way to determine whether or not you are drinking too much.

Since introspection is so notoriously difficult and subject to error, alcohologists have developed objective questionnaires to help people decide if they drink too much. These questionnaires can help you decide for yourself the status of your drinking. They are quite helpful. Try the one developed by Johns Hopkins University (Table 2-1) now. There are several others at the end of this chapter.

Some of you don't have drinking problems. But you do have feelings. Try to identify with the monologuists' feelings and you will find that you will understand problem drinking better. You will probably see your loved one reflected in one of our drinkers.

ANDY, A DAILY DRINKER

Andy, our first ruminator, is a pretty average guy. He doesn't have unusual emotional problems, nor does he have a family history of alcoholism.

Table 2-1
Johns Hopkins University Drinking Scale

Ask yourself the following questions and answer them as honestly as you can:

1. Do you lose time from work due to drinking?   Yes ____ No ____
2. Is drinking making your home life unhappy?   Yes ____ No ____
3. Do you drink because you are shy with other people?   Yes ____ No ____
4. Is drinking affecting your reputation?   Yes ____ No ____
5. Have you ever felt remorse after drinking?   Yes ____ No ____
6. Have you gotten into financial difficulties as a result of drinking?   Yes ____ No ____
7. Do you turn to lower companions and an inferior environment when drinking?   Yes ____ No ____
8. Does your drinking make you careless of your family's welfare?   Yes ____ No ____
9. Has your ambition decreased since drinking?   Yes ____ No ____
10. Do you crave a drink at a definite time daily?   Yes ____ No ____
11. Do you want a drink the next morning?   Yes ____ No ____
12. Does your drinking cause you to have difficulties in sleeping?   Yes ____ No ____
13. Has your efficiency decreased since drinking?   Yes ____ No ____
14. Is your drinking jeopardizing your job or business?   Yes ____ No ____
15. Do you drink to escape from worries or troubles?   Yes ____ No ____
16. Do you drink alone?   Yes ____ No ____
17. Have you ever had a complete loss of memory?   Yes ____ No ____
18. Has your physician ever treated you for drinking?   Yes ____ No ____
19. Do you drink to build your self-confidence?   Yes ____ No ____
20. Have you ever been in a hospital or institution on account of drinking?   Yes ____ No ____

Three YES answers indicates a probable problem drinker.
From 4–7 indicates definite early alcoholism.
From 7–10 indicates an intermediate phase of alcoholism.
Above 10 indicates advanced alcoholism.

"Am I drinking too much?" The thought comes and goes. I put it out of my mind. I enjoy drinking. Those beers after work with the boys are relaxing, convivial; they don't hurt anybody. So why worry about it? And I really like wine with dinner; it enhances life and makes coming home festive. And parties. Well, parties are fun. So why do I sometimes wonder "Do I drink too much?" . . . The kids bring home all that health stuff from school, but kids are like that — rigid and all too ready to judge, especially their parents. It really hurt when Kathy said, "The dog asks to go out when you get home. You're so loud and harsh. You always sound angry." How does she expect a Daddy to sound, like a choir boy? Then there was that big fight with Ann. But she hardly drinks. A toast at weddings; a half a glass of wine with dinner and not even that a lot of nights. Ah, women, they're all New Year's Eve drinkers like Mother. Well not all. I got upset when Ann said, "The part of you I like hard isn't your head." That was clever, but hell, everyone has trouble getting it up once in a while. She shouldn't have said that. "Give me another beer, bartender." I have to stop this brooding. There's nothing wrong with my drinking.

Do you identify with Andy? Do you find yourself wondering about your drinking? Do you find such thoughts pressing back into your mind in spite of your attempts to dismiss them? Are your wife and children unhappy with your drinking? Do you find yourself alternating between defensiveness and suspecting that something is wrong with your drinking? Do you discount other people's objections to your drinking on the grounds that "they really don't understand because they don't drink or don't drink much?" Do you find that you are having sexual difficulties you never had before? Do you have some identification with Andy's drinking pattern? With his thoughts and feelings about it? Do you think that Andy may have a problem with alcohol? If you answered yes to several of the above questions, your relationship to alcohol resembles Andy's and if you think that Andy has a problem then simple logic must lead you to conclude that you, too, drink too much.

Andy is a decent sort of fellow; he cares about his family; he has done reasonably well in his career. He didn't used to be troubled by feelings of inferiority, didn't have unusually low self-esteem, and didn't suffer crippling anxiety or depression. Yet he developed into a heavy hitter and he is worried about it. Andy appears to be a guy who developed a drinking problem by drinking. There is no alcoholism in his family and he probably doesn't have any of the varieties of genetically transmitted susceptibility to alcoholism. Perhaps some aspect of his personality attracted him to alcohol. It seems to be a social facilitator for him. Perhaps he was shy as a young man and drifted into daily drinking as a way of overcoming his shyness. In a sense, it doesn't really matter whether it was shyness or some other trait he didn't like that Andy tried, consciously or unconsciously, to overcome with alcohol. Whatever it was, it started him drinking on a regular basis. He drank, then he drank more, and now he is starting to suffer because of alcohol. He has become psychologically dependent on alcohol, and its addictive properties are likely to lead him to drink even more. If you, like Andy, are a daily drinker who is starting to run into flack about your drinking, try not to react too defensively. You are reacting that way because you're scared — something that is very important to you is threatened. Try to sidestep your reflex reaction and calmly assess what is happening to you. Can you do that?

Andy drinks too much. He is certainly a problem drinker. There are worse problems associated with drinking but his are bad enough. One way in which drinkers compare instead of identify is to zero in on how much worse the other drinker's problems are. In this way, your drinking is not threatened. But as AA says, the key word is "yet." I haven't "lost a job," "been in jail," "destroyed a marriage" . . . yet. Although these dreadful things haven't happened to Andy . . . yet, he is already suffering plenty. By his own admission he has family problems, he has sexual problems, and he is beset by anxious worry.

Andy is drinking too much in several senses. Although I agree with AA that "it isn't how much you drink, but what it does to you that counts," Andy is drinking too much just in terms of quantity. He drinks every day. He drinks before he comes home and after he gets home. He is almost certainly underestimating how much he drinks. Most people do. *In estimating how much you drink assume that you are counting low,* since you almost certainly are. Then figure in a multiplier of, let's say, two. Two? Yep! And that's conservative. Andy's drinking too much is not drinking to drunkenness. He doesn't do that. Yet, his drinking is drinking too much in the sense that it makes him unhappy in a variety of ways. That is problem drinking. Andy is definitely at risk for alcoholism. He may or may not have crossed what AA calls the invisible line into overt alcoholism. Hundreds of thousands of folks are just like Andy. Otherwise normal guys or gals who have become dependent on alcohol for whatever reason and who are now moving toward alcoholism. Could you be one of them?

MURIEL, A RELIEF DRINKER

Muriel drinks to raise a little hell and to deal with frustration. She enjoys tying one on. Does she drink too much?

> What a hangover. Am I glad Jim drove home. It's bad enough for a guy to get a DWI—for a woman, it's the pits. I really wanted to tie one on last night. The headache is worth it. It's a great release. I don't do it very often. Do I do it too often? . . . There's so much stuff on TV about alcoholism. . . . I don't think so. Five or six times a year. Sometimes I just want to raise hell. Flirt a little, dance dances I wouldn't dance sober. Jim almost killed me the time I stripped at the New Year's Eve party. I'm glad I did that. We still laugh about it. I'm uptight and letting my hair down felt great. Jim said, "Can't you let your hair down without letting your pants down?" I still wake up laughing about that. Another time we charged a flight to

Bermuda and called his mother to take care of the kids. I only missed one day's work. Jim likes to get high too. Life's just too damn dull when we're sober. Getting high is great. Last night was too much, though. It's kind of blurred. It takes more to let go now. Still, life is so short I don't want to miss anything . . . the other kind of drinking I don't like. The kind when I say, "Screw it, I'll tie one on tonight." I do that when I'm frustrated or fed up, or disgusted, or really angry. Jim does that too. Well, what's sauce for the goose is sauce for the gander. If guys can get away with it why not women? Last Saturday was one of those. Job was a horror, Jim was uptight, and my mother was on the warpath so I said, "Baby, tie one on." I did, too.

How's that total up? Six or seven hell-raisers and three or four screw-its a year with an occasional drink in between. Seems all right? Should I cut back? Never had a problem with booze that a couple of aspirins couldn't cure, so why should I? Still, I must be worried. Otherwise I wouldn't be thinking all this. . . . I know what I'm going to do—strip at this New Year's Eve party stone cold sober. Wish I could, but I couldn't do that if my life depended on it . . . Well, I'll just watch it. I'm going to stop for a while and when I go back it won't be so often or so much. Time to wake Jim and get ready for tennis.

Muriel is an occasional, or maybe not so occasional, relief drinker. She drinks to get relief from frustration and tension. She calls this screw-it drinking. Muriel also drinks recreationally, using alcohol for its disinhibiting effect. She calls this hell-raising drinking. Muriel is not yet in serious difficulty because of her drinking. She is not drinking alcoholically and it is questionable whether she is a problem drinker. Possibly Muriel can cut back and avoid becoming a problem drinker. Of the three ways of drinking too much, Muriel is not drinking alcoholically, may be drinking problematically, and is drinking too much in the sense of getting drunk. There is no way to know if her borderline drinking problem will progress into full-scale problem drinking or alcoholism. If there were alcoholism in her family, she would be on a slippery path. Muriel needs to look at the cost/benefit ratio and see if she is getting more pleasure than pain out of her drinking. Does your drinking bring you more pleasure than pain?

Since Muriel is drinking too much in the sense of getting drunk and having miserable hangovers, she could try not to drink to drunkenness. But that would be a problem for her since she often wants to get blasted. What she doesn't want is to feel god-awful in the morning. Do you feel the same way? Do you identify with Muriel? There are more Muriels than Andys, literally millions of them, so you may very well identify with her.

Of the four factors — heredity, environment, pharmacology, and personality — that contribute to drinking too much, it is Muriel's personality that most puts her at risk for trouble with alcohol. I am going to assume that there is no alcoholism in her family.

She lives in an environment where heavy drinking is an accepted way of life and that is certainly a risk factor. She must also contend with alcohol's habituating and addicting properties, but it is her personality that puts her in danger of problem drinking.

Muriel is high-spirited, outgoing, and vivacious. She is a risk taker and on the rebellious side. She has a good relationship with her husband and holds a responsible job. She is in touch with her anger and isn't excessively anxious. If she is masking a depression, she is doing a very good job of it. Muriel is an extrovert and has lots of energy; she plays tennis with a hangover. Her major emotional problems are lack of a better way than drinking to handle frustration, and experiencing herself as sexually inhibited. She feels overcontrolled although most people would judge her undercontrolled. She very much wants to let go and raise hell, but feels that she can't do so without alcohol. This is a highly doubtful proposition. *You can do anything sober you can do drunk.* I know you don't believe that, but it's true. I have seen people do all sorts of things sober that they thought they couldn't do without some "liquid courage."

Muriel has many personality traits that show up in children and adolescents who later become alcoholic. Social scientists like to follow a population from childhood through adulthood so they can determine what people were like before they developed conditions such as alcoholism. There are only a handful of studies that cast light on what people are like before they become alcoholic. These longitudinal studies uniformly show that prealcoholics (i.e., those who later become alcoholic) on the average, are outwardly confident, even overconfident, undercontrolled, devil-may-care, unbridled by convention, and prone to acting out their conflicts. This is interesting since people say they drink to feel uninhibited. It appears that the uninhibited drink to feel uninhibited. That seems strange, but it makes sense. The people who get in trouble with alcohol are the ones for whom being and feeling unrestrained is most important. Drinking too much is a form of unrestrained behavior to begin with, one which permits yet more and even wilder unrestrained behavior. Muriel is like that—she enjoys letting loose; it is one of her most cherished values. Muriel has more than a little of the stuff that shows up in the longitudinal studies. If a person whose personality is as attractive as Muriel's is at risk for trouble with alcohol then "who shall 'scape whipping," you say, echoing Hamlet. "If you're depressed, watch it; if you're not depressed, watch it. It seems that nobody is safe." Since anyone, regardless of personality, can run into difficulties with alcohol, I have to agree with you. However, people who are at the extremes are the ones who are the most prone to problem drinking: the uptight, hold-it-all-in depressives and the hell-with-the-consequences, let-it-all-hang-out rebels. Underneath the two types may share more than meets the eye. However that may be, it is important for you to know that people like Muriel who are gregarious, outgoing, basically emotionally healthy, have a strong need to disinhibit, and are more or less socially defiant are at considerable risk of developing problems with alcohol especially if they run with a heavy-drinking crowd. If you're like Muriel, you probably don't believe that, but the research evidence is compelling.

Muriel needs to cut back on her drinking. At least she says so, and who am I to disagree? Do you identify with Muriel? If so, you might consider taking a rest — stopping for a while or cutting back — but the key thing is for you to realize that you are on the verge of problem drinking. If you identify with Muriel, you are drinking too much at least on occasion, and you can easily move from having fun with alcohol to suffering because of your drinking. That cost/benefit ratio can easily flip to the deficit side. A drinking pattern such as Muriel's does not necessarily lead to alcoholism, but there is definitely a risk. If you drink like her, you are living dangerously. If Muriel tries to cut back and cannot she is in trouble. The same is true for you. If you have been drinking like Muriel and you can cut back successfully, fine; enjoy your drinking. Prost! L'Chaim! If you cannot, you have a problem. If you cut back successfully but then find that your drinking is creeping up seemingly against your will, then you are definitely drinking too much.

WARREN, A DEPRESSED DRINKER

Warren retired a few years ago. Like many retirees, he isn't having much fun, and like many retirees, he is drinking far more than he ever thought he would.

> It's funny, but I never drank much. Never really cared for it. Mary and I would have a cocktail before dinner if we went out, but half the time I didn't even finish it. It was more the idea of it — seemed festive, and sure, I'd have a drink or two at a party, but it never was very important — wasn't my thing. Sometimes months would go by without my even thinking of a drink let alone taking one. It's different now. Ever since I left Zander Manufacturing I've been stopping at Pete's Tavern in the afternoon. Never thought I'd have any problem with retirement. I couldn't wait to get out of there. The last five years I was counting the hours. Golf, bridge, travel, more time with Mary, no schedules, no boss — no more

pencils, no more books, no more teachers' dirty looks. Ha! Ha! You never do grow up. I have enough money. There's lots of things I like to do, so why do I sit here every afternoon drinking beer? No harm in it I suppose — something I never did before. What is retirement for if not to try something new? Wonder if I'm depressed. But why should I be depressed? I'm free now — money, time, no real problems. I suppose I do miss some of the boys . . . and Ralph. Losing Ralph, that was hard — so hard for Mary. Just like that — one slick in the road and it was all over at 24. I always hated that motorcycle. But that was ten years ago; I'm over that. The other kids are doing great and the grandchildren . . . well, I guess I'm as much of a fool as the other grandfathers, but they're the best. "Pete, Give me another beer." Nice sitting here looking out at the rain and sipping beer. Pete's a great guy and there's the TV and the regulars. I like most of them. Never feel lonely here. Funny though, I'd probably be sitting here if it was beautiful out. Maybe not, might be at the club playing golf. Don't play as much as I thought I would. I always hated the drinking in the clubhouse. People acted so stupid after a while. They used to laugh at me when I ordered chocolate milk. But that was good-natured. People liked me. It's different now. I can't wait to get to the clubhouse and sock down a beer. Maybe I was missing something all those years. Drinking is fun. Relaxes you. Mary never says anything when I drink at home, but I know she doesn't like it — I can see it in her eyes. Good sport though, even says, "Can I get you another beer, dear?" I'm glad I got into beer. Cheers you up. I guess I need cheering up now. Damned if I know why. Never felt the same about the job after I was passed over for V.P. seven years ago. Those bastards might have made some allowances for the fact that I was down over Ralph. I was just a time server after that. Glad I'm out.

"Pete, I think I'll have one more — can't play golf on a day like this." Cheers you up but it does make you tired. Maybe I'll try to cut down. "Pete, did I ever tell you about the time I took the kids fishing in the Rockies and we got caught in a snowstorm in July? Sure, take care of that customer, I'll tell you about it later." Better watch it, I have to drive home in the rain, but what the hell, I'll have a last one. Damn Doc Fisher and his liver enzymes; he put these thoughts in my mind. Why shouldn't I drink a little now that I have the time? Well, maybe I should cut down a little, it does make you tired.

When it comes to their relationship to alcohol, Warren, Muriel, and Andy are quite different. Perhaps you are more like Warren than like Andy or Muriel. Are you a person who was a casual drinker most of your life but who now finds yourself drinking often, regularly, and enough to make you think about it? Warren, unlike Andy, was never much of a drinker. It is highly doubtful that genetic factors play a significant role in his present drinking behavior. There is no problem drinking in his family. Warren is drinking too much because he is having difficulty negotiating a new life stage and can't adjust to the changes attendant upon it. Warren mistakenly believes that alcohol will facilitate the adjustment. Do you find that you're suddenly drinking differently? That alcohol, seemingly coming out of left field, is now a major or even dominant factor in your life? Warren is having difficulty adjusting to retirement, but retirement isn't the only transition that can shake people up, sometimes to the point where they drink to cope, or seemingly cope, with that transition. Graduation, marriage, becoming a parent, promotion or success in a business or profession, divorce, job loss, and relocation are transitions that are sometimes extremely stressful. Success may seem an odd one, but many studies show that any change in fortune, for better or worse, can be highly stressful. So if there has been a major change in your life that is difficult to come to terms with and you find that you're drinking more perhaps without even wishing to, then you may find much to identify with in Warren's ruminations and you may see many similarities between his drinking pattern and yours.

DEPRESSION, LOSS, AND DRINKING

Warren is not only having an *adjustment problem,* he is also *depressed.* Depression does not cause problem drinking, but using the sauce to self-medicate depression does frequently result in problem drinking and sometimes leads to late-onset alcoholism. Warren is dangerously close to late-onset alcoholism and is clearly already a problem drinker. He sort of knows this, but won't allow himself to fully know it — that would threaten the drinking now so dear to him. Do you identify with any of this? Do you suspect that you are depressed and are drinking to feel better?

Depression has many causes, both psychological and somatic. Drinking doesn't help relieve any form of depression be it caused by a problem in the chemistry of the nervous system or by a disappointing love affair. On the contrary, it makes it worse. Warren was depressed before he started drinking heavily. Far more frequently, *people become depressed because of their drinking.* Both patterns exist. Warren had suffered a terrible loss, the tragic death of his son Ralph. He never really got over it. However, he fooled himself, not deliberately or even consciously, into thinking that he had put his loss behind him. Ralph's death was a long time ago and "that was over." It wasn't. Unresolved mourning inevitably leads to depression. In fact depression is often a direct consequence of the failure to mourn. Because alcohol anesthetizes feelings, you can't mourn if you are drinking excessively. Have you lost someone you loved deeply, tried to put your loss out of your mind, and found that you are drinking more? Perhaps much more? Depression is often masked and not directly experienced. Instead there is a loss of zest for life and beloved activities — like Warren's golf — feelings of boredom and vague dissatisfaction. Difficulty in sleeping, especially early-morning awakening, loss of appetite, and loss of sexual desire are also symptoms of depression. Prolonged feelings of sadness, as well as feelings of helplessness and hopelessness are additional signs of depression. Think about it. Were you overtly depressed, or did you have a masked depression before your drinking escalated? If so, you are drinking to treat your depression, although you may not be aware that you are doing so. It won't work. Alcohol doesn't alleviate depression; it exacerbates it. Drinking to medicate a depression is always drinking too much.

DRINKING AND BLOWS TO SELF-ESTEEM

Warren suffered a terrible blow to his self-esteem when he was passed over for promotion. The technical term for such a hurt is a *narcissistic wound.* Narcissistic wounds are injuries we experience very deeply, down where we live. They are injuries to our core selves. Vocational roles are central to our self-concepts; they are a vital part of our core. If career disappointment and hurt go too deep, we are lacerated to the core. Such was the case with Warren. Have you experienced such narcissistic wounds? Did you minimize or discount them when you were really hurt to the quick? Looking back, can you remember rejections, for that is what they are, blows to your self-esteem that were so painful that you couldn't let yourself feel them? Did they precede your starting to drink heavily? One response to narcissistic injury is *narcissistic rage*—anger of monumental proportions. That feeling may have been so frightening to you that you had to stuff it. Push it right down out of your awareness. Unconscious rage does not go away. It is turned against the self and causes depression.

Narcissistic rage is murderous. It is a response to a threat to your core self. Since you feel that someone is trying to kill a vital part of you, it makes perfect sense that you would want to kill them. An eye for an eye, says the primeval moral code. If you can't allow yourself to experience your rage because that would be too dangerous, or if you experience it but can't express it, as Warren couldn't to his employer, then your rage goes underground. Now without being aware of it you are murderously angry at yourself. Rage against the self may be so intense that suicide results. Alcoholic drinking has been called a form of *chronic suicide.* Such drinking is an expression of self-hatred based on internalization of rage. Warren became depressed in this way and started to use alcohol to anesthetize his pain. His drinking was both an expression of his self-hatred and a passive, indirect expression of his hatred for the Zander Corporation and the people who screwed him there. Do you identify with Warren here? Is your drinking partly self-hatred and partly a feeble expression of your rage?

We have mental images of ourselves and others. Sometimes we are aware of these self and object representations, as they are called, and sometimes we are not. They may be conscious, or they may be unconscious. Normally, your mental image of yourself is distinct from your images of other people. As psychologists say, you have firm boundaries. However, when you are very upset — overwhelmed by strong feelings — your mental images of yourself and others become confused. Your boundaries blur. If you are very angry at somebody, and your internal representation, your mental image of him, is blurred and confused with your internal representation of yourself, then you will be angry at yourself. This is different than turning anger against yourself, but the result is the same. Warren was confused in this way, and it worsened his depression. This, in turn, resulted in his drinking more. Unfortunately, *alcohol blurs boundaries,* so once again the attempted cure, drinking, makes the problem worse. In fact, this cure is worse than the disease. Damn, that booze just isn't what it's cracked up to be! Professional help, on the contrary, can greatly assist people to reestablish firm boundaries. Warren could certainly use some. You probably can't tell if you have this kind of internal, unconscious confusion, which alcohol always makes worse. For now, just concentrate on determining if you're drinking too much.

Warren might have handled one blow, the death of his son. He might have handled two blows, the death of his son and being passed over, but he couldn't handle three blows. The emptiness, the loneliness, and loss of purpose in retirement did him in. Alcohol will complete the job if he doesn't stop. Does any of this ring a bell for you? Narcissistic blows are often dismissed. The hurt and rage go underground and fester. Most of us don't like to think of ourselves as so vulnerable to hurt, and, of course, being excessively vulnerable is a problem. There are people who are grievance collectors and who nurse resentments. Such grievances and resentments can then be used to justify, rationalize, one's drinking. Some problem drinkers are grand masters at finding such seemingly rational reasons for drinking. It is possible that this is your pattern. However, for the moment don't be too harsh in judging yourself—later you can figure out if you are overreacting or collecting grievances. The issue right now is recognition. Harsh self-judgment only gets in your way. The real question is whether you identify with Warren's hurt and his reaction to it. Do you?

Warren is not a grievance collector. Warren is sensitive all right, but he certainly had been injured. His problem lay in how he handled his hurt, not in excessive touchiness. When his promotion was denied he didn't let himself feel hurt, just as he couldn't endure fully feeling his son's loss. Then, *totally without conscious awareness of the connection,* he turned to drink to anesthetize and indirectly express those feelings. Now he has a drinking problem of increasingly serious proportions in addition to his other difficulties. The same may have happened to you. Has it?

DRINKING BECAUSE YOU CAN'T BE ALONE

There is another reason Warren drinks too much. Warren is lonely. Loneliness is a universal human problem; the question is, how do we handle it? Drinking is one way. Do you drink to assuage and alleviate loneliness? People often go to bars looking for companionship. They seldom find it. There is a sort of pseudointimacy in a tavern—occasionally even some real intimacy. For Warren the promise of companionship was not fulfilled. The bartender rebuffed him. Feeling even lonelier he ordered another drink. Has that ever happened to you? Do you go to bars because you are lonely? Do you leave feeling even more lonely? That happens to people all the time. Feeling rebuffed, or just plain lonely, it is so natural to turn to alcohol for companionship. At least your drink is reliably there and always available. Alcohol seems to alleviate loneliness. Before you know it, alcohol has become your best friend. AA knows this. There is an AA rubric, HALT, which means don't get too *h*ungry, *a*ngry, *l*onely, or *t*ired. AA members escape loneliness by attending AA meetings, where there are always plenty of people. You have a very real need for companionship, for human contact and relationship. When this need isn't met, you feel lonely. The only cure for this kind of loneliness is people. Alcohol won't fill the bill. But aloneness is a part of the human condition. It can't be avoided. Unendurable loneliness can result from an inability to be alone peacefully, rather than from lack of companionship.

Let me tell you about a wonderful man named Donald Winnicott, who was first a pediatrician and later a psychiatrist and psychoanalyst, who rode a motorcycle and wrote poetic, illuminating papers. One of his most beautiful papers is called "On the Capacity to Be Alone" (1958). In it he postulated that the ability to be alone is a developmental achievement based on a paradox. It develops from the experience of the small child being alone in the presence of another. If you have been fortunate enough to have had the experience of being alone joyfully self-involved in play in the presence of a loving, supportive, but nonintrusive parent, you can probably enjoy being alone. The nonintrusion, the letting alone, or to use Winnicott's language, the "not impinging" is just as important as the "being with." You need both. Being alone under such circumstances is a good experience. If you have enough of it, the other person slowly becomes a part of you or, as the psychoanalysts say, becomes internalized. Then you can be alone without being lonely because you carry your mother or grandmother, or father or grandfather, or whoever loved you with you and in you. If on the contrary, you either didn't have such a person to spend time with you, or to put it differently, you were pushed to a premature independence, *or* mother or her substitute couldn't let you be, was too anxious or too uptight to let you alone, then you will have failed to develop the capacity to be alone to its fullest. Being alone will be painful and difficult. An experience to be shunned, perhaps by drinking.

Being alone in Winnicott's sense is not isolating oneself; it is not an avoidance of people. It is something positive. It is not hiding, or hiding out because of fear. Avoiding people because you are afraid is defensive isolation. That is not what I am talking about. Being alone in Winnicott's sense is a vital human capacity. It is necessary for growth, for self-actualization, for creativity, and for a sense of completeness as a separate person. Being alone is so much a part of life that we usually take the capacity to be alone for granted. But amazingly it is far from being a given; it is something we acquire only slowly and only if we are fortunate in our early experience.

Warren either hadn't developed or had lost this capacity to be joyfully alone. Something was missing inside. One way to make up for something missing on the inside is to supply it from the outside. Warren's beer drinking was, in part, just such an attempt at self-cure. Beer was not only a substitute for human companionship; drinking it was an attempt to internalize a loving presence. Do you ever find yourself doing this—using alcohol either as a companion or as a way of being alone comfortably? Drinking for these purposes, if it is more than very occasionally, is drinking too much.

I will have more to say about using something such as alcohol from the outside as a way of attempting to remediate the lack of something inside. The technical term for such a deficiency is "failure of internalization"—it means that something went wrong and something that should have become a part of you has not done so. Unfortunately, the attempt to fill an inner emptiness with alcohol never works. It is like trying to self-medicate depression. In one case, you get more depressed, in the other you become even emptier. The reason this happens is that problem drinking inevitably impoverishes rather than enriches and one is left with an empty bottle, an empty world, and an empty self. Trying to fill an inner emptiness with alcohol is like trying to heal a gastric fistula (a hole in your stomach) by eating. It is an exercise in futility.

We have seemingly wandered far from Warren and his late-onset drinking problem. But have we really? Can you identify with drinking to alleviate a barely conscious or all-too-conscious depression, to express rage passively and indirectly, or to be able to be alone? If you can, even if you've never had a problem with alcohol in the past, you are drinking too much now.

Before we leave Warren, I want to point out that Warren is starting to have physical problems related to his drinking. Doc Fisher is worried about Warren's liver enzymes. As we age, it takes less alcohol to damage our bodies, but physical difficulties secondary to drinking can arise at any age. If you are starting to have physical problems relating to your drinking, you are unquestionably drinking too much.

VICKY, A "MAD HOUSEWIFE"

Vicky is a closet drinker. She never goes to bars. She just stays home and sips a little wine. She could hardly get in difficulties that way, could she?

> Those kids are driving me out of my mind. I'm going to have a glass of wine while I'm making dinner. I lost it yesterday. I never spanked Susie that hard before; her backside was purple. I get so angry I want to scream. A little Chianti will do me good. I shouldn't have hit her that hard; I don't want to do that again. This wine is great. "Shut up you kids, or I'll give it to you again." Sally told me that she takes a glass of wine or two when she feels like she's going to lose it. It does mellow you out. Tomorrow I'll have Sally over and we'll have wine and cheese together. I'll have another glass. "Yeh, do whatever you want. It's okay. Mommie won't get mad." I don't like feeling sorry for myself, but kids aren't people—not really. I need people to talk to. Tom's gone all day and I don't see Sally so often. They're really good kids, just a

little naughty now and then. I feel awful about what I did yesterday. Am I turning into a child abuser? When I have the wine I don't get so worked up. Tom doesn't like it, though. He says he can't stand coming home to a sloppy wife. I just sip wine while I'm making dinner. What's wrong with that? . . . Mother never drank around the house. Mom would be wild if she knew I hit Susie. She wouldn't like the wine either. Maybe the Valium is better. It doesn't smell. Come to think of it, I'm using a lot of Valium. Tom doesn't like that either, but he isn't home alone in this hot house all day. I'm getting a little . . . confused. I'm starting to feel high. A little too high. Maybe I shouldn't have had the Valium on top of the wine; I mean the wine on top of the Valium. I wish Sally was here or Tom would come home. I don't like the way I feel. I feel like crying. I love those kids so much, why am I such a bitch to them sometimes? I don't want to be. I'm so moody. It must be awful for them. I'm so angry and anxious most of the time. The Valium stops that for a while. It helps, but not like wine. I get so sad when I drink wine. I can't cry in front of the kids; I'll go into the bathroom. I don't like the way I feel. Oh shit, the stew is burning. Tom will kill me. I better hide the wine and brush my teeth. I'll take an extra Valium. I'm not going to drink alone anymore. Only when I have Sally over. Tom doesn't mind that so much. If only I wasn't so angry and resentful I wouldn't sip so much Chianti. It is good, though. Okay, I'll drink, but not alone, and I'll hold the Valium down. Oh hell, here's Tom and there'll be another fight.

Ever feel like Vicky? Trapped? Angry? Afraid of your spouse? Enraged at your kids? Wanting to kill and feeling terrible about feeling that way? Drinking to numb or *anesthetize rage* is real popular. Vicky, the "mad housewife," does just that. Lots of other folks do it too. Very few people are comfortable with anger. They were told at an early age that it isn't nice to boil over with rage. Women have even more trouble dealing with anger than men. They are more likely than men to have been taught that expressing anger is "bad." So you hold it in, or try to, like Vicky. Sooner or later it gets away from you and you hit the kids, scream at the repairman, kick the cat, or just cry with rage. Vicky is an *extremely* angry lady. Are you that angry? Vicky hates herself for being so angry. Do you identify with her self-hatred? Vicky has no idea why she is so angry. The only thing she knows is that she can't stand it. Did you ever feel the same way? Since she can't stand it, Vicky has to do something to stop it, and she only knows two ways to do that: mellowing out with Chianti or taking a Valium.® Vicky does one or the other, and sometimes she does both. They give her some relief, but unfortunately it soon wears off leaving her feeling even worse. Do you identify with the feeling worse part?

If you're drinking to quell your rage you're drinking too much. An occasional "drop dead" martini may not be the best way to express anger, but it has its uses. The same cannot be said for the routine use of alcohol to express/repress anger. Routine numbing of rage with alcohol or tranquilizing drugs has nothing to recommend it. Although it masks it, alcohol fuels rage. Then you have to drink more to quell the rage induced by your last drink, and before you know it, you're on a merry-go-round.

Drinking and "Losing it" with the Kids

Vicky hits her kids. If she is not a child abuser, she is getting close to it. She knows this and hates herself for it. One reason she drinks is to tranquilize herself enough not to react to the kids. Usually it works the opposite way: the kids get beaten when their parents are drunk or hung over. If you hit your kids when you're drinking, don't. It's all too easy to lose control and regret it afterward. *Child abuse and problem drinking are highly correlated.* Although Vicky hits her kids when she is sober, she does so because her nerves are raw from the previous day's drinking. Although you don't believe it, children are actually easier to handle sober. Children of recovering alcoholics who were abused when their parents were drinking almost never report being mistreated after their parents get sober. One reason that the kids won't get on your nerves as much when you are sober is that you are far more likely to deal with things as they come up and to set reasonable limits rather than let them get out of hand and then react with uncontrolled rage. Another reason is that the kids have a more available and more consistent parent to relate to. If you're having lots of problems with your kids and you drink to tolerate them or to not react to them, then you're drinking too much. That is simply not a good reason to drink. You don't have to go to Vicky's extremes to identify with her. Maybe you yell at your kids instead of hitting them and then drink to calm yourself down. Essentially it's the same thing. You have a situation you don't know how to handle, you become intensely angry, and you drink to quiet the anger. If that's your pattern, you're drinking too much.

Vicky also drinks because she's lonely. It isn't primarily that she lacks the capacity to be alone, although this too may be a problem for her. Rather, the problem is that she simply doesn't have enough human contact. One reason she is so angry with her kids is that they can't give her the kind of companionship she craves. Loneliness is painful. It can be intolerable. Many, many people drink to assuage loneliness. Are you one of them? I'm not talking about feeling empty inside, just feeling plain lonely. So lonely you can't stand it. Many things make Vicky angry, but nothing angers her more than not having people to talk to. She blames her husband for her loneliness, but she has never told him so. Chianti has become her friend. Has alcohol become your best or your only friend? Has your liquor cabinet become your social club? It's so easy to wind up lonely because you're home drinking instead of out with people. Of course, you're drinking in the first place because you're lonely. Using the sauce as a friend easily leads to yet another vicious circle, another version of the merry-go-round.

That happened to Vicky. She really doesn't have enough stimulation and she makes sure that she doesn't find any by staying home and drinking. Perhaps you identify with Vicky's drinking because she is lonely and being lonely because she drinks. Do you?

Circumstances are against her, but she makes things worse with the wine and the pills.

Vicky, like most problem drinkers, bargains. She doesn't want to give up drinking so she makes deals with herself. She sets limits, conditions for her drinking. She won't drink alone; she'll take less Valium. Have you found yourself bargaining like Vicky? If you have, drinking has become too important to you. Social drinkers don't have to make deals with themselves about the conditions of their drinking. They just drink and enjoy it. Setting conditions— not before five, only wine, not with pot, no more gin, and so forth— are signs that something is wrong with your drinking.

Alcohol and Tranquilizers

Vicky takes Valium, a minor tranquilizer. There are many other minor tranquilizers including Librium®, Miltown®, Ativan®, and Xanax®. They are all antianxiety drugs; they make people more tranquil. Some of them are also muscle relaxants. "Major" tranquilizers are not really tranquilizers at all. They are antipsychotic drugs, not antianxiety drugs. They are properly called neuroleptics. Thorazine® and Mellaril® are examples. They are almost never used for recreational purposes; there is no high and people don't get hooked on them. Not so for the minor tranquilizers. They are all addictive. You need more and more to get the same effect; that is, they build tolerance, and there is a definite withdrawal. Valium and the other minor tranquilizers are "downers." Pharmacologists classify them as sedative-hypnotics. Pharmacologically Valium, Librium, ethyl alcohol (the kind you drink), phenobarbitol, and the other barbiturates are in the same category—they all sedate and as the dosage goes up put to sleep—hypnotize. That is why they are called sedative-hypnotics.

AA says of these tranquilizers that they are martinis in powdered form. AA calls their misuse "sedativism"—addiction to downers of whatever sort. Sedativism is a disease just like alcoholism is a disease. *Cross-addiction* to alcohol and minor tranquilizers is extremely common. Vicky is cross-addicted. Do you use pills to come off the sauce? Do you take tranquilizers when you aren't drinking? If you do you are a sedativist. You are drinking too much if you have to use downers when you aren't drinking. Your nervous system is constantly being depressed, if not by alcohol, then by prescription drugs. Alcohol and tranquilizers are a dangerous combination. It is far easier to get hooked on the combination than on alcohol alone. Minor tranquilizers are medicines; they have many legitimate medical uses. Staying calm between drinks isn't one of them. They used to be prescribed indiscriminately. This is less true now, but it still happens. If you identify with the booze-downers syndrome you definitely need help. Try to look at your pill use as objectively as possible. Is it the case that you are frequently under the influence of either a pill or a drink?

Vicky started drinking too much because she felt trapped and didn't know how to get out. Now she is hooked, although she doesn't know it. All she knows is that she is miserable, guilty toward her children, filled with self-hate, and in conflict with her husband. She can't rationally express her dissatisfaction or do anything about it because the very solution she chooses, wine and tranquilizers, prevents her from doing so. Can you identify with any of this? Is it possible that you could do something to improve a miserable or otherwise intolerable situation if you quit or cut back on your drinking?

Vicky had one problem. She couldn't deal with her feelings of rage, sadness, and despair. She didn't know how to improve her situation. *Now she has two problems:* sedativism and not knowing how to express her feelings. There is no alcoholism in her immediate family and genetic factors probably play a minor role in her drinking too much. Her personality, her emotional inhibition, and her fear of confronting her husband with the impossibility of her isolation were the major factors that drove her to the sauce. She drinks too much largely because she can't express her feelings, especially her angry ones. The rest is circumstantial. Her only friend is a heavy wine drinker who served as a model for sipping away the day; her doctor is an ass who prescribes Valium to shut up complaining women, and her husband is the kind of guy who doesn't want to see anything wrong. He prefers to look the other way—unless dinner is burned. The sheer pharmacological power of alcohol and Valium in combination closed the door on Vicky, leaving her addicted.

Vicky's story is extremely common. Hundreds of thousands of women have lived it. It seems so easy for Vicky to rationalize her drinking. But her rationalizations don't really work for her. She doesn't quite believe them. She is a mass of quivering guilt, conjuring up her mother's disapproval as a stick to beat herself with. Do you try to justify your drinking in the ways Vicky justifies hers? "I'm lonely"; "It makes me feel better"; "I don't want to yell at the kids"; "I can't stand the anger, the sadness, the pain." If you can identify with any of this, think about Vicky and how transparently she is conning herself. Is it possible that you are conning yourself in the same way?

PEGGY, A BLACKOUT DRINKER

Peggy, our next ruminator, is on the fast track. She's young, bright, well educated, and in the right place at the right time. Opportunity knocks, yet she is miserable. Alcohol and drugs play an all-too-important role in her life.

> Who's this guy? Jesus, it's the third time this has happened. Well, they do it pretty much the same way so what difference does it make? I feel awful. Went to Smith for this? Shit, I'll have to do something to change my life. I'm really out of it. Never got that smashed before. Have to stop using grass when I drink, or maybe it's the coke—coke sucks. I'll stick to margaritas and this won't happen. He's really out. Jesus, he isn't even circumcised. Never had one of those before. I wonder what it felt like. Probably real primitive, I must have loved it. Maybe he'll wake up and we'll go around again. Not with this headache. I think I'm going to puke. One more night like

this one and I think I might pack it in. Oh hell, I'm too young to check out. Maybe some coke will straighten me out. No, I'm not doing any more of that. Just clean up and get dressed, kid. There's some beer in the fridge. I'll have a bottle—just like a Hemingway character. Beer in the morning; death in the afternoon. Stop this melodrama, so you slept with some hunk in a blackout. Who hasn't? I'll douche when I get home. Just get the hell out of here, okay? Jesus, I'm scared. I don't like what's happening to me. I have a great opportunity at Wallace Publishing and act like a slut. Only when I drink, though. Sex isn't all that great, especially if you don't even remember it. Could screw up my job, too. Feeling better now. That beer really helped. Well, I am having a hell of a good time. I'll cut the coke and either drink or smoke but not both. A little lipstick sure makes a difference. "Oh, hello there, I was just leaving." Nothing like being young and carefree. Why don't I stop for a margarita on the way home? Never hate myself after a few of them. Stop this doom and gloom guilt shit. It's still the weekend, isn't it? Weekends are to have fun. No coke or grass today, though. Everything will be all right. I know it. Maybe I should lay off the booze too. Naw, leave that for Mother Theresa. "So long, fellow. I'll be down at Tony's if you want to join me later. I like the margaritas there."

Do you have memory lapses? Do you have holes in your experience of yourself and the world? Did you ever wake up and wonder what you did or said last night? If you have, I'll bet that it happened after drinking and that it doesn't happen when you aren't drinking. In fact, I'll give you pretty good odds that you only *blackout* when you're under the influence. Peggy had a whopper of a blackout, as such memory lapses are called. You don't have to wake up in bed with a stranger or find the police at your door investigating a hit-and-run to have had an episode of *alcoholic amnesia.* "Amnesia? That's serious stuff, isn't it? Not like forgetting the end of a party. That's not serious is it?" you ask. I can only reply that you have to decide that for yourself. But amnesia is amnesia and not remembering what you did or said is *always* deeply disturbing. People joke about it, laugh about it, dismiss it as part of the "game," but underneath the jocosity is anxiety or even terror. So upsetting is the experience that people drink to blot it out, which may very well lead to another blackout. Peggy did that. She was so upset by what she woke up to that she assumed a cynical, hard-boiled attitude, far from her true feelings, and picked up a drink. Did you ever dismiss things you had apparently done while under the influence with cynicism, black humor, or an assumed hardness? Did you ever reach for a drink, like Peggy's beer, to quell your morning-after fears?

Peggy is on the coke, pot, booze merry-go-round, but booze is her real love. She tries to protect her drinking by putting the blame for her difficulties on other drugs. "If only I don't smoke pot or snort coke or use acid, then I can drink without worrying about it." Looking at her behavior from the outside this seems like blatant nonsense, but to a person like Peggy caught up in the fast-lane vicious circle, such reasoning seems perfectly logical. Do you live in the fast lane? Have you become caught up in a similar maze? Peggy is certainly drinking too much. If she hasn't crossed the line from problem drinking to alcoholism she is perilously close to it. "Better things for better living through chemistry" said the old Du Pont ad. Peggy could subscribe to this slogan wholeheartedly. She is "chemically dependent." If it's not alcohol, it's pot or coke. Such polydrug use is more the rule than the exception these days. If you're under age 35 and have a problem with alcohol it is probable that you also have a problem with other drugs. If you do, you may still value alcohol the most. It's your "drug of choice." The other stuff is ancillary. That's the way it is for Peggy.

Do you drink in the style of Peggy? If you go from drink to drug to drink, you do. If you black out you do. Memory loss is a symptom of Alzheimer's disease, senile dementia, and other dread neurological diseases. Why self-inflict such a symptom? There's something a little, or not-so-little crazy about doing that, isn't there?

Blackouts need not be total. They can be partial — greyouts — the sort of foggy, soupy, hazy recollection in which you are not too sure what really happened. Greyouts are *not* a normal response to drinking. If you grey out with any frequency, you are drinking too much, at least on the nights that they occur.

Drinking to Feel Together

One reason that blackouts or greyouts are frightening is that they are interruptions in the experience of self. First you are there, then you aren't there, and finally you are there again. That's weird stuff and can be more upsetting than not knowing what you did or didn't do the night before. Paradoxically, people drink because drinking is integrative, makes them feel more together — more cohesive. Sometimes it also helps people feel more connected, better integrated with their fellows. So the very stuff that you sometimes use to confirm your "togetherness," your experience of yourself as cohesive and enduring, leads to the very opposite experience. Now, far from feeling together, you reach for more cement (booze) in a futile attempt to feel together again. America's greatest playwright, Eugene O'Neill, who was an alcoholic, wrote, "Man is born broken. He lives by mending. The grace of God is glue." For O'Neill's tormented protagonist, as for so many drinkers, the glue was "God's good creature rum."

Drinking to feel more connected is exactly like drinking to alleviate depression, becoming more depressed from the drinking itself, and then drinking yet more to alleviate the depression caused by the drinking. *Vicious circles* seem to be characteristic of problem drinking; we have encountered them time and time again in our examination of drinking behavior. In each case there is an attempt at self-cure . . . of anxiety, of depression, of the lack of capacity to be alone, of not feeling together . . . and in each case the attempt is futile. The cure makes the problem worse. Are you beginning to see that drinking too much isn't a form of depravity, of badness, or a moral lapse? Rather, it is a mistake, almost like a mistake in arithmetic. It's your logic, not your soul that's causing the problem. Drinking too much is often based on a mistake — the mistaken belief that alcohol will heal or cure some inner deficiency or conflict. It never does. Can you identify with any of this? Do you drink in an attempt at self-cure?

Why Peggy Drinks

Peer Pressure and Drinking

Peggy drinks for many reasons. One of the most powerful is *peer pressure*. Adults tend to think of peer pressure as something that influences teenagers. The kid got into drugs because he got into the wrong crowd. It has nothing to do with us adults. So you think. But that's plain untrue. We are all deeply influenced by our fellows. Your peers profoundly affect your behavior. They are models and to a greater or lesser degree you want their approval. To some extent you choose the people whose approval is important to you, but not entirely. Circumstances and unconscious needs determine much more of your "choice" of associates than you believe. You are not as free as you like to think.

Peggy runs with a crowd that drinks and drugs one hell of a lot. It is a life-style that works for some people; it is not working for Peggy. Perhaps you run in such a crowd. Everybody seems to have fun but you. Don't be too sure. They may not be having all that much fun. I have my doubts. Peggy had fallen in with a literary Bohemian crowd in college. Typically they were ambitious, convinced that they would write great novels and profound poetry. Some of them may, but for the most part they were dreaming the dreams of youth. They tended to be arrogant, unconventional, and contemptuous of ordinary folks. They spent a lot of time telling each other how great they were. Peggy desperately wanted to be one of them. She identified with their values and with their life-style. They drank a great deal of wine, and not a little bit of the hard stuff. Peggy joined right in. She loved drinking and what it did for and to her from the first sip. It was love at first taste. It took away her insecurity and bought her acceptance in the aspiring-poets clique. Her new friends served as models for heavy drinking. They gave her permission to drink as much as she wished and rewarded her for doing so. Since Peggy liked to drink anyway, she took full advantage of that permission. The feeling of *belonging,* of being part of an elite club, which went with her drinking, strongly reinforced it. Pot smoking was just as much a badge of membership as wine drinking in her literary circle. Although she didn't like it as much, Peggy was soon drawing on a joint with as much relish as the single published member of the clique. Drinking and drugging were romanticized by Peggy's friends. She came to share in this romanticization. As she says, she's "Just like a Hemingway character." She forgets, or unconsciously identifies with, Hemingway's suicide, a suicide intimately connected with his alcoholism.

Do you identify with any of this? Not necessarily with aspiring to be a poet, but with wanting to belong to a heavy-drinking exclusive "club"? Remember, identify with feelings, rather than comparing circumstances. Do you see drinking as something magical, the very special possession of your circle? Is membership contingent on drinking? Do you ever feel like a Hemingway character or another fictional character because you drink like them, heavily, that is? If so, you are drinking for the same reasons that Peggy drinks, and you rationalize, excuse drinking too much in the same way that she does.

Of course Peggy selected her friends, chose a peer group that drank heavily. But that's not the whole story. She went to college at a time when pot smoking was virtually a graduation requirement and shortly afterward entered a viciously competitive profession just as coke came in. Almost all of the young people she was thrown with drank and drugged. So once again her peers expected her to act in a way she wanted to anyway. But Peggy would never have found cocaine on her own. By now she was often depressed. Coke took care of that and it was the "in" thing to do. She did it, early and often, as Tammany Hall is said to have recommended to its voters on election day. *Environment* played a crucial role in Peggy's early entry into the fast lane. Is that true for you? Everybody she associated with was into alcohol and drugs. For all her bravado, Peggy badly needed approval. Outwardly brash, inwardly she was jelly. Taking a drink or smoking a joint was an easy way to get that approval. Sound familiar? Did you drift, for whatever reasons, into a heavy-drinking crowd where using was expected and rewarded? Were you also outwardly self-confident, but inwardly insecure, looking for the security of belonging? Insecurity plus peer pressure, that's powerful stuff. The rest was pharmacological. Drink more, smoke more, and before you know it, you need it. Throw in some coke and you're in real trouble. That's what happened to Peggy. Has something like that happened to you?

Don't disidentify with Peggy because you don't use drugs. You may have gotten into the same sort of mess without them, but that doesn't change the fact that you're drinking out of insecurity, out of the need to belong.

Peggy also drinks to assuage guilt. Peggy is a "closet puritan." She talks like a streetwalker, but the truth is that she is very uncomfortable with her sexuality. She has *never* had sex cold sober. Have you? This may sound like a strange question, but millions haven't. I have had many patients who had never had sex sober, who were unaware that they needed to drink to go to bed until I drew their attention to it. They were closet puritans without knowing it. Peggy drank in order to have sex and she didn't know it, at least not consciously. She had gotten high in order to lose her virginity and she continued to have a drink or smoke pot to go to bed with her college boyfriend. There were other relationships all tinged with fear and then she found anonymous sex. Leaving college and moving into the adult world was overwhelming for Peggy. The real literary world, the publishing game, wasn't like her college lit crowd. It was faster, tougher, smarter. If she barely felt safe in college, she now felt terrified. Again, she didn't let herself know it. Instead, she drank and drugged and before long started taking men home with her. Her conquests were reassuring. They were more about being with somebody and being wanted than about sensual pleasure. In the short run they shored up her tenuous self-esteem, but she was never really comfortable with any of it. Her guilt became unmanageable and she picked up a drink, a joint, or a line of coke to escape that guilt. Before she came down, more likely than not she was in bed with someone else only to awake even more guilt-ridden. What could she do at that point? Drink, of course, and the merry-go-round would start again. Driving ambition; deep-seated insecurity, masked and denied; relentless, repressed feelings of guilt; and a peer group that's heavy into the sauce and other stuff—what else do you need to get hooked? Nothing except the addicting power of alcohol and other drugs. Do you identify with Peggy's feelings of desperate striving, buried fear, and crippling guilt? If you do and you hit the sauce hard, watch out, you are on a slippery path. Peggy's behavior is extreme, but *her pattern is quite common*. In asking yourself if you can identify with her, ignore the details and look at your feelings and the pattern.

Peggy's drinking and drugging is driven by yet another fear, a sadly contemporary one, the fear of AIDS. So terrifying is this possibility that Peggy dare not let her fear come anywhere near the surface. It is erased with margaritas and joints. In this case, burying her head in the sand may literally be fatal. The very ways in which she avoids her terror results in more unsafe sex, and her unconscious terror intensifies. This is one you don't want to identify with, but if you are taking chances with AIDS while high, you need to know it, face your fear, and start protecting yourself.

Peggy differs from Andy and Warren in an important way. She is far more insecure, lacking self-esteem, and driven to prove her worth, in short, far more emotionally troubled than either of them. Do you identify with Peggy's emotional pain? Peggy's emotional difficulties were there before the booze and the drugs. She was a troubled young lady to begin with, and she has no chance at all to deal with her emotional problems unless she gets sober. Neither does anybody else. In a sense, it doesn't matter whether or not your emotional difficulties existed before you started drinking heavily. In either case you can't effectively work to overcome them while you continue to drink. Peggy's personality didn't "cause" her alcoholism, but it *was* an important factor in her getting hooked. Personality, environment, and the pharmacology of alcohol—that's what did it to Peggy. The same factors may have done it to you. Did they?

Peggy's drinking and drugging was also motivated by rebellion. It was compensatory for feelings of low self-esteem *and* it was a way of thumbing her nose at the "straight" world. Is your drinking partly a way of thumbing your nose at your parents, your spouse, your boss, at society at large?

MAX, A PRIMARY ALCOHOLIC

Max has lots of alcoholism in his family. He thought that it could never happen to him.

> I never thought that I would drink like my father. I hated him when he was drunk. I felt so ashamed when he made a fool out of himself. Who wants an asshole for a father? I was sure I'd never do that to my kids and, damn, I'm doing it. Dad could get mean when he drank. I hated all the fighting and screaming and cursing and Mother crying, though she could get pretty mean too. I guess she just couldn't stand Daddy drinking. I don't get mean; I just act like an asshole. Why the hell do I do it? I never had any trouble with booze when I was young. Got drunk Saturday night at the fraternity when I was in college, but everybody did that. After I left the service and married Helen, it really leveled off. I guess it's just since I turned forty I started forgetting, and getting sloppy, and acting foolish. Hardly drank at all in law school, with what the G.I. bill gave to live on I couldn't. Well I'm a member of the bar now — sure am. I don't want to stop drinking; it's too big a part of my life. Sober as a judge, they say — well, I haven't seen too many sober judges and even fewer sober lawyers. Everybody drinks. I just have to learn to drink better. To hold my liquor like a man. Why couldn't Dad do that? He was great when he wasn't drinking. That early stroke must have had something to do with his

boozing. As the years went on, he drank more and more. Didn't his Dad die of liver trouble? Someone on Mom's side, too. A lot of booze in the family. God damn it, I'm not going to stop drinking. How could I practice law? Half my business in conducted over martinis. What I have to do is set limits. No more than one at lunch. That was Dad's trouble — he drank before five. No more of that for me. As soon as I feel it hitting I'm going to stop. They all drink wine these days. I'll switch to wine coolers. That's the answer. Boy, do I feel better, no reason to have to go down the tubes like Dad. All I have to do is stay away from the hard stuff.

Max is denial incarnate. He is full of rationalizations and strategies for drinking safely. Alas, none of them are going to work, for Max is an alcoholic. He has the disease of alcoholism. His alcoholism is not advanced, but his isn't exactly a light case either. His disease will progress if he continues to drink. Unless arrested it will eventuate in premature death. Max's form of alcoholism is powerfully mediated by his genetic endowment. He came into the world with a predisposition to develop alcoholism. Either Max metabolizes alcohol differently from normal drinkers or it affects his nervous system differently or both. This cannot be changed; it is a biological given.

C. Robert Cloninger (1983) studied the heritability of alcoholism by tracing the drinking histories of children of alcoholics who were adopted by nonalcoholics shortly after birth. He found that these adoptees developed alcoholism at a much higher rate than the general population and concluded that there was something genetic that predisposed them to alcoholism. Cloninger found that there are two ways in which a predisposition to alcoholism can be inherited. One is called male-limited susceptibility to alcoholism. It occurs only in males and is highly heritable. It is characterized by early onset, severity, and antisocial behavior. Max does not suffer from male-limited susceptibility to alcoholism. The other is called milieu-limited susceptibility to alcoholism and affects both men and women. It is less heritable and requires environmental provocation to become expressed in alcoholism. That is, people with this kind of predisposition develop alcoholism only if they live in a heavy drinking environment. It develops slowly and is not associated with antisocial behavior. Max has this type of milieu-limited susceptibility to alcoholism. Regardless of whether the factor that led to it becoming manifest was growing up with an alcoholic father or the heavy drinking in his professional circle, he has it now. Although biological factors play less of a role in milieu-limited than in male-limited susceptibility to alcoholism, they are there. There is something biologically amiss in Max's reaction to alcohol.

Scientists have used the term *primary alcoholism* in a variety of ways. I am using it to mean that the alcoholism comes first and is not secondary to some other condition such as major depression. If someone is suffering from major depression and tries to self-medicate it with alcohol, the depression will get worse and the self-medicator runs the risk of developing *secondary alcoholism*.

In the scientific literature the term primary alcoholism usually implies that the alcoholism is genetically transmitted, heritable, and has a biological basis in liver metabolism and/or neurochemistry. So used, primary means not only first, but also caused in a particular way. Cloninger's male-limited susceptible alcoholics are clearly primary in that sense. Their alcoholism is partly heritable and has something to with aberrant enzyme systems or the like. I do not wish to convey any special theory about causes of alcoholism when I say primary. I only mean to say that drinking is the primary problem. Max, who is a Cloninger milieu-limited alcoholic, is also a primary alcoholic in the sense that I am using the term. His susceptibility to alcoholism has a genetic base, but that is not the whole story. Environmental factors and the way in which he handles his emotional conflicts play an important role in Max's drinking too much.

Max grew up in an alcoholic household. No child grows up in an alcoholic home without being scarred. Some alcohologists argue that parental alcoholism does not contribute to alcoholism in any way other than the transmission of genetic susceptibility. They cite research evidence and give elaborate statistical rationales to support their point of view. I don't find this believable. I have worked with hundreds of adult children of alcoholics and I have never met one who has not been emotionally damaged by his or her parents' alcoholism. Like Max, they often become alcoholic themselves. Like Max, they "never thought that they would drink like their fathers" — or their mothers. Yet . . . they do. Has this happened to you?

Part of the reason that children of alcoholics are prone to alcoholism is genetic, but only a part. The rest is unconscious identification. One of the most powerful psychological defense mechanisms is *identification with the aggressor*. It was first described by Anna Freud (1938), daughter of Sigmund. Identification with the aggressor plays a large role in human life as witness the ways in which oppressed peoples identify with their oppressors. To grow up in an alcoholic home is to grow up with chaos, unpredictability, and often violence. Identification with the aggressor is an attempt to feel some sense of control in a situation in which you are powerless. If you can't beat them, join them. The process can be conscious, but usually it isn't; it is something you do without any awareness that you are doing it. Did you unconsciously identify with your alcoholic parent and become hard drinking yourself in spite of how much you hated his or her drinking? Early models are powerful, they are hard to escape. Do you identify with this aspect of Max's drinking?

You were probably puzzled when I told you that AA believes that, "Alcoholism is the disease that tells you that you don't have it," and that AA also maintains that "Alcoholism is a self-diagnosed disease." Both statements are integral parts of AA's folk wisdom, yet they are contradictory. As in so much of AA's folk wisdom, polar opposite perceptions and insights are expressed by a pair of mutually contradictory slogans. This seems to make no sense. If I combined the two slogans, the result would read, "Alcoholism is self-diagnosed by people that know that they don't have it." If that were the case, alcoholism would be a rare disease indeed, in fact, it would never be diagnosed. You ask, "A highly prevalent disease which is never diagnosed — isn't there something wrong there?" Yes, there sure is, but as with so many of AA's contradictory pairs of slogans, the paradox is more apparent than real. At a deeper level the paradox disappears and the two statements reconcile.

The German philosopher Hegel understood this reconciliation of paired opposites very well. He taught that in any attempt to elucidate the truth about anything, one first arrives at a partial truth, which he called the *thesis*. Being limited, an expression of only one aspect of reality, the thesis generates its opposite or *antithesis*. Thesis and antithesis then interact to generate a more comprehensive truth, the *synthesis*. Thesis-antithesis-synthesis. In our case, "alcoholism is the disease that tells you that you don't have it" is the thesis, while "alcoholism is a self-diagnosed disease" is the antithesis. What then is the synthesis? It would go something like this. "It is only when denial is overcome and the sufferer admits to himself or herself that he or she is suffering from alcoholism (self-diagnosis) that the cure becomes possible." In other words, denial is very much there, but it is only when denial breaks down sufficiently for self-diagnosis to occur that anything helpful can happen. If one's alcoholism is diagnosed by somebody else, this in itself is futile since the "cure" involves self-care, and self-care necessitates self-awareness—awareness of one's alcoholism. So at a deeper level, AA's seemingly contradictory statements about the diagnosis of alcoholism are reconciled in such a way that the insight contained in both contribute to the possibility of successful treatment.

By now you must be saying that this doesn't make much sense. "Thesis-antithesis-synthesis stuff and nonsense. On the one hand you tell me that in spite of the fact that alcoholism is the disease that tells you that you don't have it, it must be self-diagnosed. On the other hand, you have rather precisely diagnosed Max's alcoholism. How does that fit together?" I think it does. Let me explain how. In some cases you can look at something from the outside and see quite well what it is. In Max's case, he tells of his father's and grandfather's deaths from the complications of alcoholism, and that his mother's relatives' health also suffered because of their drinking. He also relates that he forgets, gets sloppy, and acts like an asshole when he drinks. His ruminations provide more than enough evidence for an outside observer to conclude that Max has a serious problem with alcohol. If that outside observer also has scientific knowledge of alcoholism, he or she could accurately conclude that Max is alcoholic. However, *none of this will do Max one particle of good if he himself does not come to see and acknowledge that he has a serious drinking problem.* We who look on can provide him with information and reflect back what he himself discloses, but unless Max himself can manage to look behind his fear and see what he in a sense already sees, our efforts will be futile. In the end, only Max can diagnose his alcoholism in a way that means anything, so alcoholism remains a self-diagnosed disease.

My purpose in telling you all this is to help you self-diagnose your alcoholism or problem drinking if you have it. So once again I am asking you to identify, in this case with Max and his drinking. Do you have alcoholism in your family? Were your parents or grandparents or brothers or sisters seriously hurt by their drinking? If so, and if you are drinking more than minimally, you are drinking too much. You are susceptible to alcoholism because your genes program your liver to produce a variant of the enzyme alcohol dehydrogenase, the enzyme that metabolizes alcohol, or your neurons do something slightly different than normal drinkers' neurons do with alcohol, or some yet unknown oddity characterizes your body's reaction to alcohol. If you drink very circumspectly, you may have no problem, but you are at risk and must be extremely cautious.

Alcoholism is frightening. Mere mention of the word sends chills up your spine. Don't let the word *alcoholism* stand in your way. Just ask yourself if you drink too much in the way Max does. Look at his pattern—youthful drunkenness minimized in memory, a period of trouble-free social drinking that gave pleasure, membership in a professional circle where heavy drinking was the norm, and finally, growing problems with alcohol. Max misperceives how much his associates drink; heavy drinkers usually do. Is it possible that you overestimate how much the people around you drink? Max is also highly selective in choosing only the heavy drinkers in his professional circle to socialize with. That's exactly what heavy drinkers do. Could this be something you do without being aware of it? Minimizing your own drinking, assuming that others drink at least as much as you do, and avoiding those who do not puts you in good company. Doing so is well-nigh universal among problem drinkers. Think carefully; it is so easy to do these things without knowing that you are doing them.

How about Max's symptoms? Do you identify with any of them, such as the forgetting, the change in the effect alcohol has on you, the emergence of behavior you regret the next day, acting foolish? How about the rationalizations? *Everybody drinks — I can't be in business if I don't drink. It's okay as long as I don't drink before five. No more hard stuff, I'll stick to wine coolers. Only one at lunch.* All of this is an attempt to control what is not in control, your drinking. Social drinkers don't have to control their drinking. Do you identify with Max's attempts to control his drinking? If you do, you are probably drinking too much.

LARRY, A NEUROTIC DRINKER

Larry drinks like a fish. He is Jewish and he believes that Jews are immune from alcoholism. Of course, they aren't. Larry is a tormented man, guilt-ridden and torn by conflict.

> My grandfather was a religious fanatic — I once dreamed I told him to shove the Torah. Good thing it was a dream, my mother would have gone crazy if I ever said that to him. Sure liked his schnapps, though. He could kill a bottle of slivovitz without batting an eye. It didn't seem to bother him, he lived to 90. Zaddie was the only one in the family who drank at all. Mom and Dad and the rest hardly ever drank except for bar mitzvahs and weddings. None of them understands drinking, that's why they are always harping on my drinking. *"Shicker iz a goy,"* so a nice Jewish boy like me shouldn't drink. They should only know what I *really* do. Pick up men and have sex with them. Lots of them. Wherever I can find them and that's

usually in a bar. Everybody is coming out — if I came out it would probably kill my parents, so let them harp on my drinking, it's a lot better than, God forbid, they should know I am gay. Didn't Maimonides prescribe stoning for homosexuals? Everybody else is marching in gay rights parades and is proud of it. I'm not, for me it's a dirty secret. My boss doesn't know; investment bankers in pin-striped three-piece suits are supposed to have a wife, kids, dog, and picket fence. I have a dog. I'm not high enough up to be one of the decadent rich, then it would be okay, but I'm not exactly invisible either, so I have to hide my private life — not that there is much of that since AIDS. Oh God, what a horror! No wonder I drink so much. I used to drink to score, now I drink because I don't dare cruise. Life stinks. It's a cheat. At least I can drink and I only drink the best stuff. I can afford that. Rare vintages, aged brandies — even that isn't much fun anymore, but I still do it. It's all I have except for the dubious pleasures of my job. Well, Jews don't become alcoholic, so I am not going to deny myself the only pleasure I have. But I sure wish I didn't feel so damned awful the next day.

Larry is another closet puritan, although his puritanism isn't the only thing in the closet. Closet puritans abound in our "liberated" age and come from all sorts of religious backgrounds, including the secular. Peggy, who woke up with a man she didn't know, belongs to the Protestant branch of closet puritanism; Larry belongs to the Jewish branch. There isn't much difference. Guilt is pretty much guilt although its manifestations vary somewhat from culture to culture. I have spoken about the use of alcohol to anesthetize anxiety and depression; alcohol can be used to quell any painful feelings. Guilt is extremely painful; it can be intolerable. Have you experienced such unbearable guilt? Have you used alcohol to make it bearable? Alcoholics and problem drinkers are often accused of being without a conscience, of lacking a moral sense. From this point of view, the problem is that drinkers don't feel enough guilt. Drinking behavior *is* self-centered, which seems to confirm this, but I have found, quite to the contrary, that alcohol abusers tend to have overly strict and punitive consciences. They are harshly self-punitive. In fact, their drinking is, whatever else it may be, a way of punishing themselves. This is true for Larry and for Peggy. "Drinking to punish myself. That's a crazy idea." Is it? I know that you find it a strange concept, but could it be true that you drink to punish yourself?

Guilt and Drinking

Guilt is tormenting, but it doesn't necessarily lead to treating others better. People are often treated abysmally by those who are feeling guilt toward them. You need to be angry with those you have hurt, then you feel less guilty—after all, they really deserved whatever it was that you did to them. For example, if you hurt somebody you love by your drinking, then you find reasons to hate that person so you no longer need to feel guilty. Do you identify with this? It is common enough.

Now let me turn the screw a bit. Suppose you feel guilty about something you have done to yourself, drinking destructively, for instance. Then you will treat yourself especially well to compensate for the self-inflicted damage, right? Wrong! What usually happens is that you treat yourself even more abominably to justify the damage you have already inflicted on yourself. "You really deserved it, you bastard," is the unconscious thought. "In fact, you deserve yet more punishment." Additional self-punishment takes the form of drinking more. This accomplishes several things—the alcohol anesthetizes the guilt as it does all feelings and sensations and at the same time it punishes you yet more. Perhaps you know that you are doing this, but far more likely it is an unconscious process. It may surprise you that one can feel guilt about damage inflicted on the self, but this is so. You may be punishing yourself, consciously or unconsciously, as a consequence of guilt which itself is either conscious or unconscious, and which arises out of earlier self-inflicted damage.

Your guilt may be rational, that is, make some sort of sense in relation to the sin or other transgression, real or imagined, that you are atoning for; or it may be irrational, that is, totally disproportionate to the alleged offense, which may be a forbidden thought rather than an action or even a childhood wish. Do you relate to any of these? Because guilt is often unconscious, you may not be able to identify here, in spite of the fact that I have perfectly described your behavior and its underlying motivation. Drinking too much simultaneously to obliviate guilt, punish the self, and punish those toward whom one feels guilty is extremely common. Needless to say — or maybe not so needless — it is not a good reason to drink. In fact, if you are drinking to deal with your guilt — about drinking or anything else — you are drinking too much.

Larry is wracked with guilt. He not only punishes himself; he enlists his mother, his father, a medieval Jewish sage, a punitive God, and his boss to help him beat himself. Ostensibly he repudiates each of these figures and consciously he is at war with each of them. But he keeps calling them to mind as potential tormentors. They are sticks with which he beats himself. This doesn't stop him from being enraged at each and every one of them. In fact, he feels rage of murderous proportions. Murderous? Yes. Well, what happens to murderers? They are almost as bad as homosexuals and we know what Larry thinks is recommended for them. Larry feels such rage that he wants to murder; he then equates the wish with the act and feels that he *is* a murderer as well as a sodomite, and that he deserves whatever punishment is meted out to him. At the same time he rebels, but he is a failed rebel. He can't break with his family, his tradition, or his society. On the contrary, they constantly haunt him. Their values are too much a part of his mind — they have become internalized — so the war between Larry and the world around him is also a war within him. Psychologists call this kind of unresolved internal conflict a neurosis. *Larry is a neurotic drinker trying to self-medicate a neurotic conflict.* This is one that's hard to see since one or both sides of the conflict are probably outside of your awareness; that is, unconscious. Instead of being aware of this conflict, you feel anxious, depressed, guilty, or just plain awful and don't know why.

So you may drink too much in a futile attempt to manage your neurosis without even knowing that you are doing so.

On the other hand, it is easy to mistakenly blame your drinking on emotional pain, which is actually caused by drinking. So be careful here. Professional help is often needed to sort out what is cause and what is effect when it comes to emotional pain and alcohol, but for now just concentrate on the possibility that you are drinking to deal with emotional conflict and/or emotional pain. If you are, you are drinking too much regardless of whether your drinking is "caused" by your conflict or your conflict is caused by your drinking.

Larry's conflicts are a special kind centering around his being gay. Don't let the particulars of Larry's conflict stop you from recognizing that you are drinking in a futile attempt to resolve a conflict, if that is what you are doing. The nature of your conflict isn't important in assessing your drinking. What is important is that you have one and don't know a better way than drinking to handle it. Of course, if you are gay or lesbian and not comfortable with it, you will have a special identification with Larry.

Larry is bitter; he is also pathetic. His blasphemies are childish, his anger is ineffectual and largely turned against himself, he is tormented by guilt and shame, and he lives in constant fear. His homosexuality has a good deal to do with this, but it is really his attitude toward his homosexuality and his way of handling it that is the problem. That is not to say that society's attitudes toward homosexuality don't powerfully affect Larry. Of course they do. Are you gay or lesbian? If so, you have a whole set of special problems to deal with. Emotional burdens over and above those we all have. Gays are prone to alcohol abuse, to drinking too much. There are several reasons for this. One is guilt—identification with the aggressor, with all those who disapprove of homosexuality: parents, family, church, society. Another is the cruising scene, which is largely a bar scene. Anonymous sex is certainly not the only form of gay sex, but it is common among gay men, and most of us, gay or not, are uncomfortable with anonymous sex and that's where the booze comes in. A few drinks and the uncomfortable becomes comfortable. With the AIDS epidemic anonymous sex has become dangerous and homosexual men are fearful. One way, albeit not a very good one, of dealing with fear is to drink. Guilt, shame, fear, and a social life set in bars certainly makes one vulnerable to drinking too much. It did Larry. If you are gay, feel guilty about it, and make the bar scene, you are at risk for problem drinking and alcoholism. Do you identify with the fear of AIDS and with Larry's bitterness over a constricted sex life? Do you identify with Larry's drinking too much to reduce his guilt, his fear, and his bitterness? If you are drinking for any of these reasons you are drinking too much.

Spirits and Spirituality

Larry is preoccupied with religion. He obsesses about it. He can neither let it go — be a comfortable nonbeliever — nor practice his religion. His dilemma is a common one. He is enormously rageful at his religious grandfather and at Judaism. He dreams that he tells his grandfather to shove Judaism's most sacred symbol. Deep religious conflict characterizes many alcoholics. Carl Jung, the great Swiss psychologist, had something very interesting to say about this. How he came to say it is an interesting story.

One of the founders of AA, Bill Wilson, was in the last stages of alcoholism when a friend, Ebby Thacker, rang the bell. Bill, who was drinking around the clock, was delighted to see his old drinking buddy. Naturally, Bill offered Ebby a drink; unaccountably he refused it. Bill was shocked. To make matters worse, Ebby was stone cold sober. Curiosity overcame disappointment and Bill asked Ebby what the hell was going on. Ebby told Bill of his encounter with Roland H., an American businessman who had gone to Zurich to be treated by Jung. Roland was in a mid-life crisis, but his basic problem was booze. He was analyzed by Jung and left Zurich convinced that he understood himself, his conflicts, and his motives so well that he would never get drunk again. A short time later he arrived back on Jung's doorstep in worse shape than ever. Jung told him that there was no hope. He would either drink himself to death or die in a sanatorium. Roland begged the renowned doctor for help. Jung just puffed on his pipe and shook his head sadly. Finally he relented and told Roland that there was one way that he might be saved from destruction by alcohol. If he were to have a spiritual awakening, he would be freed from his obsession with alcohol. What was needed was a profound psychological reorganization, which could only come about through some sort of a conversion experience, a virtual rebirth. It would take the emotional intensity engendered by such an experience to bring about the psychological reorganization that was required for recovery. That was Jung's view.

Roland left Zurich in despair. Some months later Roland attended a meeting of the Oxford Movement, a sort of upper-class revival movement named for the university where it began. During the meeting Roland had his spiritual awakening. He joined the Oxford Movement and did not drink again. Upon his return to New York he ran into Ebby, who was drunk as usual, and told him his story. Ebby was touched by Roland's peacefulness and serenity. He, too, joined the Oxford Movement and became sober. Shortly thereafter, he decided to visit his oldest drinking buddy, Bill Wilson, and tell him how he had achieved sobriety. Bill had hit bottom, the state of despair that often precedes recovery from alcoholism. He admitted himself to a private drying-out hospital, where he had been many times before. This time it was different. While in the hospital, Bill had a conversion experience of his own. He never drank again and went on to found Alcoholics Anonymous. Ebby Thacker didn't make it, he died of alcoholism.

Many years later Wilson wrote to Carl Jung and told him about his recovery and its indirect connection with Jung. Jung wrote back that alcoholism was an attempt to reach spiritual goals through the use of spirits. "You see, 'alcohol' in Latin is *spiritus,* and you use the same word for the highest religious experience as well as for the most depraving poison. The helpful formula therefore is: *spiritus contra spiritum*" (1973, p. 623). The spiritual against the spirits.

I believe that Jung is onto something here. Many people who have trouble with alcohol are indeed looking for some sort of answer in the bottle. Their drinking is a kind spiritual quest. Because alcohol blurs psychic boundaries, it can promote feelings of connectedness, indeed, of merger, with both other people and with the ultimate nature of things—Nature, God, the Life Force, or what have you. Drinking to feel united with people or with the divine is called integrative drinking. One might say that alcohol enables the mystical. It is for this reason that alcohol plays a part in so much religious ritual. I don't wish to romanticize a fatal disease, but it is true that people sometimes seek the same sort of solace and relationship with the omnipotent in alcohol as they do in religious experience. Rationalists and those who furiously reject established religions are particularly prone to covertly try to satisfy the very same needs people satisfy through religion by the consumption of alcohol. Are you one of those people? Have you sought the spiritual in spirits? If so, you may be looking in the wrong place and drinking more because you can't find what you are seeking in the bottle. This is a far from uncommon route to drinking too much. Do you drink too much for these reasons? Since heavy drinking impoverishes emotionally *and* spiritually, the more you drink the more spiritually empty you become and the more alcohol you have to consume in your futile quest for spiritual fulfillment. This is yet another vicious cycle associated with drinking. Are you caught up in this one?

To return to Larry. Larry has a love-hate relationship with his religion. He can neither renounce it nor enjoy it. His very hatred constitutes a bond that he cannot sever. Many problem drinkers are in a similar bind. They are at war with a punitive God. More Catholics than Jews have this conflict, but that doesn't matter. The inner experience is the same. As Buck Mulligan says of Stephen Daedalus in James Joyce's novel *Ulysses,* these drinkers "have the Jesuitical streak injected backwards" (1914, p. 7). Alcohol makes you high—it transports you out of yourself, as does intense religious experience. Larry uses alcohol to repudiate a religious identity— "*Shicker iz a goy,*" drunks are gentiles—and simultaneously as a religious equivalent, a form of spiritual fulfillment. Drinking is the only fulfilling experience he has left and it is rapidly failing for him. Do you drink to repudiate an identity, to rebel, or to mock the values of your parents, of your religion, or of society? Larry does all of this. It doesn't bring him any happiness.

There are many aspects of Larry's drinking too much that you may identify with: his bitterness and futile attempt to assuage it with alcohol; his unsuccessful rebellion enacted in his drinking that simultaneously punishes him for that rebellion; his use of alcohol as a sexual substitute now that AIDS has radically restricted his sex life; his use of alcohol to quell guilt and shame; his use of alcohol to resolve a neurotic conflict; and his use of alcohol to still a fear that will not stay quiet. Do you identify with any or all of this? Larry drinks for about every reason except to relax and have a good time now and then as normal drinkers do. Is that true for you also?

I want to point our yet another aspect of Larry's drinking and the way he thinks about it, namely, that he uses his membership in a minority group not known for alcoholism in the service of denial. This is all too easy to do. "I don't drink too much, at least not in an alcoholic way, because I am Chinese, a woman, too young, from a good family, too old, Jewish, small-town, Italian, well educated, left-handed, or what have you." Do you identify with this sort of rationalization? Do you protect your drinking this way? If you do, that in itself is pretty good evidence that you are drinking too much. Otherwise why would you need to tell yourself that Jews, Chinese, or Italians aren't problem drinkers?

ROSE, A SUICIDE RISK

Rose is self-deluded. Her despair is bottomless, yet she denies it, just as she denies that she drinks too much.

> Why is it that in moments of quiet contemplation my thoughts turn with a certain inevitability to the consumption of spirits either in the contemplation of the not-to-be-long-delayed consumption thereof, or to obsessional rumination over the frequency and quantity of that consumption and its effects on my productivity and sense of well-being? There can be no real question but that which has been fermented inspires and vivifies me. It adds a certain excitement to my life and what, after all,

can be the harm in an afternoon glass of what my colleagues and I have taken to denoting "faculty sherry"? The English department practically runs on sherry. After all, what is poetry other than intoxication? Intoxication of the spirit — chills running down my back as Blake's lines run through my head. A sip or so of wine intensifies that. There can be no question of Dionysian abandon in my case. In fact, the penultimate occurrence of a somewhat excessive consumption was on the occasion of my presentation of my paper "Covert Eroticism in Beowulf with Particular Reference to the Relation between Grendel and His Mother." Odd that I should have been nervous at that meeting. I am, after all, a professional orator. I usually drink only wine at the Language Association meetings; however, at this the most recent occurrence of, perhaps I do have to so admit, overdrinking, martinis played their role. Ah, martinis — divine magic, so slightly green reflected clarity, penetrating the gleaming stemware. Yet, at the same time so much more scintillating than sherry or claret, or the dry, dry Mosel I so covet — covet? Yes, I must admit covet — during languorous summer afternoons. In winter there is the martini at lunch in the Faculty Club, the afternoon sherry, the martini before dinner, the red or white with dinner, and the brandy postprandially. I have to concede a certain constancy in my consumption, but in total it is not so very much. Is not so much too much? I do not believe so. Paper after paper written in the warm afterglow of sips and scents and through an almost subliminal fascination with glass and ice, tray and shaker. It is part of my life-style, which is, after all, sedate, academic, productive, satisfying. Lonely though. There have been a few, but never one, but love is an experience that I have not really needed and so, except in moments of slightly tipsy melancholy, I have not regretted not having it.

I must concede that things have changed. My

productivity wanes, my moments of melancholy intensify and deliquesce through my already damp soul and, in short, I am no longer happy. Do I drink a bit more to recover my former state of inner peace? Or do I drink in an attempt to transcend known states and discover an as yet undiscovered bliss? Or is my increased consumption an attempt to compensate for a diminution in the intensity of my life? I do not know. Perhaps happiness is over for me. Whichever of these contingencies, if any, is in fact the case, dinner without wine is not civilized and I am, whatever else I may be, civilized. So I pour another sherry and turn my thoughts outward to my lecture on the influence of Anglo-Saxon poetry on the romantics.

Rose is a bullshit artist. Her self-deception is so total that it endangers her life. Her life is a secret from herself. She drinks around the clock, has long since ceased to be productive, and is increasingly melancholy — depressed. She can rationalize anything in service of her denial. "Faculty sherry," which she seems to think is in some miraculous way different from ordinary sherry, is certainly harmless. Martinis could be part of the problem, but they are practically works of art, so there can't be anything wrong there, the English department runs on alcohol, and it isn't civilized to have dinner without wine. What a con job. So easy for us to see, but not for her. Is it possible that you are conning yourself in this way? Do you identify with Rose? With her lugubriousness, with her blindness, with her desperate attempt to shore up her self-esteem with pretensions and pomposity? There are many styles of doing this. Yours may not be an academic one, but remember, identify with the *feelings,* don't compare. Do you use your intelligence against yourself as Rose does?

Rose truly believes that her drinking starting at lunch and ending with her passing out after dinner is not heavy, although she does have some instantly repudiated doubts. People who drink far too much commonly deny it and assume that everybody drinks more or less as they do. They need to believe this. Could you be radically miscalculating how much normal drinkers drink? Could your consumption be vast while you believe it to be moderate? Do you think Rose drinks too much? If so, is it possible that you too are in denial?

Rose is what psychiatrists call a schizoid personality. That means that she is so fragile and so afraid of people that she can't let them get close to her. She copes with this in two ways, one adaptive and one self-destructive. Her relationship to literature, which in her early years was imaginative and insightful, is the adaptive one, and her relationship to alcohol is the self-destructive one. You may not be a people person and you may feel guilty about it. That may simply be your temperament or you may have had such unsatisfying early childhood relationships that closeness is just too scary. As long as it isn't too extreme, being a loner can be all right—it depends what you do with it. If being a loner makes you unhappy, psychotherapy can help, and there can be advantages in being a loner. Creativity is, after all, a lonely business. Many loners turn to alcohol for warmth and closeness. Are you one of them? Turning to alcohol for warmth and closeness is a mistake, although a very understandable one. Alcohol is a very unreliable friend, one not worthy of your devotion. John Barleycorn turns on his friends. If you are drinking, like Rose, as a form of substitute closeness, you are drinking too much.

If you are isolated, essentially alone, and drinking very heavily, you are at risk for suicide. You are depressed and don't know it. Just like child abuse and spouse abuse, suicide is highly correlated with problem drinking and alcoholism.

Rose is tragic. A brilliant woman who has become vain, pretentious, and empty with the progressive inner impoverishment that inevitably occurs as an alcoholic career progresses. She has no meaningful human relationships; she must drink to give papers, whose quality is far below what she is capable of; her teaching, once enlivened by her passion for literature, now limps along; and she is sitting on an abyss of despair. Rose is the kind of person who is found dead one day to the shocked amazement of colleagues, who say, "How could she have done it—I never knew she was so unhappy. The last few years she drank too much, but nobody thought very much about it—she was so witty and creative. I guess nobody was close to her, but everybody liked her. There will be a lot of tears at the memorial service."

HANK, A GUY WHO JUST CAN'T DRINK "NORMALLY"

Hank is preprogrammed to self-destruct when he drinks. He knows this, but he can't stop trying to drink like everyone else. He isn't having much success in that endeavor.

> What happened last night? I took the crew out for drinks and that's as far as I can take it. How did I get this black eye? The first time I got high, way back in tenth grade, it was a disaster. Wrecked Jim's house and his parents went bananas. I'm not a kid anymore. I can't get away with this shit. Why? Why can't I drink like other people? I'm general manager on a million-dollar construction project and I act like a drunken sailor. Nothing like this ever happens when I don't drink. I like my life. I'm good at what I do. You can't work construction without drinking. Especially if you're the boss. The men expect you to set them up. But they don't expect you to brawl. That's for kids. It's outrageous. Everybody can drink but me. Car accidents, fights, in jail twice, lost a couple of jobs and I don't know how many girls. I didn't have a drink for two months and then last night I did it again. Am I nuts? I can just see this crew if they thought I was seeing a shrink.
>
> Dad had the same problem, but he stopped when he was young. I hardly remember him drinking. But he was in the clothing business. Who cares if a shopkeeper drinks or not? Nobody. It's not like that for me. My crew expects it. What the hell am I supposed to do, put soda pop in my beer bottle? . . . I wonder who I hit? This can't go on. I

guess I don't have to drink until the Christmas party. That gives me six weeks to cool out. No reason I can't nurse a beer all night. Nobody will notice. Figured it out, didn't I? No different from a problem on the site, all I have to do is think it out. Hell-raising makes sense for a kid; it doesn't for a thirty-five-year-old. It's not fun anymore. I wonder if it ever was. Sometimes I wonder if I go crazy because I'm a pussycat sober. Some pussycat, I can put a guy through the wall cold sober, so that's not it. . . . I'm smarter than I thought. I doped it out. All I have to do is nurse the same drink all night. I can't wait for that Christmas party. I'll show them that I can drink like a gentleman.

Hank drinks too much because he has the type of alcoholism that is most preprogrammed. He is wired to self-destruct if he drinks, yet drinking is irresistibly attractive to him. He reacts to alcohol differently than other people. It does strange things to him. Hank's problem lies in his genes. He handles alcohol differently from normal drinkers and problem drinkers whose problem drinking isn't biologically based. Of all the drinkers whose thoughts we have eavesdropped on, Hank's drinking too much is the most biologically determined. He suffers from male-limited susceptibility to alcoholism. There is something about his liver or his nervous system or both that does something different with alcohol. Most male-limited susceptibles are in much worse shape than Hank. They quickly get into serious difficulty, often with the law, and have an awful time getting out of it. Their prognosis is not good. Hank's way of reacting to alcohol used to be called *pathological intoxication,* which is an accurate description of what happens to him when he drinks. Do you identify with Hank's story and the troubles that his drinking lands him in?

Hank is a *periodic drinker.* Unlike Warren, Max, Vicky, and Rose, Hank is not a daily drinker. In fact, considerable periods of time elapse between his benders. Unfortunately, it doesn't matter how long the gaps between his drinking episodes are, try as he will,

Hank can't drink like other people. Oh, he may on occasion, but usually it's the same shit over again—blackouts, fights, God knows what.

Do you share Hank's drinking pattern? Do you identify with him? What characterizes Hank's pattern? Its most salient feature is *trouble with alcohol from the start*. Hank first drank in tenth grade and went on a rampage. Your experience doesn't have to have been so extreme for you to have Hank's problem, but some sort of going wild, of losing control, must have characterized your early drinking. If you, like Hank, are a male-limited susceptible, you went well beyond the usual teenage hell-raising. Maybe not every time, but all too frequently. Pay special attention to fights, destructiveness, drunk driving, and memory lapses. If these characterized your early drinking, and it hasn't gotten much better, you are suffering from the most biological of alcoholisms. Adolescent drinkers raise all sorts of hell, but they stop behaving that way by their mid-twenties. If you did not, that is ominous.

This business of going out of control is the crux of the matter. Everybody drinks to loosen control, to disinhibit, but they don't drink to lose control totally. Emil Jellinek (1960), who established the disease concept of alcoholism, cited loss of control as the single most significant defining characteristic of what he called *gamma alcoholism*. Gamma alcoholism is chronic and progressive. Loss of control means that the drinker who has lost control of his drinking cannot predict what will happen once he picks up a drink. Social drinkers sometimes drink to get drunk and that is a choice; gamma alcoholics try not to get drunk and get drunk anyway—that is not a choice. Have you lost control of your drinking in this sense of not being able to predict your behavior when you drink? If you have, you are drinking too much.

Hank is definitely drinking alcoholically. He would not accept this diagnosis, but almost anybody, professional or nonprofessional, would conclude that there is something radically wrong with Hank's drinking. Most would characterize what's wrong as alcoholism. I would characterize it as episodic—periodic, male-limited susceptible alcoholism. Jellinek labeled episodic drinking to oblivion *epsilon alcoholism,* to distinguish such drinking from the more constant and progressively deteriorating drinking characteristic of gamma alcoholism. Classification schemes are abstractions; people don't neatly fit into pigeonholes. For instance, Hank has some Jellinek epsilon traits as well as the Cloninger biological susceptibility. Classification schemes help sort out the very complex phenomenon of drinking too much, but none of them is definitive or universally accepted. I brought Jellinek and his scheme in to emphasize the loss-of-control issue. For your purpose, determining if you are drinking too much, two points are important: (1) that loss of control, early or late, is a sign of something very seriously wrong with your drinking, and (2) that drinking episodically or periodically rather than continuously is perfectly consistent with drinking alcoholically. Episodic drinking to drunkenness, especially if it involves loss of control, is very serious. It always means that you are drinking too much.

Hank has tried, and continues to try, to control his drinking. He tries to control the frequency of his drinking, the speed of his drinking, what he drinks, and the amount of his drinking. I predict that he will not succeed. If you have a similar drinking history you will not either. Most people learn to drink more or less well, so a common problem-drinking pattern is to have early trouble with alcohol, learn to handle it, and then to lose control again. Hank has spent his life trying to drink well, but he simply cannot. He does not have the right neurochemistry to do so. Most male-limited susceptibles quickly move from periodic drinking to daily drinking, thereby becoming gamma alcoholics. Hank is an exception having so far avoided the progression to daily drinking. Hank is obviously an exceptionally capable and determined person who is risking everything he has achieved by continuing to drink. If you are such an exception — one who has had severe trouble with alcohol, still has it, but who puts some sort of controls on drinking that allow worldly success — you are putting everything you have in jeopardy. You are drinking too much if you drink at all.

Hank doesn't so much want to drink, as to not *not* be able to drink. Not to be able to drink would be a terrible blow to his pride. "Real men" drink. He rationalizes this. His profession requires it; it is part of his public image; his father could stop because he did a different type of work. Hank is defiant. "I'll show them. . . ." Do you identify with Hank's not wanting not to be able to drink? Hank wants to and doesn't want to drink. "I can't wait for the Christmas party." Hank even prefers being crazy to being alcoholic, although he doesn't like that idea either. Many drinkers prefer to believe that they are crazy rather than consider that they might be drinking alcoholically. Are you one of them? If you are, you can't tell whether or not you're crazy unless you stop drinking. You don't know what's underneath your booze-induced irrationality. The chances are excellent that you aren't crazy.

Hank also wonders if he isn't too passive, a pussycat when sober, and speculates that he drinks to vent his rage. Well, he may be too passive, although I doubt it, but passive or not, he isn't one of those people who drinks to vent his rage. What happens with Hank is that the alcohol causes his fury and mediates his unrestrained expression of it. Hank is something of a tough guy sober or drunk, but he is only violent when he's drunk. Hank's is a retrospective justification. He is trying to find a *psychological* reason why he gets in trouble when he drinks and there isn't any. The real problem is *biological*. Hank doesn't even know if he is angry. He may or may not be, but that is beside the point. Even Hank doesn't believe the justification he spins for himself. Many people try to rationalize or justify their drinking in just this way. "I can't express myself sober." . . . "I can't express my rage without drinking" are some of the rationalizations they use. Sometimes something very strange then happens: people stop drinking, and lo and behold they have very little rage to express. Their rage was caused by their drinking. You must be asking, "Dr. Levin, doesn't that contradict what you said about repressing anger?" No, it doesn't. The world, or at least that aspect of it involving alcohol, is very complex and as I noted, seemingly paradoxical There are people who drink because they can't express anger in any other way, and there are people like Hank who are angry because they drink, and there are people for whom it works both ways. If you identify with Hank's explosive rage while under the influence, carefully consider whether your rage is engendered by your drinking—by alcohol itself. Over and above rage that comes from the trouble your drinking brings upon you, and over and above the rage that is your self-hatred projected outward, there may be something biochemical in your reaction to alcohol that makes you crazily angry like Hank. Then you lash out and get in fights or do something else you regret.

CAUSES OF BIOLOGICALLY MEDIATED ALCOHOLISM

Hank has a type of biologically mediated alcoholism. What precisely is biologically wrong and how is it genetically transmitted? Scientists don't have exact answers, but they have discovered some intriguing things. Male-limited susceptible alcoholics have abnormally low levels of the enzyme monoamine oxidase. This enzyme plays a vital role in the nervous system as it is involved in the maintenance of the proper balance of neurotransmitters. Even more interesting is the fact that their children have the same deficiency. It is also known that young males with family histories of biological alcoholism show certain cognitive deficiencies on psychological tests and that their performance improves with a few drinks. That makes drinking highly attractive to them. These children of alcoholics also suffer from *stimulus augmentation* — the tendency to experience stimuli in an exaggerated and overly intense way. Stimulus augmentors experience the world as threatening. Alcohol improves things for them. A few drinks reduces stimulus augmentation, again making drinking a highly attractive activity.

There is also something called *static ataxia,* the tendency of the body to sway when standing still. Moderate doses of alcohol reduce body sway in the male children of some alcoholics; it increases it in "normals." This suggests that alcohol does something different to some alcoholics, the ones who have a genetically transmitted disorder, than it does to normal drinkers. Although environmental factors may play a role in causing cognitive problems, the static ataxia and stimulus augmentation found in these alcoholics and their children researchers believe to be predominantly genetic phenomena and a manifestation of vulnerability to alcoholism.

The liver enzyme alcohol dehydrogenase (ADH), which metabolizes alcohol, has variations in its molecular form. These variant forms may alter the way in which alcohol is metabolized, thereby playing a role in the genetic susceptibility to alcoholism. Atypical forms of ADH may be caused by prolonged, heavy drinking, but scientists believe that some of those who have genetically transmitted alcoholism start life with "odd" ADH.

Finally, abnormalities of the electrical pattern of the brain have been found in the nonalcoholic relatives of alcoholics, particularly in their children. Drinking lessens these abnormalities, making drinking highly attractive, which puts these children at risk for alcoholism.

If you drink like Hank and have similar problems when you drink, it is highly probable that you are biologically prewired to self-destruct if you continue to drink. This is true regardless of whether you are a daily or an episodic drinker. That's a frightening thought, but for now just look and see if you identify with Hank. In the succeeding chapters I will tell you how to cope with your disability.

As you have seen, all kinds of people drink too much. You have met anxious, depressed, angry, withdrawn, hell-raising, and gregarious drinkers. Each of them drinks too much in his or her own unique way. I have invited you to identify with them and to see if anything about your drinking or the motivation for it is like theirs. Although problem drinking must be self-diagnosed, the perceptions and reactions of others are ingredients in a self-diagnosis. So is scientific knowledge. That is why I analyzed each of our drinkers' drinking from an outside, objective standpoint as well as presenting each drinkers' inward, subjective experience. You can use both to decide if you drink too much. The real hindrance to accurate self-diagnosis of problem drinking is fear—fear that such a diagnosis means that you are weak, evil, degenerate, not a man, a debased woman, a sinner, or any of a thousand other horrid things. Additionally, there is the fear that you will lose a friend, alcohol, if you admit that you are drinking too much.

Many drinkers get to the point where they feel that they can't live with the stuff, but they can't live without it either. It is quite possible to literally believe that you can't live without alcohol. You may not believe that intellectually, yet believe it emotionally. That kind of fear—the fear that you won't be able to make it without the sauce—makes clearly and calmly looking at yourself and your drinking extraordinarily difficult, but it is possible. Try not to worry about shame, about what other people will think, or about changing or stopping your drinking. You don't *have to do* anything in particular if you discover that you are drinking too much. You will simply know something very worth knowing about yourself. So try to peek around your fear, be as detached and as scientific as possible, and see if you can discover whether or not you drink too much.

I am going to close this chapter by asking you to take the Michigan Alcoholism Screening Test (see Table 2-2) and the short, simple, but highly revealing questionnaire developed by Alcoholics Anonymous (Table 2-3). Your scores on them and on the Johns Hopkins scale you filled out at the beginning of the chapter will give you additional data on which to base your decision on whether or not you drink too much. You might also take into account the presence or absence of other objective signs of drinking too much. These include: Monday morning absences, depression that has no apparent cause and does not improve with treatment, otherwise unexplained social withdrawal, deterioration in social or vocational functioning, and the onset of irrational fears.

Table 2-2
Michigan Alcoholism Screening Test (MAST)

Points

0.	Do you enjoy a drink now and then?	Yes ____ No ____
(2) 1.	Do you feel you are a normal drinker? (By normal we mean you drink less than or as much as most people)	Yes ____ No ____
(2) 2.	Have you ever awakened the morning after some drinking the night before and found that you could not remember a part of the evening?	Yes ____ No ____

Table 2-2 (continued)

(1)	3. Does your wife, husband, a parent or other relative ever worry or complain about your drinking?	Yes ____	No ____
(2)	4. Can you stop drinking without a struggle after one or two drinks?*	Yes ____	No ____
(1)	5. Do you feel guilty about your drinking?	Yes ____	No ____
(2)	6. Do friends or relatives think you are a normal drinker?	Yes ____	No ____
(2)	7. Are you able to stop drinking when you want to?	Yes ____	No ____
(5)	8. Have you ever attended a meeting of Alcoholics Anonymous (AA)?	Yes ____	No ____
(1)	9. Have you gotten into physical fights when drinking?	Yes ____	No ____
(2)	10. Has drinking ever created problems between you and your wife, husband, a parent, or other relative?	Yes ____	No ____
(2)	11. Has your wife, husband (or other family members) ever gone to anyone for help about your drinking?	Yes ____	No ____
(2)	12. Have you ever lost friends because of your drinking?	Yes ____	No ____
(2)	13. Have you ever gotten into trouble at work because of drinking?	Yes ____	No ____
(2)	14. Have you ever lost a job because of drinking?	Yes ____	No ____
(2)	15. Have you ever neglected your obligations, your family, or your work for two or more days in a row because you were drinking?	Yes ____	No ____
(1)	16. Do you drink before noon fairly often?	Yes ____	No ____
(2)	17. Have you ever been told you have liver trouble? Cirrhosis?	Yes ____	No ____
(2)	18. After heavy drinking, have you ever had Delirium Tremens (DTs) or severe shaking, or heard voices, or seen things that really weren't there?**	Yes ____	No ____
(5)	19. Have you ever gone to anyone for help about your drinking?	Yes ____	No ____

Table 2-2 (continued)

(5) 20. Have you ever been in a hospital because of Yes ____ No ____
drinking?

(2) 21. Have you ever been a patient in a psychiatric Yes ____ No ____
hospital or a psychiatric ward of a general
hospital where drinking was part of the
problem that resulted in hospitalization?

(2) 22. Have you ever been seen at a psychiatric or Yes ____ No ____
mental health clinic or gone to any doctor,
social worker, or clergyman for help with any
emotional problem, where drinking was part
of the problem?

(2) 23. Have you ever been arrested for drunk Yes ____ No ____
driving, driving while intoxicated, or driving
under the influence of alcoholic beverage?

(2) 24. Have you ever been arrested, or taken into Yes ____ No ____
custody, even for a few hours because of
other drunk behavior?***
If YES, how many times? _____

SCORING

    * Alcoholic response is negative
    ** 5 points for the DTs
   *** 2 points for EACH arrest

5 points or more:	Alcoholism
4 points:	Suggestive of Alcoholism
3 points or less:	Subject is not Alcoholic

Table 2-3
Alcoholics Anonymous' Twelve Questions

1. Have you ever decided to stop drinking for a week or so, but only
   lasted for a couple of days? Yes ____ No ____
2. Do you wish people would mind their own business about your
   drinking—stop telling you what to do? Yes ____ No ____

Table 2–3 (continued)

3. Have you ever switched from one kind of drink to another in the hope that this would keep you from getting drunk? Yes ____ No ____
4. Have you ever had an eye-opener upon awakening during the past year? Yes ____ No ____
5. Do you envy people who can drink without getting into trouble? Yes ____ No ____
6. Have you had problems connected with your drinking during the past year? Yes ____ No ____
7. Has your drinking caused trouble at home? Yes ____ No ____
8. Do you ever try to get "extra" drinks at a party because you do not get enough? Yes ____ No ____
9. Do you tell yourself you can stop drinking any time you want to, even though you keep getting drunk when you don't mean to? Yes ____ No ____
10. Have you missed days of work or school because of drinking? Yes ____ No ____
11. Do you have "blackouts"? Yes ____ No ____
12. Have you ever felt that your life would be better if you did not drink? Yes ____ No ____

If you answered YES to four or more questions, you are probably in trouble with alcohol.

The questions from *Is AA for you?* are reprinted with permission. Use of this material does not imply affiliation with AA.

CHAPTER 3

More about Alcohol and Other Drugs

People drink for pleasure. At least that's what they say. They also drink because it's expected, but it's enjoyment that primarily motivates drinking. The pleasures of drinking are manifold: the sensual pleasures of taste and smell, flavor and bouquet; the ambience, the elegance of the stemware, and the rarity of the vintage; the camaraderie of the tavern or the chic company of the country club. Some drinkers derive pleasure from belonging; drinking is part of a way of life to which they aspire. Others drink without really knowing why; drinking is just part of their lives. Taste, smell, texture, color, sociability, snob appeal, and life-style all play their role, but by far the most potent source of pleasure in drinking comes from the *effect* alcohol has on the mood of people who drink it. It is the feelings induced by alcohol which are its ultimate allure.

Beverage alcohol, whatever its form, contains *ethyl alcohol,* also known as *ethanol.* Ethyl alcohol is the active ingredient in wine, beer, rye, scotch, bourbon, gin, vodka, saki, and brandy. Ethyl alcohol is a chemical and it is a drug. It is produced by fermentation, a natural process in which sugar is converted by the action of yeast into ethyl alcohol and carbon dioxide. Wine is produced by fermenting grapes, beer by fermenting malt and barley, bourbon by fermenting corn, vodka by fermenting potatoes, and saki by fermenting rice. Just about everything fermentable has been used to produce alcohol. After fermentation, beverage alcohol is aged. The alcohol you drink contains water, ethyl alcohol, colorings and flavorings, by-products of fermentation called congeners, and sometimes bubbles of carbon dioxide. Varying amounts of sugar make it more or less "dry." The fermented product may be *distilled* to increase its strength. Distillation is a process that removes water and concentrates the alcohol. Rye, scotch, and gin are distilled liquors.

WHAT IS ALCOHOL?

Ethyl alcohol is an organic compound. Organic compounds are chemicals that contain carbon. Each molecule of ethyl alcohol also contains hydrogen and oxygen. There are many alcohols; they vary in the number of carbon atoms they contain. The alcohol you drink, ethyl alcohol, has two carbon atoms. Methyl alcohol, the poison in the "bad hootch" of prohibition, has one carbon. The ethyl alcohol molecule has been called a dirty little molecule because it is small and gets into all of your cells easily. That is one reason it is so toxic. It is perfectly soluble in water and fat which makes it even easier for alcohol to get around in your body.

Although you don't think of it that way, alcohol is a drug, an extremely potent one. Before alcohol the chemical can become alcohol the drug, it has to get inside your body and into your cells, particularly your brain cells.

Although alcohol can be inhaled, injected into a vein, and someone has probably frozen it for use as a suppository, it is almost always drunk. It is usually poured from the bottle into a glass, although if you are a heavy drinker, you might skip this step. When you swallow it, your drink passes through your lips, enters your mouth, stimulates your taste buds and olfactory receptors, passes through your pharynx (back of your mouth), and goes down your gullet (esophagus) into your stomach. As it does so, you taste and smell it. You experience the sensation of the drink going down. If it is strong enough, there is a burning sensation. Perhaps you like this. Alcohol is an irritant and irritates all the tissues it passes over. Because it does, heavy drinkers risk disease of the lips, tongue, mouth, pharynx, and esophagus. If you are a heavy drinker and a heavy smoker, your risk is compounded. Prolonged heavy drinking can cause cancer of these organs.

In large doses alcohol is a poison. It can damage the body in many ways. As I discuss the way alcohol gives you pleasure, I am also going to point out the deleterious effects of alcohol on various organs. It is *not* my intention to make every sip of wine or glass of beer the occasion for an anxiety attack. On the contrary, it is my belief that alcohol used wisely is a harmless source of pleasure. However, if you drink the stuff, it makes sense to know what alcohol can do to you that you don't want it to.

Nothing happens to the alcohol on its way to the stomach. Once there, however, it is quickly absorbed into your bloodstream. Alcohol requires no digestion; your body accepts it just as it is. Because the alcohol molecule is small as molecules go, it readily passes through your stomach lining into your "system." How quickly it does so depends on how much food you have in your stomach. Drinking with a meal hits you much more slowly and gently than belting it down on an empty stomach. Twenty percent of the alcohol you drink is absorbed from your stomach; the rest gets sopped up in your small intestine. Your stomach is sensitive to alcohol and stomach upsets are notorious accompaniments of hangovers. Heavy drinkers increase their risk of gastritis, ulcers, and stomach cancer.

Once those small molecules of ethyl alcohol are in your bloodstream, they travel to every organ and tissue in your body. Their smallness and solubility in water and fat give them ready access to the cells which comprise those organs and tissues. Thus, alcohol affects every cell in your body, but the primary effect of alcohol, the drug, is on your nervous system.

What Makes You High?

It is the effect of alcohol on your nervous system that makes you high. The nervous system is made up of units called neurons. Neurons are cells specialized to transmit information. They do this by a complex electrochemical process. During this process they "fire"—emit a bleep. The pattern and frequency of these bleeps encodes information, enabling your nervous system to serve as your body's communication system.

Neurons don't quite touch each other; they are separated by a gap, or *synapse*. Information is conveyed across the synapse by chemicals called neurotransmitters. The nervous system is made up of wires (neurons) and juices (neurotransmitters). The wires are not exactly like the wires in your home because they don't passively transmit, rather they play an active role by firing. Alcohol slows down the firing of neurons; it also interferes with the release of neurotransmitters. In short, alcohol depresses the functioning of both the wires and the juices. Although it does this to all nerves, alcohol's most powerful effect is on the brain. Because it depresses the brain function, pharmacologically alcohol is classified as a *central nervous system depressant*. It is for this ability to depress the function of the brain that people drink it. Strange, isn't it, that a depressant is so associated with pleasure? How can this be?

The nervous system is extremely complex, containing both up (excitatory) and down (inhibitory) circuits. The job of inhibitory circuits is to "keep the lid on things." They are dampers. Alcohol affects "down" circuits at lower doses than it does "up" circuits. Inhibiting (depressing) an inhibitor is excitatory. The cerebral cortex, the part of the brain responsible for "control," is inhibitory and this is the part of the brain first affected by alcohol. When you drink, alcohol first depresses inhibitors and you experience disinhibition and mild euphoria. As you drink more and the dose increases, there is a progressive depression of all of your brain circuits. Your entire nervous system starts to shut down and this is what makes you high.

I said that alcohol is a central nervous system depressant, and it is, but I could equally well have said that it is a *sedative-hypnotic*.

Sedatives sedate, while hypnotics put you to sleep. The family of sedative-hypnotic drugs includes barbiturates (downers), minor tranquilizers such as Valium and Librium, Quaaludes, and general anesthetics. Alcohol is the oldest tranquilizer, although it is not a very good one.

The various sedative-hypnotic drugs work differently, but their effect is the same—they all relax, sedate, and finally produce sleep. Paradoxically, sleep disturbances are extremely common in heavy drinkers because drug-induced sleep is not the same as natural sleep. If you stop drinking, you may have trouble sleeping until your body readjusts.

The initial effect of sedative-hypnotics is relief from anxiety, followed by disinhibition, sedation, hypnosis (sleep), general anesthesia, coma, and death. Death? Yes, if you drink enough, the respiratory centers of the brain shut down and so do you. Another way to look at the effect of progressively higher doses of alcohol is expressed in this rubric: Jocose, Bellicose, Lachrymose, Comatose!

Relief from anxiety, disinhibition, devil-may-care, kick-up-your-heels-euphoria is what you seek when you drink. Sometimes you find it and sometimes you don't. The superego (Freud's term for the conscience) has been described as that part of the mind which is soluble in alcohol. When you drink, the restraints of the superego disappear and guilt-induced anxiety vanishes. No wonder alcohol is so popular in our guilt-ridden culture. A few moments of devil-may-care, kick-up-your-heels abandon is precious to most of us. Many folks can't enjoy sex, get angry, or raise hell without a few drinks. Are you one of them? Whatever overrestraints you suffer are momentarily shunted aside when you sip wine, drink beer, or savor a cocktail. Add a magical setting, compelling ritual, and boon companions, and the allure of drink is irresistible.

People drink for both the exciting (disinhibiting) and the sedative effects of alcohol. They like the up and they like the relaxation. Which is more important to you? Normal drinkers don't drink to pass out. Nor do they drink to slur or stagger, or vomit, or fall down. You probably don't either. These things happen because the effects of alcohol are dose-related and the difference between mild euphoria and drunken oblivion is only a few drinks. As you drink more, your motor coordination, your judgment, your ability to think clearly, and your emotional state all deteriorate.

Alcohol Is Addictive

Alcohol is both a central nervous system depressant and a sedative-hypnotic; it is also an *addictive drug*. That may surprise you — drug addicts are people who shoot heroin or smoke crack in dark hallways, aren't they? Not necessarily. By far the most prevalent addiction in America is addiction to alcohol. When I say that alcohol is an addictive drug, I mean two things: (1) Alcohol builds tolerance, that is, you become tolerant to the effects of alcohol; and (2) there is a withdrawal when you stop drinking. By tolerance, I mean that it takes more to get the same effect. That nice warm relaxed feeling that used to come with the first Old Fashioned now comes with the third. This happens for two reasons: neurons accommodate to alcohol and it takes a higher concentration of alcohol to slow them down, and the liver metabolizes (burns up) alcohol more rapidly. Social drinkers get used to drinking and learn to hold their liquor, but they don't build much tolerance. Not so for heavy drinkers. Withdrawal isn't a problem for social drinkers either, although a severe hangover is partly a withdrawal symptom.

When you stop drinking, you stop depressing the nervous system. There is a rebound effect and the nervous system becomes hyperactive. It is as though you pushed down a jack-in-the-box and then released it. That's why you feel shaky the morning after. Withdrawal can be serious, even life-threatening, if you drink heavily for a prolonged period and suddenly stop. Psychological dependency, needing a drink to do or feel whatever, precedes physiological dependency. It usually takes a long time to become physically addicted to alcohol, but it is easy to become psychologically habituated to it. Alcohol is insidious. Many a social drinker without serious emotional problems has been hooked without suspecting what was happening to him or her.

BODILY DAMAGE ASSOCIATED WITH HEAVY DRINKING

In high doses, especially if it is consumed over a long time span, alcohol is a poison. Because its small molecules get everywhere and, unlike opiates, don't have special receptor sites to hold on to them, alcohol can raise havoc with any organ in your body. Alcohol's favorite targets are the nervous system, the liver, and the heart.

The Nervous System

Prolonged heavy drinking damages the nervous system in manifold ways. Neurons are destroyed by the direct toxicity of alcohol, and heavy drinking causes clumping (agglutination) of red blood cells in the capillaries of the brain, causing microstrokes. Over time, these twin actions can do tremendous damage resulting in *alcoholic dementia,* (wet brain). Alcoholic dementia is caused by destruction of the cells of the cerebral cortex. Your brain contains spaces filled with cerebrospinal fluid. CAT scans of even relatively young heavy drinkers show less cortex and more space. The more you drink the bigger the "holes" in your brain get. The symptoms of alcoholic dementia are similar to senility: memory loss, disturbed thought, emotional disturbances, and, in severe cases, motor impairment.

The other parts of the brain can also be damaged by alcohol. Such damage can be fatal. To make matters worse, heavy drinkers are often malnourished and this can also damage the brain. Lack of thiamine (Vitamin B_1) is a complication of alcoholism. Untreated it is fatal. Even treated, it may result in severe brain damage. Enough of these horrors. Hopefully you don't have to worry about them, but you should know that they can occur.

What about the ordinary heavy hitter? You are a man or woman who goes to work every day, eats more or less regularly, but belts them down after five. You also suffer neurological impairment. Your thinking is fuzzy, your judgment dull, and your emotions volatile. All of this is caused by alcohol, not by your personality. You don't believe this. Yet it is true. If you regularly drink heavily, you are not playing with a full deck. Fortunately, these are derangements of function, not of structure. They are caused by alcohol's deleterious effect on your neurochemistry, not by structural damage to your brain that is irreversible. Heavy hitters who haven't taken things too far clear up when they stop drinking. So would you.

Prolonged heavy drinking and vitamin deficiencies can also damage the nerves that go from the brain and spinal cord to muscles and glands. Sufferers first develop difficulties in walking. If they continue drinking, all sorts of other unpleasant things occur. This, too, is reversible as long as the damage is not too extensive. The treatment is to stop drinking and eat well.

The most common neurological symptom of alcohol abuse is the *blackout*—amnesia for periods of time while drinking. Many social drinkers experience blackouts and dismiss them. Underneath their casual dismissal is anxiety. "What did I do? Did I tell the boss to go hang herself or, God forbid, hit a kid with the car?" Such things happen. Blackouts are often the earliest sign that drinking has become a problem. They should be taken seriously. They are a sign that something is wrong with your drinking. Usually nothing worse than mooning the neighbors happened during the time you can't remember, but you don't really know.

The Liver

The liver plays a vital part in the body's processing of alcohol, so it is not surprising that the liver is frequently damaged by excessive drinking. Once alcohol is in your body, it would just stay there and do its thing to your nervous system forever unless something happened to it. Something does happen to it. It gets metabolized. Metabolism is the process by which food stuffs, including alcohol, are burnt (oxidized) to obtain energy. The end product is excreted. In a limited sense alcohol is a food. It is metabolized to obtain energy, but these are empty calories. They contain no vitamins, minerals, or proteins.

The metabolism of alcohol — the way your body gets rid of it — is often confused with the effect of alcohol. They are completely different. The effect is the result of alcohol's action on the nervous system; the conversion of alcohol into energy and waste products — its metabolism — is quite a different process and takes place in the liver.

Liver cells contain an enzyme, alcohol dehydrogenase, which metabolizes alcohol. There are several stages that alcohol passes through before it is finally converted to carbon dioxide and water and these are excreted. In the process, energy is released.

Your liver is your body's chemical factory, where metabolic processes take place. When your liver burns alcohol, it needs a co-enzyme, nicotinamide-adenine dinucleotide (NAD), to do the job. NAD is needed for all sorts of metabolic work. If it is used up metabolizing alcohol, it takes time to replace it, and the normal chemical work of your liver is interrupted. Heavy drinking, especially prolonged heavy drinking, not only distorts liver chemistry, it adversely affects the chemistry of the entire body. Not surprisingly, such drinking can, and often does, lead to liver disease. Heavy drinkers usually have fatty livers. If you have a fatty liver, it is enlarged and you can probably feel it pressing against your ribs. A fatty liver isn't exactly good, but it's not so bad either. If you have one and stop drinking, it will return to normal. If you continue to drink, alcoholic hepatitis may ensue. This destroys liver cells and sometimes the drinker. The destroyed cells are replaced by fiber. If this happens to enough of them, the result is cirrhosis. *Alcoholic cirrhosis* is one of the most common and the most serious medical complications of alcohol abuse. Bad stuff indeed. It can be fatal.

Once metabolized, alcohol is no more. The by-products of its metabolism are excreted by the lungs and kidneys. Not all of the alcohol is metabolized; about 95 percent is. The rest is excreted unchanged through the lungs. That is why breath mints don't work — you're breathing the stuff out.

Other Organs

Excessive alcohol consumption can damage any part of your body. Some of that damage would be the direct result of the toxicity of alcohol and some of it would be indirect — the result of alcohol messing up your body chemistry. Alcohol-related anemia is common. So is high blood pressure. Damage to the heart and muscles is also possible. Digestive problems including malabsorption are common in heavy drinkers. Even those who eat well, and few do, may suffer malnutrition because the food never gets from their guts to their bloodstreams. Many heavy drinkers suffer chronic diarrhea. It is amazing how many folks who thought they had dysentery were completely cured when they stopped drinking. Inflammation of the pancreas — pancreatitis — an excruciatingly painful, potentially fatal disease is another possibility.

I could go on. But enough, you get the idea. Chronic heavy drinking takes a terrible toll on your body. All of it — including the sex organs. The sex organs? I'm afraid so.

Alcohol and Sexuality

According to Masters and Johnson (1970), the most common cause of sexual dysfunction — impotence in the man and failure to achieve orgasm in the woman — is alcohol. "But Dr. Levin, I thought you said that alcohol is disinhibiting and makes people sexy. I agree with Ogden Nash, 'Candy is dandy, but liquor is quicker.' " In low doses, used occasionally, yes. In large quantities, and used often, quite the reverse. There is a famous experiment in which college girls were shown erotic films while being allowed to drink as much as they wished. Their vaginal pulse pressures, a measure of sexual arousal, were measured. The more they drank the less aroused they were although they reported the opposite. Similar experiments with men have demonstrated an inverse relationship between firmness of erection and alcohol intake. So it seems that high and hard are opposites. Perhaps Shakespeare put it best, "Drink provokes the desire, but takes away the performance." Long-term heavy drinkers may suffer far worse sexual impairment. Excessive use of alcohol can permanently damage both the testicles and the ovaries, and liver damage can lead to feminization in men. Alcohol can damage a fetus. In fact, heavy drinking during pregnancy is a major cause of retardation. It is wise not to drink at all during pregnancy.

Alcohol and Nutrition

You have learned that heavy drinking can cause malabsorption of food and that the thiamine deficiency suffered by some heavy drinkers can do awful things. All sorts of other vitamin and mineral deficiencies are found in heavy drinkers. So if you like to drink and do it often, make sure you don't drink on an empty stomach and that you eat a balanced diet. Daily multivitamins are also a good idea. If you find yourself preferring drink to food, it's time to think about your drinking. That's a sure sign that you are drinking too much.

Alcohol's Effect on Thought and Feeling

Alcohol loosens you up. That's true of both your thoughts and your feelings. The devil-may-care, euphoric feelings of the first few drinks are pleasant. You don't worry so much about being strictly logical and that can be a relief. After a while you don't even worry about making sense and you may not make sense. Again, that can be okay. Or it may not be so okay. Emotionally you may be far more expressive than usual. Again, fine up to a point. After that, emotions, like thoughts, become confused, less organized, and more primitive. Problem drinking leaves the drinker chronically somewhat befuddled and emotionally volatile, a state that can last well into sobriety.

Alcohol and Depression and Anxiety

Alcohol is the oldest tranquilizer. A drink or two certainly quells anxiety. Beyond that it causes it. By the third drink, alcohol brings about the release of adrenalinelike chemicals which make you nervous and anxious. So drinking a lot frequently causes fear and anxiety rather than tranquilizing it. Lots of folks drink to quiet their anxiety. Chemically it just doesn't work. If you add guilt and worry about drinking, then things become even worse. Pharmacology and psychology combine to make you uptight.

What about depression? Well, if alcohol beyond a couple of drinks is a terrible antianxiety agent, it is an abysmal antidepressant. Being a depressant, it makes depression even worse. It doesn't seem that way to you because alcohol anesthetizes your feelings including your depressed ones, but underneath your numbness, your depression is getting worse. The same is true of anxiety. Underneath the numbness, it too is getting worse. If you're angry and your drinking is an angry act, that may give you temporary relief from your depression—even if you don't know that your drinking is angry drinking—but that doesn't help for long and is usually followed by guilt and remorse. Drinking to self-medicate depression is popular. Lots and lots of folks do it. It plain doesn't work. Alcohol makes depression worse, period.

OTHER RECREATIONAL DRUGS

There is a Yiddish expression, a *dreikopf* (dray kupf), from *dreidel,* a top, and *kopf,* head. A *dreikopf* is someone who makes your head spin. It is used to characterize people who manipulate, confuse, and bewilder. Before you know it, a *dreikopf* has your head spinning like a top. Drugs are like that. They promise all kinds of satisfaction, but all they do is make your head spin. They are *dreikopfen.* If you are like most other Americans these days, you have at least a passing acquaintance with recreational drugs other than alcohol. That's especially likely to be the case if you are under forty. If you drink too much and use drugs, you are almost certainly drugging too much.

Recreational drugs fall into a few major categories: marijuana and hashish; central nervous system depressants (sedative-hypnotics); central nervous system stimulants; opiates and other narcotics; and psychedelics (hallucinogens). Central nervous system depressants are called downers on the street; central nervous system stimulants are called uppers. Alcohol is a downer, although you don't think of it that way. You will find it helpful to know something about each type of drug and what it does to your body, your mind, and your emotions.

Marijuana and Hashish

Marijuana is the second most popular recreational drug after alcohol. Marijuana and hashish contain *tetrahydrocannabinol* (THC), a psychoactive agent. A psychoactive agent changes how you think and feel. Marijuana is illegal although this doesn't seem to stop anyone from using it. Many people smoke pot without becoming dependent on it. However, this is far from always the case and psychological addiction to THC in its various forms is quite common.

Marijuana and hashish are prepared from the hemp plant, *Cannabis sativa*. Marijuana is a mixture of the crushed leaves, stems, and flowers of male and female *Cannabis* plants; hashish is the resin obtained from the flowering tops of the female plant. Hashish is considerably more potent than marijuana. The pharmacological and psychological effects of marijuana and hashish are almost entirely due to the action of THC. Marijuana and hashish are usually smoked, although sixties college students baked hashish and marijuana into cookies and brownies and ate them. Marijuana has many pet names, including reefer, grass, and pot. It is usually rolled into a cigarette called a joint. Hashish is usually smoked in a pipe. Their psychological effects vary a good deal with set and setting, that is, your expectations and the environment partly determine how you experience the drug. In low doses, THC is a sedative-hypnotic. It induces feelings of relaxation, drowsiness, and well-being. Smokers seem to enter an anxiety-free drifting state resembling a pleasant daydream. Marijuana, unlike alcohol, does not disinhibit aggression, and violence while high on pot is rare. Many users report intensified perceptions and enhancement of sensory experiences. They report that food tastes better, that music is more acutely experienced, and that sex is more enjoyable. In large doses THC is a psychedelic, inducing hallucinations and changes in body image.

Prolonged heavy use can result in toxic psychosis. "Losing it" in this way is terrifying and usually profoundly shakes the smoker. The pot you buy today is twice or three times as potent as the pot used in the sixties and this makes pot smoking far more dangerous than it used to be.

THC increases pulse rate and reddens the eyes. The mechanism by which THC asserts its effects is not known. THC is metabolized by the liver and the metabolites are excreted in the urine and feces.

Frequent heavy marijuana use leads to psychological dependency. If you smoke on a regular basis, you risk getting hooked. Whether or not physiological dependency develops is controversial; however, abrupt cessation of prolonged heavy marijuana smoking results in withdrawal symptoms. Chronic marijuana usage is associated with respiratory illness including bronchitis and asthma, with suppression of the body's immunological system, and with reduced levels of testosterone, the male sex hormone. Heavy marijuana or hashish smoking leaves residues in the lungs. Recent research suggests that this residue may be carcinogenic. THC, like all psychoactive drugs, crosses the placental barrier and enters fetal tissues. Its effects on the fetus are unknown. Therefore, *it is unwise to smoke pot during pregnancy*.

Chronic pot use results in apathy, social withdrawal, and impairment of goal-directed behavior. Impairment of short-term memory also results from chronic use. Being hooked on pot is no bargain. As in any addiction life gets narrower and emptier as the smoker loses interest in anything else. I once "cured" a teenaged pot head by shocking him into seeing how constricted his life had become by saying, "You prefer pot to getting laid." He heard that and started going after young women instead.

Central Nervous System (CNS) Depressants

All central nervous system depressants disinhibit and relax in low doses and induce sleep in high doses. They assert their pharmacological effects by depressing synaptic transmission in the central nervous system. They slow the information flow in the wires of the nervous system and retard release of the neurotransmitters that convey that information across the gaps between the wires. Sedative-hypnotics come in pill form and are usually taken orally. Their effect in low doses is a feeling of euphoria and well-being. As dosage increases they assert their hypnotic effects and sleep results. In yet higher doses they act as anesthetics and can cause death. There are several types of downers; they all do pretty much the same thing.

The Barbiturates

The barbiturates are a class of chemical compounds derived from barbituric acid. The most common are pentobarbital (Nembutal®); secobarbital (Seconal®); amobarbital (Amytal®); phenobarbital (Luminal®); and thiopental (Pentothal®). The primary medical use of the barbiturates is to induce sleep. You may be hooked on sleeping pills and be barbiturate dependent without realizing it. That happens often.

Sleep is complex and has many stages. Sleep induced by barbiturates is not normal sleep. It is deficient in the stage of sleep in which dreaming takes place. If you have access to downers and are anxiety-prone, it is all too easy to get hung up on them. Barbiturates are addictive both psychologically and physiologically. Severe, even life-threatening, withdrawal effects result from suddenly stopping prolonged heavy use of barbiturates. This is not a drug to go "cold turkey" on without medical advice.

The combined effect of more than one sedative-hypnotic drug is much greater than the sum of the effects of each drug. Each drug potentiates the other resulting in a *synergistic reaction*. This is the reason that consuming barbiturates and alcohol is dangerous.

The effects of barbiturate abuse are very similar to those of alcohol abuse. As dosage increases, signs akin to drunkenness appear, including cognitive and motor impairment. Both thinking and walking become sloppy. Psychological dependency followed by physiological dependency develops with protracted use, and life becomes progressively impoverished as obtaining and using the drug becomes all-important. People who would be horrified at the thought of becoming alcoholic sometimes become barbiturate addicts.

Cross-tolerance develops between central nervous system depressants and cross-addiction is extremely common. Cross-tolerance means that you need more alcohol, for example, to get the old effect because you have built tolerance to phenobarbital or some other downer. That is, once you build tolerance to one central nervous system depressant, you build tolerance to all of them. Cross-addiction means that you are addicted to more than one drug. Cross-addiction may be to various kinds of downers or it may be between alcohol and downers. AA speaks of "sedativism," the use of down drugs of whatever sort to alleviate or mask psychological pain. AA calls such pill use, "taking a martini in powdered form."

Nonbarbiturate Downers

The nonbarbiturate drugs that get people in trouble include Miltown, Librium, Valium, Dalmane®, Tranxene®, Xanax, Ativan, and Quaaludes®. Miltown is a trade name for a drug called *meprobamate*. Librium, Valium, Dalmane, Tranxene, Xanax, and Ativan all belong to a class of drugs called *benzodiazepines*. The drug *methaqualone* is marketed under the trade name Quaalude.

MEPROBAMATE

Meprobamate was introduced in the fifties as a tranquilizer. Under the trade names Miltown and Equanil, it became a bestseller. It is less popular now, but it is still around. Miltown and Equanil were introduced to replace the barbiturates and were supposedly safer. Experience has shown this not to be the case. Sedativists will take any downer, and Miltown abuse is certainly not unknown. If you buy drugs on the street, you don't know what you are getting and you may have been taking meprobamate without knowing it.

BENZODIAZEPINES

The benzodiazepines are a class of sedative hypnotic drugs in very widespread use. They are minor tranquilizers. That is, they have sedating effects and are antianxiety agents but they do not have antipsychotic properties like the major tranquilizers. This distinction between the minor and major tranquilizers is extremely important. The minor tranquilizers, Valium, Librium, and Xanax, are sedative-hypnotics that are used as antianxiety agents. They build tolerance and have withdrawal symptoms. The major tranquilizers are not tranquilizing in this sense; they are correctly called neuroleptics. They are antipsychotic drugs. They work quite differently. What they do is to block receptor sites for the neurotransmitter dopamine. Their ability to do this makes them extremely valuable in treating serious mental illness. They eliminate or reduce hallucinations and delusions. They do not build tolerance, have withdrawal symptoms, or get people high. They are not martinis in pill form. Thorazine®, Stelazine®, Mellaril®, and Haldol® are some brand names of neuroleptics. There is another class of psychotropic medication, drugs that change thought, feeling, or mood, called antidepressants. Elavil® and Tofranil® are examples. They do not build tolerance, have withdrawal symptoms, or get you high. They are extremely useful in treating some forms of depression.

The first of the minor tranquilizers, Librium, was introduced in 1960. The chemical structure of the benzodiazepines is quite different than that of the barbiturates, but pharmacologically they are quite similar. They are somewhat more specific as antianxiety agents and they are less hypnotic; that is, less sleep-inducing. Their primary site of action is the hypothalamus, a part of the brain concerned with emotionality. They depress the respiratory center of the brain less than the barbiturates and are, therefore, less likely to result in a fatality if you overdose on them. They produce the same feelings of disinhibition, euphoria, release from anxiety, and feelings of well-being as do the other sedative-hypnotics (in low doses). In higher doses, the same impairments in memory, in judgment, in cognitive functioning, and in motor coordination occur. Contrary to early reports, prolonged use does result in tolerance and physiological addiction. Withdrawal from these drugs, especially Valium, is particularly severe. They can definitely be drugs of abuse. If you use Valium or Librium to deal with hangovers, you are playing a dangerous game. *Cross-addiction to alcohol and benzodiazepines is very common.* Like other prescription drugs, Valium and Librium are abused by people who abhor "drug addicts." Dalmane and Halcyon® are prescribed as sleeping medicines. They too mix poorly with alcohol.

METHAQUALONE

Methaqualone, marketed as Quaalude, enjoyed a vogue as a "love drug." Actually it is a sedative-hypnotic of average strength that has no aphrodisiacal qualities. It is strikingly similar to the barbiturates in its psychological and behavioral effects. It has been taken off the market, but they are still available on the street, where they are known as "ludes." People usually drink when they take ludes. All that does is get you down faster.

CNS Stimulants

The CNS stimulants are among the most frequently used drugs. The amphetamines and cocaine are wildly popular. They are used by dieters to reduce appetite, by students to stay up to study for exams, by the depressed to self-medicate their emotional pain, and by party goers to get high. The recreational use of these drugs is risky. A considerable percentage of recreational users become hooked.

In low doses, CNS stimulants elevate mood, produce euphoria, increase alertness, and reduce fatigue. In high doses they produce irritability, tension, anxiety, psychotic behavior, and convulsions.

Like a vast majority of psychoactive drugs, CNS stimulants assert their effects in the synapses. Neurotransmitters carry nerve impulses across the synapses. There are many different neurotransmitters in the brain. Among the most important are a class called *catecholamines.* Adrenaline and its relatives are members of this group of neurotransmitters. CNS stimulants act by increasing the amount of available adrenalinelike substances in the synapses of the brain. Amphetamine and its derivatives do this by increasing the release of them into the synapse. Amphetamine also mimics these neurotransmitters by directly stimulating the neurons. Cocaine blocks the reuptake of adrenaline-type neurotransmitters.

Both amphetamine and cocaine make more of these neurotransmitters available to stimulate nerve cells and your system gets hopped up. Once a neurotransmitter is in a synapse it would go on acting forever unless something happened to it. Two things happen to it: (1) it is actively pulled back into the neuron that released it, which is called reuptake, and (2) it is destroyed by enzymes in the synapse. Cocaine acts by blocking reuptake, but this leaves the transmitter remaining in the synapse subject to enzymatic destruction. The enzymatic destruction of these vital brain chemicals is responsible for the crash, the intense depression that follows a cocaine spree, and for the craving, which persists for a long time.

The Amphetamines

Amphetamine is widely used. It has legitimate medical uses in the treatment of narcolepsy (sleeping sickness) and some forms of epilepsy. Its relative, Ritalin®, is used in the treatment of hyperactivity in children. Why a stimulant should be an effective treatment for hyperactivity is something of a mystery. One theory that has been put forward to explain this paradox is that these children are depressed and that their hyperactivity is a desperate attempt to ward off their depression. Amphetamines have been widely used as diet pills because they suppress appetite. Unfortunately your body very quickly develops tolerance to the appetite-suppressant effects of amphetamine. The dosage must then be increased to achieve the same degree of appetite suppression. Many people have been hooked on uppers in this way. There is no medically sound reason to use amphetamine for weight reduction. In the (not very) long run, they are ineffective and they have real potential for abuse.

Amphetamines used to be used for the medical treatment of depression. They no longer are. However, they are widely used as a *euphoriant* both recreationally and in the self-medication of depression. Amphetamine in low doses improves psychomotor, intellectual, and athletic performance to a slight extent. Many people use it for this purpose. Unfortunately, you soon have to increase the dosage, and fine motor control is lost and performance does down.

Benzedrine (Bennies) is the mildest of the amphetamines. The amphetamine derivative dextroamphetamine (Dexedrine®, Dexamyl®, or dexies) is more potent, and methamphetamine (Methedrine or Speed) is even more potent.

Amphetamine mobilizes the fight/flight/fright reaction, the body's response to threat, resulting in increased blood sugar, decreased blood flow to internal organs, increased blood flow to muscles, increased respiration, and dilated pupils. Speed prepares you to meet an emergency, even though there isn't one. Amphetamine also increases mental alertness and elevates mood. Subjectively this is experienced as sharpness and euphoria. No wonder uppers so easily generate a craving to repeat the experience and are so notoriously psychologically addicting.

At high dosages, amphetamine produces tremor, restlessness, agitation, and sleeplessness. Tolerance quickly develops and more and more is needed to get the same sensations. "Speed freaks" inject amphetamine into their veins. They experience a rush said to be like a whole-body orgasm. Unfortunately tolerance soon builds to this effect also and "mainliners," as they are called, engage in a futile search to reexperience the quintessential high that they so vividly remember. Heart palpitations, extreme anxiety, and drug-induced psychosis are some of the benefits of shooting amphetamine.

Amphetamine withdrawal results in prolonged sleep, radically increased appetite, and profound depression. The depression following a prolonged amphetamine run, or spree, can be intolerable, and the user feels impelled to take more of the drug.

Speed and alcohol is a popular combo. It quickly becomes a

merry-go-round. Drinking to come down and using uppers to recover from hangovers is a setup for getting hooked.

Cocaine and Crack

Cocaine is strikingly similar to amphetamine in its physiological and psychological effects although far more powerful and far more dangerous. Cocaine is a white powder that can be introduced into the body in several ways. It may be sniffed and absorbed by the vessels of the nasal passages, a practice known as "snorting"; it may be treated with an alkali, usually sodium bicarbonate, and smoked, a practice known as "freebasing"; or it may be dissolved and injected directly into a vein, a practice known as "shooting" or "mainlining." Crack is a form of relatively cheap cocaine that is smoked. It is coke that has already been cooked (freebased) and is ready to be smoked. It is rapidly addicting and not what it's cracked up to be. Before the passage of the Federal Food and Drug Act (1914) cocaine was present in Coca Cola™, where its stimulant effect helped make Coke™ extremely popular. Cocaine is a potent local anesthetic and it is used for that purpose in ophthalmology.

Freud (1900) discovered the euphoric properties of cocaine and wrote about them both in his correspondence with his fiancée, Martha Bernays, and in professional journals. He wrote about it as a "wonder drug," uncritically praising its ability to alleviate low spirits. He used the drug for many years. Freud also discovered the anesthetic effects of cocaine, but his friend Carl Koller published first and received the credit (Gay 1988). It is interesting that Freud was misled by ambition, by the need for self-aggrandizement, in his erroneous judgment of cocaine. Freud's ambivalent feelings about cocaine play a large role in his masterpiece *The Interpretation of Dreams* (1901).

Cocaine is an extraordinarily potent central nervous system stimulant especially when freebased or injected. It does all the things that amphetamine does, only more so. High doses of cocaine can produce convulsions. I once treated a man who reported that he *enjoyed* the convulsions he sometimes had when he shot cocaine. In fact, he looked forward to them as a kind of grand climax of his drug experience, and mainlined coke in the hope of having one. He worked as an operator of a Van de Graff generator, an apparatus that generates very high voltage electricity. His whole life was an attempt to reach maximum voltage. He did not remain in treatment and I don't know what became of him. Drug-induced psychoses occur at far lower doses of cocaine than amphetamine. Cocaine is metabolized by the liver much more quickly than amphetamine and its effects last only a short time. Short-acting drugs call for more and that makes them highly addictive. Psychological habituation occurs readily, tolerance develops rapidly, the crash is extremely painful, and craving lasts weeks and even months after your last "run." Cocaine devotees frequently use alcohol to come down when they get too high. Alcohol is also used to medicate cocaine-withdrawal "crashes." Alcohol actually makes the depression worse, but it masks it for the moment. This is soon followed by a new round of freebasing or mainlining and the cycle starts again. The cocaine-alcohol user thus attempts to fine-tune moods and feelings through the use of technology. Have you attempted to fine-tune your moods with alcohol and other drugs? Do you attempt to exercise omnipotent magical control over your emotions? It is all too easy to become a coke-alcohol addict.

Are you frightened by my use of the word "addict"? You and your friends may occasionally use cocaine, but you certainly aren't addicts. That may be true, but cocaine is so addictive, particularly if it is freebased or in the form of crack, that you can be hooked almost without noticing it. Anyone who is on the coke-alcohol merry-go-round is addicted however much they may deny it. If you are smoking crack and drinking, you are both drugging and drinking too much.

Cocaine is an "in" drug, extremely popular with yuppies. Its status as a glamour drug makes it attractive to the upwardly mobile. The glamour is all glitter. The truth is that people who are into stimulants are warding off feelings of inner deadness and emptiness.

The Opiates (Narcotics)

Opium is a naturally occurring substance that is obtained from a plant, the poppy, *Papaver somniferum*. It is a narcotic. Narcotics have both a sleep-inducing (sedative) and a pain-relieving (analgesic) effect.

Opium has been used since antiquity for the relief of pain and the treatment of cough and diarrhea. It was also used recreationally, and addiction to it was well known in classical times. Wars have been fought over it. Opium is a crude extract that contains many pharmacologically inert substances. Opium was used in patent medicines until the Harris Act (1914) put these substances under strict control. In its original form, Lydia Pinkham's remedy for "female complaints" was alcohol laced with opium. Needless to say, it was wildly popular.

Opium contains many biologically inert compounds. The biologically active portion consists of two substances: morphine and codeine. Morphine is a powerful pain reliever and a potent anti-diarrhetic agent. Codeine shares its basic chemical structure with morphine, but it is much less potent. It is used mostly as a cough suppressant. Heroin is a synthetic derivative of morphine. It was originally developed to treat morphine addiction.

The opiates are used in a variety of ways. The resin may be smoked or like cocaine its derivatives may be finely powdered and snorted. This is the usual introduction to the drug. The opiates may also be injected under the skin (skin popping) or into the veins. Some people mix heroin and coke and shoot it. This is called a speedball, and it is not recommended for those who wish to live a full life span.

Although the reaction varies, most people experience a sense of euphoria and well-being, feelings of warmth and contentment, and feelings of great power when they take opiates. These feelings are followed by an enjoyable dreamlike state and by sleep. Some experience a rush, similar to, but more powerful than, an orgasm. Although opiates are used medically to manage physical pain, they also make people indifferent to psychological pain, which explains much of their appeal. It's that old self-medication routine again.

Opiates act by binding with specific receptor sites in the brain and in the intestinal tract. These receptors appear to be designed to receive opiates. This seemed strange before the discovery of naturally occurring opiatelike substances, the *enkephalins,* in the body. Exercise releases enkephalins and can give you a natural high.

Morphine and heroin are rapidly metabolized by the liver and excreted by the kidneys. They disappear from the body in four to five hours, which means that a narcotics addict must constantly renew his supply. Tolerance to the analgesic, euphoric, and sedative effects develops. Tolerance can be incredibly high, so the user needs ridiculous amounts to get high.

Withdrawal from opiates is painful, although not dangerous in the way that withdrawal from alcohol is. Withdrawal symptoms include agitation, restlessness, craving, intense anxiety, fever, vomiting, flulike pains, rapid breathing, chills, and violent diarrhea. They last about a week. Because they are bound to receptor sites, opiates do much less damage to the body than alcohol.

Psychedelic Drugs (Hallucinogens)

Psychedelic drugs are drugs that alter sensory experience and alter consciousness. The experience induced by these drugs is called a trip. They induce hallucinations, alter the experience of time, and change the conception of the self. They may cause what psychiatrists call "derealization" and "depersonalization." That is, they put the reality of both self and world into question. Chemically they differ widely, but all of them either mimic, or modify the action of, a neurotransmitter. Their effects are primarily psychological. They are not physiologically addicting, but they do produce tolerance and they may induce psychological dependence in susceptible individuals. Their long-term effects are unknown. Repeated use may cause brain damage. Heavy users sometimes experience flashbacks, involuntary trips that occur months or years after their last dose of the drug. Addiction to these drugs is rare. Their use is self-limiting and most people return to alcohol or pot or uppers as their drug of choice. Bill Wilson, the co-founder of AA, experimented with psychedelic drugs toward the end of his life, but he neither became addicted to them nor returned to alcohol. The use of these drugs may lead to psychotic episodes in already shaky individuals. Although psychedelic drugs are less popular than in the sixties and seventies, bad trips still account for a significant number of psychiatric hospital admissions.

The use of psychedelic drugs has a long history. They occur naturally in a variety of plants and herbs that have been used medically, recreationally, and ritually. They have been used to induce ecstatic or mystical states as part of religious rituals. The best known of these naturally occurring substances are the mystical mushrooms of Mexico and the peyote cactus of the American southwest. The mushrooms contain psilocybin and psilocin, both of which have been synthesized and are available on the street. The "buttons" of the peyote cactus are chewed to obtain its active principle, mescaline, which has also been synthesized and which is also available on the street. In the late fifties, the novelist and student of mysticism Aldous Huxley wrote a book called *The Doors of Perception* (1954) reporting his experience with mescaline. He regarded it as a shortcut to mystical insight. The book was widely read and the drug enjoyed a vogue among rebellious youth. Mescaline is structurally similar to the neurotransmitter norepinephrine (NE). Mescaline, like NE, induces behavioral arousal, but unlike NE, it also alters perception, changes the experience of time, and induces hallucinations.

Lysergic acid diethylamide (LSD) is an extremely potent synthetic hallucinogen. It is the most widely used of this class of drugs. It is usually taken orally. It too received a great deal of publicity in the sixties when its use was advocated by Timothy Leary. It is believed to act by altering synapses using the neurotransmitter serotonin in such a way that sensitivity to sensory input is augmented. Psychologically its effects are similar to those of mescaline; however, unlike mescaline it produces those effects in almost infinitesimal doses. The hallucinations and alterations of consciousness produced by LSD are particularly intense and vivid. It can produce bad trips, flashbacks, and psychological dependence.

Problem drugging and addiction are strikingly similar to problem drinking and alcoholism. It's the old story of a friend turning into an enemy with the victim being taken by surprise. Denial, knowing yet not wanting to know that drugs have become a problem, is the problem. Once denial is overcome the "cure" is relatively easy.

If you are an occasional experimenter, I wouldn't worry too much. But if you are using pot or coke or Valium to manage the effects of drinking too much, you need to look at that very carefully. In the last chapter, Peggy was on the alcohol-coke roller coaster, and Vicky was on the tranquilizer-wine seesaw. Did you identify with either of them? Having read this chapter, you know what the various drugs can do to your mind and body. Are you suffering from any of the adverse effects of drugging too much?

Another problem with drugs and alcohol is that one leads to the other. So if you are using both drugs and alcohol and you have concluded that you are drinking too much, then you are also drugging too much. You can't deal with one without dealing with the other.

CHAPTER 4

Hitting Bottom

By now you know a great deal about the effects of alcohol on your mind and body, and you are struggling to decide whether or not you are drinking too much. You know that alcoholism (problem drinking) is a self-diagnosed disease, and that alcoholism (problem drinking) is the disease that tells you that you don't have it. Somehow you have to negotiate this paradox in making your decision. The AA notion of hitting bottom can help you do that. What that notion says is that the emotional conviction required to realize and act on the realization that you are drinking too much is only possible when you feel the pain that drinking is causing you.

In its literal meaning, hitting bottom is falling on your ass. Falling so far and so hard that the jolt breaches your denial and lets a little reality peek through. Figuratively, the bottom is a state of despair—like Roland H's after Jung told him that there was no hope. Hitting bottom is powerful stuff. Suddenly you realize that your drinking is hurting you very badly. Your beloved alcohol has turned on you and done you wrong. Your disillusionment is profound and it feels like there is no way out. Life would be dull, stale, and unprofitable without drink to enliven it, yet . . . yet you now know that you are drinking too much and might not be able to drink at all. You are caught in the middle, and betwixt and between doesn't feel good. If you, like many drinkers, are at the point where you literally believe that you can't live without alcohol and now believe that you can't live with it either, you are in a terrible spot. Your despair may be so intense that you think of suicide. That sometimes happens when people hit bottom. Your feeling that you can't live without alcohol is delusional; it has no basis in objective reality, but it sure has emotional reality. You genuinely believe it.

I once treated a man who was detoxified from alcohol in a hospital. He woke the morning after his discharge feeling a force pulling him toward the open window of his fourth-story room. He was ineluctably drawn to the window. Terrified, he braced his legs against the unrelenting force and halted his advance toward death. Summoning up a vestige of the life force, he managed to turn and flee his room. He ran sixteen blocks to an AA meeting, where he collapsed in a sweat-drenched panic. During the meeting a member related how he had been plagued by thoughts of suicide during his early sobriety. Drinking had been his escape and now his escape route was closed — he had nowhere to hide. Feeling trapped, he thought, "I can kill myself and escape my emotional pain." The speaker started to laugh and said, "All that seems absurd now, but it didn't then, it seemed inevitable. Thank God I came here to learn the alternatives." As soon as the formerly suicidal member began to speak he engaged my patient's rapt attention. Listening to this "sharing," his compulsion to commit suicide left as abruptly as it had appeared. They say that there are no coincidences in AA. Perhaps this is so. At any rate, this man heard what he needed to hear when he needed to hear it. I am telling you this story because it illustrates so vividly how terrifying one's bottom can be. Of course, bottoms aren't usually so dramatic or dangerous.

I agree with AA that some sort of bottom must be reached. Otherwise, the conviction necessary for recovery is absent. Bottom means the realization that drinking just won't do it for you anymore. Yet certitude that life is either impossible or not worth living without alcohol is extremely common and a major obstacle to recovery. What a dilemma to be in. Booze won't do it for you anymore and you don't know what will. "Hickey, what have you done to the booze? It doesn't have its old kick" is the lament of the down-and-out drinkers in Eugene O'Neill's great play, *The Iceman Cometh.* Many a drinker can identify with this. Has the booze lost its kick for you?

The man who felt pulled out of the window wasn't crazy although his experience was delusional. It was an enactment, an externalization, of the inner struggle between his desire to live and his desire to die. *Addictions are decisions to die on the installment plan* — a kind of chronic suicide. Since alcoholism is a progressive fatal disease, things don't get better for the drinker and the ultimate bottom is the cemetery. The cemetery is indeed the bottom for many people, but it need not be. The purpose of treatment, of education, and of this book is to raise your bottom. In its early days almost all of AA's membership were low-bottom drunks, those who had lost jobs, marriages, relationships, homes, and health. This is no longer the case. High bottom is better than low bottom — it doesn't hurt as much and it is easier to recover from. "Bottoms up" can mean raising your bottom, and not being hurt anymore by alcohol, rather than draining your glass.

Since it is an AA concept, hitting bottom was originally intended to apply to alcoholism. But problem drinkers hit bottom too. In either case, the realization that your drinking is injurious enters your awareness with emotional conviction. The only difference is in what you will need to do with that awareness. In this chapter, I am going to talk mostly about alcoholism. Don't let that bother you. If it seems to fit your case, just substitute the words "problem drinking" for "alcoholism."

AA tells high-bottom drinkers that jail, the mental hospital (the "flight deck"), bankruptcy, unemployability, cirrhosis, and DWIs are "yets." They haven't happened to you yet, but if you keep on drinking, your chances of becoming personally acquainted with your "yets" is excellent. Compulsive drinking is a ride on a down elevator, the last stop being death. You can get off at any floor. The longer you drink the worse things get.

As with so many other aspects of alcoholism, hitting bottom is paradoxical: recovery isn't possible without hitting bottom hard, yet that bottom mustn't be so low that recovery is unlikely. Is there a way to hit a bottom sufficiently deep to carry conviction yet not so deep that the road back seem insurmountable? The answer is yes.

Bottom is a state of mind and doesn't have to do with skid row, destitution, or being a social outcast. You can reach bottom in a Park Avenue apartment just as well as on the Bowery. Bottom is the moment when you realize that drinking the way you drink is no longer possible. It's the feeling that there is no more pleasure left in the bottle; the sudden insight or the gradually dawning realization that alcohol no longer gives you cessation of pain, let alone enjoyment. By now your drinking is more about relief from pain than about having fun. Bottom is finding out that the sauce doesn't take away your pain anymore, or at least not reliably. You can't count on it anymore. *Put a little notebook in your pocket and record each drink you take and what it does for you.* Is it taken to relieve pain of some sort? To ease a hangover, lighten a depressed mood, anesthetize guilt, quell anxiety? Is it fun? Are you getting any pleasure out of it? Does it work for the purpose intended? Invent your own charting system and record all of this data. This is a very hard thing to do honestly because unconscious distortion is all too easy, but give it a try and be as honest as you know how. Tabulate your results at the end of a day, a week, a month. How many of those drinks were fun? How many gave pleasure? How many dulled or obliviated pain? How many didn't do anything or made you feel worse? You may be very surprised at what you find. In fact, you may find that the booze just isn't working anymore. The moment of such a realization is a dark one. It is necessarily a time of fear, indeed of panic, since the one thing that you thought you could count on has turned out to be a strumpet.

There are two traditions that relate moments of deep despair to psychological reorganization: one is religious and one is scientific.

Every religious tradition and many philosophical systems include accounts of the lives of sages or saints who are said to have achieved some form of special insight. Some of these sages are spoken of as mystics, people who have had intense experiences of union or merger with what is variously described as God, Nature, or the Totality of Things. Mystics from the most divergent religious traditions speak of the "dark night of the soul" that precedes illumination. Such experiences have been reported by Zen Buddhist sages, Native American shamans, hasidic holy men, and Christian saints. Leaving aside the various belief systems to which these men gave allegiance, they all described a psychological process of losing hope, falling into confusion and fear, reaching a kind of terminal despair characterized by feelings of hopelessness and helplessness — the dark night of the soul — followed by the discovery of a newfound sense of hope and meaning, which resulted in a profound shift in values and sense of self. Since so many different people from such different cultures have left records of such experiences, they must be fairly common. William James, the American philosopher and psychologist, wrote a book called *Varieties of Religious Experience* (1902) in which he described what he called "conversion experiences." James's book had a profound influence on Bill Wilson and helped shape AA's view of alcoholism. William James spoke of sudden Damascus conversion experiences (an allusion to the conversion of St. Paul on the road to Damascus) and of more gradual educational conversion experiences. What James was interested in was not the religious aspect of this per se, but the psychological process. The point is, that for very many human beings, despair has preceded hope. I tell you this to give you courage, and you are going to need some courage since some degree of despair — hitting a bottom — is necessary to deal with alcoholism and problem drinking.

A more scientific view of hitting bottom was developed by Henry Tiebout, the psychiatrist who treated Bill Wilson for depression during the years Wilson was consolidating AA. The two men learned much from each other. Tiebout developed a notion he called *ego deflation*. Basing his theory on a great deal of work with alcoholics, Tiebout concluded that radical ego deflation is necessary to puncture alcoholic grandiosity. Since alcoholic grandiosity supports denial, this is a necessary step for recovery. Grandiosity means unrealistic feelings of invulnerability, indeed of immortality, "nothing including alcohol can touch me"; "the yets can't happen to me"; feelings of entitlement, "I deserve everything"; and unrealistic feelings of power (Tiebout 1957). The grandiose person feels that he or she can do anything. Do you have such feelings? If you do, your grandiosity is compensatory for your underlying feelings of worthlessness and powerlessness.

There is an intimate connection between alcoholism and grandiosity. Grandiosity and ego inflation prevent drinkers from seeing themselves and their drinking as they are—instead, drinkers see through bottle-colored glasses, which distorts their true situation. If you are like other drinkers, and the odds are that you are, your ego is getting in your way. Ego deflation in depth constitutes a surrender. Surrender is another AA concept—in the words of the first of AA's Twelve Steps, "We admitted we were powerless over alcohol—that our lives had become unmanageable." Tiebout's papers on the necessity for ego deflation and surrender have a kind of moralistic, rub-their-noses-in-it quality that turns me off, but I think that he is basically right. There is something about this business of surrendering, of admitting one's powerlessness, that is liberating. It sets people free. Once again we have a paradox: the admission of powerlessness restores power; the admission of enslavement frees; and the admission that one's life and one's drinking are out of control leads to the reestablishment of control. Surrender is the hoped-for outcome of hitting bottom. You're probably thinking, "Hitting bottom, ego deflation, surrender—what a crock—no way that stuff's for me. I'm just drinking a little too much, problem drinking at the very worst, not drinking alcoholically, so just tell me how to drink safely and don't badger me with this depressing bottom stuff." Okay, but before you close the door, why don't you see what hitting bottom was like for a few folks who aren't so very different from you. You may surprise yourself by identifying with them.

HERMAN, A RED-INK BOTTOM

Herman was a patient of mine for about a year. When I worked with him he was mildly depressed and somewhat sullen. He kept his distance and I often felt that he wasn't in the room. It was obvious that he didn't want too much connection with me. Herman had come for therapy because of his depression and because his second wife was complaining about his drinking. It was clear that he was there mostly to shut her up. He was compliant and resentful at the same time. Herman was a highly functional guy. He held an upper-middle-management position in a large manufacturing firm. He had worked in a number of similar executive jobs and it was not clear how much of his job-changing was related to his drinking. He had come up a long way starting from near poverty. He was the only member of his family to do well and was both proud and a little guilty about it. He was an excellent father, being lovingly involved with his children by his first marriage. He hated his first wife. Our work together consisted mostly of putting Herman in contact with his anger and helping him let go of his resentment of his first wife. Although he readily admitted that both his wives regarded his drinking as abnormal, he insisted that it was not, and avoided the topic as much as I would let him. When Herman terminated abruptly I was not surprised. I felt that I didn't really know him and that we hadn't made contact. Several years later Herman called and asked if he could return to therapy. It was a different person who presented himself in my office. He didn't seem at all remote now. He had hit bottom and wanted help. In a sensitive, yet matter-of-fact businessman's way, he told me how that had happened.

> Something happened this weekend. I realized I had had it with drinking. Nothing special really happened. I was drinking with the boys like I always do when it suddenly hit me that I had spent the whole weekend drinking. I thought "Jesus, no wonder my wife is pissed off, I'm

never with her." I don't know what was so hard about seeing that; it's as clear as the nose on my face, but I never saw it before. After that it wasn't hard to decide the booze wasn't worth it. Besides, I felt awful Monday morning. I've had plenty of hangovers but usually they weren't too bad, and besides, a drink or two at lunch took care of them. This one was different; I felt worse than I ever had before. Then there was an awful lot of stuff coming down at work. There's a power play going on at the top and I better be on my toes if I want to survive. I can't do that hung over. I need a full deck to make it in my business. Then my kids aren't getting as much of me as I would like. I'm a damn good businessman. I looked at the balance sheet and concluded this is a deficit situation. Then I thought, "If I'm going to turn red to black I have to stop drinking." Three days ago I quit. It's very hard; I feel rotten, so I decided to come back to counseling.

Herman's recovery was dramatic. His physical and emotional withdrawal symptoms didn't last long. Unlike many people, he experienced neither the despair and desperation nor the euphoria, the pink cloud, usually associated with early sobriety. Consistent with his low-key persistence that had taken him through night school and up the corporate ladder, he simply didn't drink once he had made up his mind not to. His first wife, who was a difficult and critical person, but with whom he had to deal because of the children, became a petty annoyance rather than an obsession. He lost his job in the power struggle at his firm, but quickly found another one. Herman's life, which had always been pretty good, became much better when he stopped drinking. His problem was alcohol and somehow his accountant's mind had enough objectivity to see the red ink just before disaster struck.

I was fascinated by Herman's turnabout. I felt a compelling need to understand what had allowed him to see that drinking was his problem. During the year he had worked with me, that was the last thing he was willing to look at. I asked him if he could share the inner process that had enabled him to finally see what alcohol was doing to him. He replied, "It was *a change of attitude;* it was my attitude that was the problem. Once my attitude changed, it was easy." "Your attitude?" I asked. "Yes. Before, I was defiant and angry, nobody was going to take anything away from me, and I thought that drinking was really important. I think the real attitude change was when I realized that drinking was no big deal. It isn't. It just didn't seem that important anymore. After that, I didn't need to be defiant. I grew up poor and I want to be rich. Nothing that gets in the way of making money is that important. I just don't care about drinking anymore." Herman's description of his bottom as an attitude change is illuminating. According to AA, "Alcoholism is a disease of the attitudes." Herman hadn't been to AA; he came to that insight on his own.

Herman's bottom was a bad hangover and the realization that two things that were important to him, family and career, were suffering because of his drinking. When he spoke of letting go of his defiance and anger, Herman was describing ego deflation. His response to his reading of the balance sheet was surrender. With his dry, emotionally detached, rational acceptance of the red ink and the need to change it into black, Herman surrendered and started recovering. Of course, the process was far more emotional than Herman would have us know, but that's not important. What is, is that it worked. Herman's case is a gentle illustration of how defeat—the red ink—becomes a precursor to victory–recovery. In fact, in the paradoxical manner of things associated with alcohol, Herman's defeat *was* his victory.

There is much for you to identify with in Herman's hitting bottom. His was a high bottom. He had lost nothing. If you haven't yet been seriously hurt by alcohol you can identify with Herman and use that identification to hit your bottom before you suffer greatly. Essentially, Herman's bottom was the realization that the game wasn't worth the candle. Is the cost of your drinking too high? Are you, too, into red ink? Such a simple realization can be your bottom. Empathy can help you see the red ink. Herman suddenly realized that his drinking left his wife lonely, and putting himself into her shoes enabled him to see what was happening to him. That led to his attitude change. Can you try to see yourself and your drinking through a loved one's eyes? From that perspective is there anything wrong with your attitude? Is your business career being hurt by your drinking? Seeing that it is can be your bottom. So can a bad hangover. Your bottom doesn't have to be horrendous. Nor need it be dramatic. Herman's wasn't, although his recovery certainly was. What it must be is deeply felt.

SALLY HITS BOTTOM EARLY, BUT HARD

Sally came to me for the treatment of a post-traumatic stress reaction. She had been in an automobile accident in which her face was badly scarred. She was deeply depressed. She later had successful plastic surgery, but when I first saw her, she had no way of knowing she would get such a good result.

Sally was young and very appealing. She had been referred by her attorney, who had not mentioned alcohol, so I was surprised when she told me that she was an alcoholic. She told me that she had been alcoholic since the age of 12 and that she hit bottom four years ago at the age of 25. I asked her to tell me about her drinking and what led her to hit bottom. She did.

> I come from an alcoholic family. Both my parents died of alcoholism. My father deserted us when I was four. I remember the last time I saw him. We were eating in a diner and I was spilling my food. He screamed, "You're disgusting," and ran out. I've always felt that he left

because I was so disgusting. I feel like a pig; I'm a compulsive overeater. I know in my head that he didn't leave because of the way I ate, but I don't know it in my heart. I still believe it.

Things got worse after Dad left. My mother drank more and more and we had very little money. Sometimes there was no toilet paper in the house, but there was always beer. Later we moved to my grandfather's. He was rich, but he grabbed my thing when my mother wasn't around. I think he was senile but he drank too, so maybe that was it. After I grew up, my mother told me she had known what he was doing to me, but was afraid to do anything about it because he would have thrown us out. She was drunk when she told me that. Why did she have to tell me? I hate her for letting it happen and I hate her for telling me that she let it happen. How could a mother do that? I have a daughter. I'd cut off his balls if a man did that to my daughter. My grandfather got more senile and I don't know exactly what happened after that. My mother was like two people. When she was sober, she was wonderful—beautiful and interested in me. But very snobby and uptight. Then, I didn't think she was a snob, I thought that she was a great lady—perfectly dressed and so elegant. I loved her so much. Then there was mother when she was drunk, sloppy and falling down. She'd sit with her legs spread with no panties and you could see everything. She'd curse and then try to play the great lady again, "Oh my dear," and all that shit. I hated her then.

I started having sex play with the neighborhood kids. Mostly with the boys, but sometimes with the girls too. Do you think I'm a lesbian? I loved sex—it felt so good and it made me feel good about myself. Somebody wanted me. I must have felt guilty underneath. Later I hated myself and all that sex play had something to do with it. I was raised a strict Catholic—once I was naked— I had just gotten out of the tub and I did an imitation of the Virgin Mary—I was about 6—and my mother really whaled my ass with a ruler. When I was about 10, my mother met my stepfather. Eddy was a complete asshole. He drank all the time too. Mother dropped me; she was more interested in drinking with Eddy. I started getting in trouble in school—at 11 I got fucked for the first time. And I mean I got fucked, not made love to, by some 20-year-old pervert. Can you imagine an 11-year-old getting fucked? I loved it, or thought I did. I hung out with all the older boys. They had cars and liquor. I can't tell you how many men I had. Big ones, small ones, white ones, black ones. And you know, I was never sober once. Every one of those guys had something to get high on— beer, pot, hard stuff. I loved booze from the first time I tasted it. It was even better than sex. I drank a lot. Any boy or man who gave me something to drink could have me. Sometimes I really liked it, but mostly I wasn't really there. I think I was really turned on by myself. My mother and stepfather raised hell when they weren't too drunk to care and finally my mother had me put away. Can you imagine that? What kind of fucking mother would put a kid in the places she put me? For God's sake, one place had bars and I was locked in. I hate her for doing that. Mental hospitals, homes for delinquent girls, the House of the Good Shepherd, the whole ball of wax. Finally I got out and met Calvin.

What a bastard he was. Oh! I forgot to tell you that when I was 15 I was team banged. They beat me too, but not as hard as Calvin did later. Oh yeah, Calvin beat me all the time. I must have been crazy but I loved him. He took me away from my hometown and my mother didn't bother me anymore. He sort of made a prisoner out of me—if I even went to the grocery store without his permission, he beat me. He always had beer and weed and other stuff and I stayed high most of the time. He's the father of my child. When I went into labor, he was stoned. He slapped me and called me a rotten whore. He wouldn't go to the hospital with me. Do you know what it's like for a 16-year-old kid to have a baby alone? Forget it.

I never cheated on Calvin but he never stopped accusing me of being with other men and hitting me. Sometimes he hit me with a wooden plank. I think I thought I deserved it — that I needed to be punished for all the things I had done. I needed Calvin to beat me. As long as he supplied drugs and alcohol, I would have stayed. It was the way he acted around the baby that made me leave. One day when the baby was about two, I ran away when he wasn't home. I couldn't stand his insane jealousy anymore; he was even jealous of the baby. A guy crazy enough to be jealous of his own kid; that's sick. Something in me said enough, you've been punished enough. Of course I kept drinking. There wasn't any more sex, just falling-down drunk every day. I went on welfare and sometimes I worked off the books. I was sort of dead. That went on for a few years and I hated myself more and more. I tried to be a good mother and I don't think I did too badly, but God was I depressed.

My stepfather was dead by then and my mother was far gone. My brother was in the Program — AA, that is. I thought he was a jerk, a real ass, an uptight loser. Who else would join those holy rollers? What I couldn't figure out was how such a raving asshole could be happy, and the damn jerk *was* happy. Even *I* could see that. He did something really smart; he didn't lecture me. In fact, he never even mentioned my drinking. Damn good thing he didn't because the way I rebelled against everything and everybody I would never have listened. What he did do was tell me what had happened to him — ran his story, as they say in AA. I didn't want to hear that shit but I heard it in spite of myself. I was getting worse; I was terrified

Calvin would come back and kill me—I guess I thought that he should, because of the way I was living, but I didn't know that then, I was just scared. I was getting sicker and sicker from drinking. It got to the point where I couldn't stand any more. If it wasn't for my daughter, I would have killed myself. I don't know why, but one day I asked my brother to take me to an AA meeting. I think it was the guilt—once I didn't have Calvin to beat me, I couldn't stand the guilt—I *knew*—I mean I really knew what it's like to have alcoholic parents. I loved my daughter—she has such a sick fuck for a father, so I wanted her to have at least one parent with her head screwed on straight. So I went to that fucking meeting. I loved it—I mean I *loved* it—like I never loved anything. For Christ's sake, I even identified with the coffee cups. When I do something I do it—I went all the way—the whole nine yards. I was sick—sick, sick, sick, from my crotch to my toes not to mention my head. I was so scared; I hadn't had a sober day in years, but I've made it a day at a time. I still can't stand the guilt and the rage; you wouldn't believe how angry I get, and the crying, I cry all the fucking time, but I don't drink, I don't drug, and I don't care if my ass falls off, I'm not going to. At least not today.

I didn't want to be like my mother. I *won't* be like her. She's dead now. I couldn't stand it when she died— she died from her drinking—she had an accident drunk, it was kind of a suicide. I knew she was dead, but I didn't know it. I couldn't let her go—not the awful way it was— if she was sober and I was sober I could have let her die, but she wasn't, so I knew but I didn't know she was dead. I never accepted it; she couldn't forgive me dead; nor I her. Then one day, I went to the cemetery. I looked at her grave for a long time. I couldn't believe she was dead; I started screaming, "Move the fucking grass! Move the fucking grass, Mother!" I screamed and screamed but she didn't move the fucking grass and I finally knew she was gone. I went to my home-group meeting hysterical. All I said was she couldn't move the fucking grass and I cried the rest of the meeting. Nobody said a word, they just let me be, they didn't try to take away my pain and I didn't want or need anybody to take it away, what I needed was somebody to be with me in that pain, and they were.

I love the fucking Program and all the crazy screwed up people there. They're like me; I'm crazy too, but I'm sober. For God's sake can you imagine what it would have been like if I was drinking when she died? Thank God, I wasn't. I hate her — I love her — I still can't let go of her although I know she's dead. I hate alcohol. I hate drinking, look what it did to her, to my father, to me. How did I get sober? I don't really know — I sort of had two bottoms — a being beaten bottom and an alcohol bottom. In that first bottom, I sort of saw myself and saw I couldn't go on exposing my daughter to that stuff; the second was luck or something. No, not exactly luck, or not only luck. It had something to do with *willingness* — I became willing to go to that meeting. Maybe I had just had enough; I didn't want any more pain for me or for the baby; she's not a baby anymore. They say, "Why me?" in the Program. When you're drinking you have the "Poor mes," so you're always asking, "Why me?" If you recover, you ask it differently. I don't know why me. The way I lived, I should be dead but I'm not. I don't know if I deserve it or not, but I'll take it.

Sally is probably harder than Herman for you to identify with, but there are important things you can learn from Sally's experience of hitting bottom. Sally turned out to be one of those patients who makes doing therapy a joy. Her life had been pure hell, yet I watched her transform herself into a wise, compassionate, accomplished, and loving woman. She just seemed to grow and grow.

Sally hit bottom young. If you are still young, you can too.

There is no need to continue drinking too much until you injure your body in middle life. If you are drinking too much, you can hit your bottom right now regardless of your age. Sally came from an alcoholic home, as do many who drink too much. She was sexually abused and abandoned in that home. Her father left physically, her mother emotionally. If you grew up in an alcoholic home, perhaps you identify with Sally's pain and with her drinking too much to quell that pain. Perhaps you can also identify with her courage.

Like so many children of alcoholics, Sally took the blame on herself, believing that her father left because of her. Have you done that? Sally's bottom was the realization that she didn't have to punish herself anymore. Her desire to be sober for her daughter brought her to that realization. Have you been drinking to punish yourself? Have you punished yourself enough? Can you let yourself feel your guilt — however unrealistic it may be — instead of anesthetizing it? Have you too had enough? If you lost a parent to alcoholism, you share many of Sally's feelings about her mother. You can't resolve them until you hit bottom.

BETTY, A POOR-HEALTH BOTTOM

Betty was an art historian, interested in the psychoanalytic interpretation of painting. She was the sort of art critic who could talk at length about the oral conflicts in the painting of Frans Hals without ever mentioning that the painting she was discussing was titled, *Man with a Keg of Beer*. Betty lived in her head. Her approach to things was cautious, intellectual, critical, and very controlling. She was a stickler for correct speech and often corrected my diction and pronunciation. Once when she spoke of something "transpiring," I snapped back at her, "Trees transpire, events occur." I had long been infuriated with her and her pedantic attitude. So I managed to be more pedantic than she. Therapists are human too.

Betty was in a state of perpetual warfare with her

husband and had stormy competitive relationships with her children. We worked long and hard together. As the months then years went on, our relationship became increasingly adversarial. She wanted to analyze dreams and I wanted to talk about her drinking.

Betty had come to me three years previously because she was concerned about her drinking. She told me that she "wanted an analyst not a hootchist." I was supposed to laugh. Betty was the kind of person who would never go to an alcoholism counselor, but was willing to see me since I had psychoanalytic training. Analysis meant intellectual respectability to her. Since she had many symptoms of emotional distress: anxiety, depression, free-floating rage, and a pervasive feeling of lack of well-being *and* admitted to drinking a not-inconsiderable amount on pretty much a daily basis, I suggested an experiment. I said, "Alcohol causes anxiety and depression so all of your symptoms may be caused by drinking. There is no way to tell unless we eliminate the alcohol. It is purely an empirical question, one of fact, so what we must do is conduct a scientific experiment. Can you stop drinking for six months so we can determine whether or not your emotional problems are caused by alcohol?" My academic approach to the problem appealed to Betty. She readily agreed and she did stop drinking for six months. The puffiness in her face and the redness in her eyes disappeared, but there was no other change. She remained anxious, depressed, and angry. Betty had not hit bottom; there had been no ego deflation, no surrender, and no attitude change. So to speak, her vacation from drinking was good for her liver, but not for her soul. She continued to want to drink, hated me for taking something away from her, no doubt felt tricked by my scientific approach but didn't know how to refuse rational authority, and was "booze fighting" every day of that six months.

Nevertheless, *I would suggest to you that if you are drinking heavily or even moderately and you are plaqued by anxiety, or chronic low-grade depression, or fairly constant feelings of inchoate rage that seems to be disproportionate to events, try a similar experiment. Don't drink, a day at a time, for an extended period, say ninety days.* Try not to make yourself miserable like Betty did. You can always return to drinking, but first evaluate how you feel at the end of your period of planned abstinence. Your comparison with how you felt while drinking won't be valid if you don't allow yourself to enjoy your sober interlude. Remember, nothing is being taken away from you; this is an experiment. You are going to evaluate the results and decide whether or not you wish to resume drinking. If you find that you cannot stop, either because you feel so bad physically or you can't tolerate it emotionally, suspend the experiment and get professional help.

Betty hated every minute of her experiment. She wouldn't have admitted that she felt better if her life depended on it. After the six months, she returned to drinking. We went through another year and a half of deepening mutually hostile therapy. I couldn't figure out why she stayed, and many times decided to terminate with her, for I had decided that she was alcoholic and going downhill. I didn't want to be an *enabler,* one who supports another's drinking too much, yet I was afraid to stop the therapy. It had become increasingly clear that Betty's relationship with me, angry as it was, had become the most positive thing in her life. In fact, she had very little else going for her. Her despair was a yawning pit waiting to envelop her; only her brittle and increasingly fragile intellectualizations kept her from plunging into that pit. In my gut, I felt that suicide awaited Betty if her defenses failed. So we were in a high-risk situation — Betty's defenses, which now included our therapeutic relationship, were preventing her from feeling sufficient despair to confront her alcoholism, yet losing them was dangerous indeed. So I continued with Betty. Looking back on it, I had also become caught up in a power struggle with this highly intelligent woman. I was going to cure her if it killed both of us. Alcohol is like that; it elicits grandiosity in all associated with it. During the final six months of her drinking, Betty felt and expressed pure hatred of me, the evil depriver, the taker awayer. Try taking a bottle away from a hungry baby or a bone away from a hungry dog and you will see something of what Betty expressed to me. Her hatred reached a crescendo at Christmas. The previous two years, she had given me elaborate and aesthetically pleasing gifts. This year she walked in with a paper containing a pickled herring that had been around too long. It reeked incredibly. No doubt the rotting herring was a self-representation, a statement about how she felt about herself, but her giving it to me was also hostile as hell, a gift of shit from which my office smelled for days. A week later Betty surrendered. The herring was her last stand before hitting bottom.

Behind all the rage and hatred of me as the evil depriver was fear. Fear that she couldn't live without alcohol. Her fear and hatred of me was also a reenactment, a second edition of Betty's relationships with the authority figures of her childhood. The technical term for such an unconscious reenactment of a childhood conflict is *transference* because it represents the transference of feelings from parents to therapist. Transference, however, is not limited to the therapeutic relationship; it occurs in day-to-day life, where it often complicates, or indeed destroys, adult relationships. It is reacting to other people as if they were figures from your early life rather than themselves. We all do this to some extent, and one purpose of psychotherapy is to make people aware of it. However, alcohol blurs and confuses things including our mental representations of others, so transference distortions are intensified by drinking. All this is true, but it was irrelevant at the end of Betty's drinking. The only thing that was relevant was her stopping drinking. She did, and this is how it came about.

The session after the herring, Betty appeared looking defeated. She was shaky and crestfallen. She said, "I stopped drinking. I just can't do it anymore. During the last few months my feet have been swelling, my face goes numb, and my liver is enlarged. I've dismissed three physicians because they thought my physical problems were related to my drinking. My present doctor is an imbecile, but he never mentions drinking. I get along very well with him. He can't figure out what's wrong with me; there doesn't seem to be any explanation of my symptoms. But you! You! You without any medical training had the temerity to suggest that the things that were happening to my body might be connected to drinking. Okay, you win. I'll stop. I have stopped. I can't take anymore. I can't stand it. I feel ghastly all the time. Enough. I give up; I don't want to drink anymore. I went to one of those AA meetings you're always harping on. It was okay. I think I'll go back. I feel dreadful, but my body isn't so tense. Okay, okay, you win. I just can't drink, period. I'll drink Perrier — that'll make you happy, won't it?" I didn't say a word.

The occasion of Betty's hitting bottom was physical. Her body couldn't take it anymore. Ego deflation for her was the realization that when it comes to drinking, mind over matter won't work. Her surrender was angry and sarcastic, but there was some humor in it. Humor is healthy; it represents perspective. Betty knew that she wasn't doing it for me this time, but she needed to pretend that she was. It was sort of face-saving for her. I let her have it. Betty's was an educational rather than a Damascus conversion experience. She didn't drink and she went to meetings. At first she was very much on the fringe, fearful and distrustful of AA, but slowly she let her guard down and became part of the group. After about four months, she told me that she no longer felt the desire for alcohol. By her eighth post-sobriety month, Betty was intensely and joyfully involved with AA. On the first anniversary of her sobriety (AA celebrates such anniversaries) she reported that her entire life had turned around and that she was the happiest she had ever been. I asked her to what she attributed this state of affairs. She replied, "It's the spiritual side of the Program. I've developed a spiritual attitude. That's hard to explain, but it has something to do with not caring if I'm the smartest one anymore. I don't need to be the smartest because I feel good about myself. I care more about other people and somehow that's related to caring more about myself. That sounds like a contradiction, but I know that it isn't. I'm not fearful anymore either. I don't need to win every argument. I guess I 'Let go and let God,' as the AA slogan has it, except I don't believe in God, but that doesn't seem to matter. That's the change. That's what makes the difference, the spiritual attitude I developed. Of course, I don't have it consistently. That's why I go to meetings besides insuring my sobriety. I have two problems: alcohol and me. In AA I get help with both."

So Betty, too, reached a point of despair, in her case facilitated by her body starting to fail her, went through a period of black hopelessness characterized by infinite rage at herself and the world, finally realized that she just couldn't drink no matter what, and surrendered. The rest was her attitude change, to what, she described as a spiritual attitude. Herman's attitude change preceded his stopping, so things were easier for him. Betty's followed, so her achievement of sobriety was more painful, albeit in the long run equally satisfying.

DAVID HITS BOTTOM IN A HOSPITAL

David is a retread. He had several years of sobriety before "slipping," and precipitously deteriorating. Skid row is called skid row for a reason and David sure skidded. His bottom was a psychiatric hospitalization. Bottom is a state of being, an inner experience, so in saying that hospitalization was David's bottom I mean that it was the occasion for that experience, not the experience itself. In these days of alcohol rehabs few drinkers wind up in psychiatric hospitals, but some do. The experience of going through a psychiatric hospitalization is traumatic. For most drinkers it is a profound narcissistic wound, a deep laceration cutting to the core of their being. It can serve as the "ego deflation in depth" necessary to penetrate grandiosity and denial. But that doesn't always happen. The experience of hospitalization may be so upsetting that the drinker drowns his or her humiliation as soon as possible. There is a bar across from the Bellevue Hospital psychiatric ward that does a booming business serving the just discharged. That post-hospital drink not only blots out the shock and disbelief that you wound up in the bughouse; it is also an expression of rage. "Screw them! I'm not crazy; I can do whatever I damn well please." Any in-patient treatment—detox, rehab, psychiatric—is a crucial event in a drinking career. It can be a fulcrum around which recovery is organized, or it can fuel the sort of feelings of rage, shame, hopelessness, and defiance that keep people drinking.

I met David some years after his hospitalization. He was a social worker who used a lot of psychiatric jargon as a defense against feelings. Intellectualization is an extremely popular defense among problem drinkers. It supports denial, "I'm so smart I can't be a drunk," and it avoids feeling too much. If you drink too much you intellectualize too much. Smarts can work against you if you use them to fool yourself. David is an intellectualizer who learned to feel. His bottom was dramatic, but his movement from defiance and denial to acceptance and serenity is something you can identify with. This is the story he told me.

Doctor, I've come to you because I'm not enjoying my sobriety, although my present unhappiness is paradise compared to how I felt during my drinking. I've been thinking about my drinking. Four years ago I wound up on the flight deck—that's AA-ese for the psycho ward. Naturally, I didn't go to just any psycho ward, I went to the University Hospital Psychiatric Clinic. I'd been drinking since high school, except for a couple of years in AA. I didn't much like AA, I was so much smarter than most of the people there. I always thought that I would drink again, but I didn't until I broke up with my girlfriend. I used that as an excuse to pick up a drink. Doctor, I am sure you've heard that alcoholism is a progressive disease—believe me, it is. It was sheer hell once I picked up that drink. I would go on a binge, not go to work, not go home, sleep in fleabag hotels, wake up shaking in the middle of the night and reach for the bottle or run past the other bums to find an open bar; then I would go to a few (AA) meetings, get sober, and go back to work. But I couldn't sustain it. Before long, I would pick up another drink and be off and running. It, or maybe I should say I, was crazy. Since I had been in AA, I knew I had to stop drinking, but I wouldn't or couldn't do it. Things got worse; my sober periods became shorter and when I drank, I drank nonstop. I couldn't get my feet on the ground. Finally I became so ill—physically and mentally—that I went to my doctor and told him I was going mad. He suggested I take a little rest. I got drunk and went to my job, where I resigned with a flourish. I drank some more and blacked out. The next thing I remember I was signing myself into the mental hospital. It hadn't taken me long to change from a dissatisfied, anxious, but functional human being into a stumbling zombie who couldn't even remember how he got to the funny farm.

By then I had found a new girlfriend. I stayed away from her when I was drinking so she hadn't seen much of me. I started to call her, but two attendants interfered. I started shaking. What had I done? Signed away my freedom. I wanted a drink; I wanted a thousand drinks; I wanted to leave. Too late! The attendants led me to the elevator. I told them that I had permission to make a call. "Permission to make a call!" Jesus Christ, what had I gotten myself into? I called my girlfriend and told her I had signed myself into the bughouse. She said, "Good, you should have done that long ago." I gathered that she had been less than delighted with my condition and I had thought that she didn't know. In AA they say the drunk is the last to know he has a drinking problem. I found out that is true. I told Annie, "I love you," and stumbled to the elevator. The attendants looked like concentration camp guards. The clang of dungeon (elevator) doors closing resounded in my ears. You raised your eyebrows, Doctor. Think I'm overdramatizing, don't you. Of course, I threw away my freedom myself, but it felt like it was taken away from me. By then I was quaking inside and out.

The elevator opened and I was in the "floor"; it was dark and gloomy. I was locked in. For the next month I did not leave there without an escort. Ever been locked up, Doctor? If you're writing that the patient suffered a blow to his self-esteem, you're right. I still shudder at those locked elevators. You can put down claustrophobia too. I felt bewildered. I couldn't remember how I had got there or what I did that day. Now it was night and the place was deserted. There were bars on the windows. A shiver ran down my spine. I was told to take a shower; that made me feel dirty. I wondered if I smelled. My dread of being locked in faded some, but my blood alcohol level was falling and I was feeling more and more shaky. Every nerve was screaming for a drink. I barely managed to shower and put on a hospital gown. My arms and legs were rubbery and not working very well. Two very young residents arrived to examine me. They asked an endless series of stupid questions, which I resented. These "kids" weren't exactly great at establishing rapport and I sure needed some rapport. I put them down because I was scared. I was in such bad shape that I had a hard time answering their questions. I thought, "Oh shit, I really did it this time, I'm brain damaged." Mercifully, the residents switched to a medical mode and gave me a physical. I found this reassuring.

I had been drinking two quarts of rye a day for quite a while and you might say that I was more than a little worried about my health. You had better get your eyebrows analyzed, Doctor, they're out of control. I can't be your only patient who drank two quarts a day. The examination ended and I fell into a stupor.

I woke feeling like death. A nurse told me to come to the day room. All I could think of was a drink and I made my way unsteadily down a seemingly endless corridor and found the day room. The people there didn't look like patients, however patients are supposed to look. I found this reassuring. Maybe this wasn't such a bad funny farm. I met my regular doctor, Doctor Kruse. I perceived him to be extremely authoritarian. He told me he was detoxifying me from alcohol and that I would be given decreasing dosages of medicine for five days and then nothing. He suggested I spend a few days in bed. I found Kruse so intimidating that I forced myself to enlighten him by telling him that alcohol strips the body of B vitamins and that I wanted vitamin therapy. Kruse prescribed the vitamins and I felt more in control. Pathetic isn't it, Doctor? Still, being able to ask for something and get it helped.

Then I panicked. Five more days and then no alcohol and no medicine. I literally didn't think that I would survive. I didn't have to deal with a drugless state for five days, yet I was going up the walls. I turned to my AA experience and decided that this was going to be tough but that I could deal with it a day, an hour, a minute at a time, and I did. My years in AA were not entirely wasted; I used the Program to get through the hospital experience and to get all that I could from it. I decided not to stay in bed and to participate in the hospital program from the start. My desperate attempt to retain a little dignity in front of Kruse and my decision to use AA's day-at-a-time concept to do what I had to do to face drug freeness were important events in my recovery. I know that it sounds corny, Doctor, but that was the point that I started to fight to get well and somehow, sick as I was, I knew it then. Knowing it was almost as important as doing it, because knowing it changed how I felt about myself. Nothing like an "observing ego," as you shrinks say, eh Doctor? Smiled that time didn't you? Seriously, as soon as I was capable of it, I tried to understand what was happening to me as it happened to me. Sure this was a defense against feelings and I can intellectualize forever, but this trying to understand also helped me a great deal. If it did nothing else, even if all the insight was pseudoinsight, it increased my self-esteem. Interesting patient aren't I, Doctor?

These vestigial feelings of self-worth and of having a coping strategy didn't last long. As I walked back to the day room, my skin crawled; my breath came hard then seemed to come not at all; I started to hyperventilate; my palms dripped sweat; my heart pounded wildly; the vessels in my temples pulsed and felt like they would pop; my legs quivered; my hands shook; my vision blurred; the lights seemed to dim. Ever have a panic attack, Doctor? Do you know Edvard Munch's painting, *The Scream?* I see you do. Well, that's what it's like. Oh why am I explaining—you're human aren't you? "Nothing human is alien to me," eh? I must stop mocking you. It's part of my cool, detached, arrogant yet proper and polite persona. In the hospital I was super polite and very controlled, under the shaking, that is. I liked to look in control. I acted super intellectual. Technical terms poured from my lips like I had four Ph.Ds. It was a pathetic attempt to retain some dignity.

I was given my withdrawal medicine — pentobarbital. It felt wonderful, like two triple whiskeys. Soon I felt drunk once again and I loved it. This was only a reprieve, but I didn't care — it felt too good.

I was soon staggering and slurring. Pat, the big, snappish, tough black nurse who had given me the medicine, tried to talk me into going to bed. I refused. She relented and I staggered from the nursing station to the day room literally bouncing off the walls. I'm glad the hospital let me stagger around. I needed to be allowed to fight. The will to do so made the difference. It's a mystery isn't it, Doctor? Why did I choose life instead of death? I don't know, but I did. God? the anabolic forces of the universe? a massive psychic reorganization? Who knows, but it happened. Somehow I was able to say to myself, "I messed up but I'm going to do it differently this time; I'm going to build on bedrock instead of sand. "Somehow I knew that I could do that although I would forget and return to panic and despair. I decided to use everything the hospital had to offer and to get everything I could from the experience. King of goody, goody, eh, Doctor? Of course I was casting myself in a heroic role and I enjoyed that. But so what, why shouldn't I have enjoyed my private version of the myth of death and rebirth?

So I bounded and staggered into the day room. Sitting there were an angry-looking bear of a bearded middle-aged man and a seventyish, stylishly dressed woman. Bill was slapping down cards from a Tarot deck with great force and looked every bit the conjurer. I wobbled across the room, introduced myself and said,

"Will you overlook my ataxia and dysarthria? They are induced by the medication that I'm taking." Sadie looked blank; Bill said, "Sure kid," and slammed down the Tarot cards harder than ever. I lunged into a jargon-filled discussion of my condition. Bill said, "Sit down and let me get a reading." I continued to play the pleasantest of gracious intellectuals who knew more or less everything and was willing to share it with all. As they say in AA, I was being a people pleaser. Bill and Sadie took it all in stride and again invited me to join them. This time I did.

I was slurring so badly that it would have been difficult to understand me if I was making sense, which I wasn't. That didn't bother Bill or Sadie. As we say in AA, we ran our stories. Bill, a lecturer on communications, was manic–depressive. He was in the hospital because his wife was afraid of him. Looking into the deep pools of hatred and rage that were his eyes I understood why. Sadie was 67 and in her third hospitalization for depression. She was very much the lady and I thought it funny that her doctor had told her to buy a set of cheap dishes and smash them. I couldn't picture that. Internalized anger doesn't do much for people, does it, Doctor? It almost killed me. Just as we were getting acquainted a chime rang. I'll always be able to hear that chime. It rang for meals, for meds, for activities, for bedtime, for everything. Structure for the structureless, I suppose. Comfort in routine. I got to hate those chimes. The day room filled up and we were lined up and marched to the locked elevators. The attendants were actually kind and friendly, but I experienced them as prison guards. Being escorted everywhere through locked doors was humiliating. I staggered as the others walked. We were taken up to the top floor, which had a gym, game room, and a screened-in roof garden. The younger patients played volleyball, while the older patients played board games. I didn't feel capable of doing anything so I went out on the roof garden and looked down at the traffic far below through the wire mesh. "At least it's not barbed," I thought, as my depression rose like waves through the waning pentobarbital.

The next four or five days I followed the hospital routine as best I could. There was individual therapy, group therapy, recreational therapy, occupational therapy, dance therapy, and community meetings. As the withdrawal medication was reduced, my anxiety returned and once again moved toward panic proportions. The slurring and staggering gave way to a sort of spasticity. I should mention that I was withdrawing from Valium as well as alcohol. My arms and legs would jump up much as if I was a dancer in the dance of the toy soldiers. It was embarrassing, although it was hard to feel embarrassed in the totally accepting atmosphere of the floor. It was also disabling. Without warning, an arm or leg would fly up. I remember sitting, playing bridge with Bill, Sadie, and "the Princess," a wealthy, uptight woman who had got herself hooked on pills and attempted suicide. I had had my last dose of pentobarbital. I could feel the drug losing its effect. I was excited about being drug-free and terrified at the same time. Suddenly, the day room grew bright and the objects in it sharply defined. It was as if the lights had gone on in a dark theater. I was fascinated. So this was what the world was supposed to look like. I was dealt a hand. As I picked it up my arm involuntarily snapped over my head and the cards flew across the room. The heightened illumination of the room now seemed sinister. My thoughts raced. I thought, "I'm going mad. This is the madhouse. I'm losing my mind. I'll never get out of here." I felt sheer terror. Yet, I picked up those cards and bid one no trump. Made the hand too. I wanted to talk about what was going on inside of me but I was afraid to. My thoughts became more confused. I jumped up, ran to my room, and collapsed. Doctor, I know part of it was physiological, but I must have been close to madness that night.

I fell into a troubled sleep. After I don't know how long, I woke to one of the strangest sensations I have ever felt. Waves of force emanated from the center of my abdomen, traveled through my body, and smashed against my skin. Rhythmic and relentless, wave succeeded wave. It felt like I would shatter. The impact of the waves against the surface of my body was so strong that I feared that I would fly off the bed. I reached up, grasped the bars of the bed, and held on for dear life. Smash, smash, smash, the waves kept coming relentlessly, inexorably. I thought of screaming out, but I didn't. Suddenly a thought occurred to me. "Good God, that's my anger, my rage, my, my, my anger coming out. This is not something happening *to* me; it *is* me—it's my rage." I held on to that thought as my last tie to reality. I repeated to myself over and over again, "It's my anger and nothing else." Doctor, it was sort of a Copernican revolution. It was my Copernican revolution. What I mean is that that thought changed the center of things for me like Copernicus changed the center of the solar system. It was I who was doing this thing, not some outside force. It took a long while for the waves of pressure to stop shattering themselves against my flesh, but the terror was gone. I fell into a deep sleep from which I awoke drained, yet somehow freer than I had been for a long time. Doctor, I suppose that you would classify what happened to me as a somatic delusion, but that doesn't matter. What does matter is that I was able to use it to "own" my anger.

The floor consisted of two long arms connected to a body consisting of the day room, the nursing station, and the dining room. During the days following the anger waves, I paced those arms, the corridors, obsessively. You are probably thinking I was going in and out of

Mother's arms to her breasts, the nursing station. Perhaps you're right on that, Doctor. It's probably of some significance that I forgot to mention that my mother was critically ill during my final binge. Responded to that one, didn't you Doctor? As it turned out Mother survived, but her illness must have had something to do with my prolonged binge.

One of the things I am most grateful to AA for is that it taught me how to mourn. When I returned to AA, I was able to mourn my father. That was an old loss and I think that my failure to come to terms with my feelings about him and his death were connected to my slip. Gratitude for being able to mourn. That's really crazy, isn't it, Doctor? I'm embarrassed by the depth of my feelings. AA puts a lot of emphasis on gratitude: gratitude for sobriety; gratitude for the Program itself. Sure sometimes that gratitude is defensive, another form of denial, but sometimes, it's genuine, at least it has been for me, and that's really important. It may sound like I'm intellectualizing again but I'm not. On the contrary, I'm choked up thinking of all I have to be grateful for.

As the days passed the spastic jerking of my extremities became less frequent. I still paced, but the focus of my concern had shifted. I became hypochondriacal and drove Pat, the nurse, crazy. Pat did not take kindly to my pestering and I considered her the floor ogre. During my hypochondriacal phase, I was very aware of my anger. At times it was so intense that I thought it might break me in half, but never after the anger-wave hallucination did I experience it as external. It was an objectless anger— free-floating rage.

I was so overwhelmed by the intensity of my rage and fear that I self-consciously tried to constrict my experience to an instance at a time. My world became more and more constricted until I was living in a succession of infinitesimal discrete moments, an infinitesimal at a time, so to speak. I did not dare look even five minutes ahead or behind; to do so engendered too much fear. I similarly constricted my spacial world. I mean this quite literally; when my anxiety was high enough I could feel my world shrinking toward an instant and a point. It was as if there was a camera in my head being focused more and more narrowly. I remember being in the gym totally overwhelmed by rage and fear and something like despair as I stared at the punching bag. Suddenly my visual field narrowed to a patch of pebbly brown. I tried to expand my visual field but I couldn't. I thought, "You really did it this time; all you can see are spots." Then I thought "So be it," and I started pounding that patch of pebbly brown with the pent-up rage of a lifetime. When I stopped, wringing wet and exhausted, my point-world gradually expanded to encompass the gym and my fellow patients. That was scope enough for me. I knew that something important had happened, but didn't understand what. I spent many hours punching that bag. It helped.

The hospital I was in did a terrific job of creating a sense of community. For all of the inevitable aloneness, there was a real feeling of shared adventure and of closeness on the floor. I liked the hospital's emphasis on being honest about your feelings and expressing them. It wasn't AA, but its values were similar. I know that I also have a lot of negative feelings about the hospital and the way I was treated like a prisoner. But my positive feelings aren't all phony or a form of denial either.

Paradoxically my period of being "stimulus bound," as I thought of it, coincided with my increasing involvement in the life of the floor. The way my perception of the world would expand and contract was almost cinematic. During my expansive periods, my relationships with Bill, Sadie, and the Princess, Jan, deepened. There was a real bond around the bridge table, a bond not without its conflicts and disturbances. I became increasingly afraid of Bill. He looked like he might kill everyone on the floor. Sitting across from him at the bridge table was no easy thing. He was threatening to sign himself out because his psychiatrist was insisting that he take a major tranquilizer. I told him I thought he was dangerous and that he should take the medicine. Amazingly he agreed. After that, we became closer and I was initiated into Tarot-card mystique. When I had a good reading, I felt elated. A recovery is made of many tiny steps, like those infinitesimals I spoke of, that accrete into something substantial and solid. Telling Bill he was dangerous was such a step for me. I'm preaching to you, aren't I, Doctor? Sadie was a lovely person who had had a lot of loss. I wished she would break those dishes. The Princess could be arrogant, but she was bright and witty. I enjoyed her. She had been in the hospital for a long time and was scheduled for discharge. She went on pass and took an overdose. Her suicide gesture greatly upset me; I thought nobody gets out of here intact. I was surprised when the Princess was discharged anyway. She was replaced by an overtly psychotic patient. When I told him I was in for alcohol abuse, he said, "Oh that, I stopped drinking years ago and joined AA—look at me now." This frightened and discouraged me more than the Princess's suicide attempt. About the same time, a late-middle-aged man was brought in on a stretcher. He was also an attempted suicide. He turned out to be a physician whose son had been killed in a South American political upheaval. He clearly did not want to live. The sadness in his eyes was as profound as the anger in Bill's. He was a charming and worldly man whose charm and worldliness were clearly automatic and emptily mechanical. He insisted on leaving the hospital. I was sure that he was going to his death.

During my "social period," I felt a great need for

approbation. After I confronted Bill, I seemed to regress. He improved on his medicine and was out on pass most of the time. The Princess was gone. Sadie offered little companionship. I felt isolated and alone. I became even more of a people pleaser; I felt that I needed the approval of every single person there. My facade turned people off, particularly Pat. Every night we had a community meeting. The night Jan left and Bill's discharge date was set, I was particularly forlorn, left behind in the madhouse. At the community meeting some blowhard droned on, monopolizing the conversation. I was furious but said nothing. I couldn't risk alienating anybody. I should tell you that a psychotic medical student had been brought in that day. Julie was a student at Einstein and kept repeating E equals MC squared. In the course of the day, she became more and more disorganized. They put her in the quiet room, an isolation cell used for out-of-control patients. The quiet room held a peculiar fascination for me. I was utterly and totally terrified by it. I was afraid of, and unconsciously wished to, lose control. Fear of confinement permeated every fiber of my being. The quiet room was a prison within a prison. I identified with Julie and her E equals MC squared and by that night all of my terrors were focused on the quiet room. At that community meeting I was not only desperately into people pleasing; I was in dread of losing control and being put in the quiet room.

So there I was, listening to a long-winded asshole ramble on. Suddenly I knew I had to say something. I was slumped down in a couch, almost buried in it. It took every bit of my strength to force myself to sit up. Sweating and shaking, I finally managed to say, "I don't like what you're doing; you're taking over this meeting; sit down and shut up." My body almost convulsed, but I had done it. I sank back into the couch. That was one of the hardest things I have ever done—it took more courage to say those few words than to accomplish many of the more significant things I have done. At the end of the meeting, Pat came over and put her arm around me and said, "You did good." I shan't forget that.

Speaking up at the community meeting opened things up for me. Julie grew increasingly agitated. I thought that she was reacting to being locked in the quiet room. Put in the quiet room because she was agitated; agitated because she was put in the quiet room. I would look hypnotically through the window of her locked door. She became more frantic. Finally they "snowed" her, put her out with massive doses of tranquilizers. Now she lay on the floor of the quiet room, unconscious, with her arm raised and splinted as an IV dripped into it. I thought, "They're killing her." I became totally absorbed in her fate. The quiet room became a symbol of all I feared and dreaded, yet perhaps secretly wanted — after all, hadn't I rendered myself unconscious with a drug, alcohol? Hadn't I sought death? That day in my session with Kruse, I said, "I'm afraid of you, you have too much power." The reference was to Julie, but I was thinking of myself. Making this comment to Dr. Kruse was difficult but not as difficult as speaking at the community meeting. Courage is cumulative — each instance of it makes the succeeding one easier.

Another way in which I opened up was by "running my story." I had learned to do this in AA. I ran my story to everybody who would listen and to some who didn't. I did it in group therapy, at community meetings, with the staff, and with my fellow patients. Each time I told my story, I learned something new.

I also opened up physically. I had been involved in recreation therapy, playing volleyball with the greatest reluctance. I played fearfully, holding my body tight and closed. I was self-protective to an extreme. Naturally my playing was awful. A few days after the community meeting, I was cajoled into playing. This time it was different. I could feel the energy flowing through my body. I became the game. I felt myself leaping into the air. I felt myself coming down hard. I felt myself taking risks. The closeness, the tightness, the self-protectiveness fell away. It was wonderful. They say that how you play the game is a picture of yourself; it's true. I was not self-conscious while it was happening, but afterwards, I processed what had occurred and that helped too.

I had a similar experience in occupational therapy. At first I was reluctant to do anything. I looked upon arts and crafts, "basket weaving," with contempt. But I said to myself, "I'll do this garbage anyway since I've decided to work the hospital for all it's worth." Commitment won over arrogance. I struggled for weeks to make a ceramic ashtray. At first it was almost impossible because my hands shook so much. Finally I finished the damn thing. I couldn't believe my reaction; I was ecstatic. I had proved that I could function in the face of anxiety. I told Pat that the ashtray was "an external and visible sign of an internal and invisible grace." She treated this bit of pretension with the contempt it deserved, but the idea behind it is valid enough. I think of that ashtray whenever I think I can't do something.

Julie stayed "snowed out," and I kept returning to her window to stare at her prostrate body much like a child compulsively putting his tongue to a sore loose tooth. One of the staff told me, "It's okay. She needs to regress." I oscillated between thinking that this was a bullshit rationalization for what they had done to her and that it reflected a really deep empathy. I guess that reflected my ambivalence toward the hospital—mistreated and understood at the same time. A few days later Julie was released from the quiet room. She and a tough street kid named Ruth immediately became friends. I remember one exchange between them. Julie asked,

"How is this nuthouse different from all other nut-houses?" Ruth answered, "It's the real McCoy." For some reason I loved the medical student and the street kid for this exchange.

I was getting better. I was given a pass to leave the hospital. As I walked out of the hospital and started to walk down the street, I felt a magnetic force drawing me back to the hospital. I don't mean this metaphorically; I mean I actually felt pulled back to the hospital. Another quasi-psychotic episode I suppose. I said, "No, this can't be happening." But it was. It felt like the force would pull me back. I fought it and succeeded in breaking loose. No doubt a projection of my desire to cling to the mother, eh, Doctor? Or was it the regressive, seductive pull of addiction? Fortunately, I had had enough regression; I feared it more than I desired it. I started to run and didn't stop until the pull was gone.

I felt a surge of joy. I was free. I bounded toward the park. I felt as if I had springs in my heels. Looking back on it, I was more than a little manicky. AA calls this the "pink cloud." I ran toward the polar bears at the zoo. They seemed glad to see me. We spoke for a while. I felt a great sense of communion with the polar bears. A psychologist wrote of the toddler's "love affair with the world." My feelings in the park were like that. Later in the day I, so to speak, stubbed my toe and ran crying back to my mother-hospital. You know, Doctor, AA's like that — a safe home base from which you can go into the world, take your lumps, and return to be comforted. We all need that, don't we?

After a while I left the park and went to my new girlfriend's. The hospital strictly regulated phone calls and visits. When she was finally allowed to visit, Ann had been very supportive. I shared as much of my hospital experience with her as I was able to. I had an over-whelming fear of being impotent sober. If you've been to

AA meetings, Doctor, you know that's a very common fear. At her last visit, I had spent an hour explaining to Ann that we couldn't make love for at least a year. I was perfectly serious. Five minutes after I arrived in her apartment, we were in bed. Everything went fine.

Several hours later, I left Ann to go to an AA meeting. I had come down off my pink cloud, but I was still feeling good. That wasn't to last long. I was excited about going back to my old group. I had bounced in and out of that meeting during my nine months of drinking. Now I was sober and hopeful. I walked into the meeting and immediately felt estranged. I couldn't connect with anything or anybody. It was horrible. I sat through the meeting, but I really wasn't there. I felt very far away. It was as if a viscous fluid surrounded me and isolated me. Again I do not speak metaphorically. I could feel that viscous medium intruding between me and the people in that room. It prevented me from making human contact. It was like being underwater. I must have been doing the distancing, but I sure didn't know that I was doing it. I left in a state of deep despair. Whatever my ambivalence toward the hospital, I felt warmth and concern there. I had counted on finding that at my AA meeting. I didn't or couldn't or didn't want to or something, but it surely didn't work. I have never felt as alone as I did on my return to the hospital. I felt defeated and profoundly depressed. I wanted to give up. I think that was my bottom. I knew that I couldn't drink anymore. It just wasn't going to work for me, but I wasn't at all sure that I wanted to live if sobriety was going to be like that.

During the following days, I went through the hospital routine mechanically. My friends had been discharged, making me feel even more forlorn and abandoned. For some reason I didn't talk about my experience at the AA meeting. Although Julie was out of solitary, I was still obsessed with the quiet room. Although I didn't know it, I had put myself into a quiet room by emotionally detaching at that AA meeting. My discharge was approaching. I thought that I would probably kill myself. I was given another pass. I didn't want to use it, but I did. With great reluctance I decided to try a new AA group. This one met at the Church of the Epiphany, a few blocks from the hospital. I was very shaky as I walked into that meeting. I didn't really expect anything good to happen. The meeting started. The preamble was read: "Alcoholics Anonymous is a fellowship of men and women who share their experience, strength, and hope with each other. . . ." Something happened. Those words sounded like pure poetry.

The speaker was a beautiful young woman, intensely and vibrantly alive. Her vivacity and sparkle certainly facilitated what was about to happen. She spoke of her years of drugging and drinking, of her progressive spiritual and emotional death. Finally she said, "I got to the point that I couldn't feel anything. For no particular reason I went on a trip across the country with some drinking buddies. As we crossed the country, my feelings became more and more frozen. We arrived at the Grand Canyon. I looked at it and felt nothing. I knew that I should be responding with awe and wonder to the sight before me, but I couldn't. I had always loved nature, now that love, like everything else about me, was dead. I decided to take a picture of the magnificence spread before me so that if I ever unmelted I could look at the picture and feel what I couldn't feel then."

At that moment something incredible happened to me. I completely identified with the speaker. I understood her frozen feelings, they were mine; I understood her wish to preserve a precious moment in the hope that someday she could adequately respond with feelings of awe and wonder to it. Something welled up in me. I began to sob, deep, strong, powerful sobs; they did not stop for the hour and a half that the meeting lasted. As the speaker told her story—how she managed to stop drugging and drinking and how her feelings had become unfrozen, my feelings became unfrozen. I was still crying when I shook her hand and thanked her. I walked out of the meeting feeling happy. Happy, Doctor. I couldn't even remember feeling happy.

As I walked down the street toward the hospital, the tears were still flowing. Now they were tears of happiness and gratitude. I who had been so formal and controlled and concerned to impress walked past staring strollers with tears streaming down completely indifferent to, indeed oblivious of, their reactions. Doctor, do you know Edna St. Vincent Millay's poem "Renascence"? It tells of a young woman who has been buried, then the rain comes washing her grave away, returning her to life. She becomes aware of "A fragrance such as never clings/ To aught save happy things. . . ." I had always loved that poem, now I truly understood it. My tears were like the rain in the poem; they, like the rain, washed me out of the grave I had dug for myself with alcohol and emotional repression. I too smelled the fragrance that never clings to aught save happy living things.

I walked into the floor feeling buoyant. As I joined the perpetual rap session in the day room, a thought came to me, "God in is the quiet room." I didn't know where it came from nor what I meant by it, but I vocalized it. I think it had something to do with feeling loved and connected and potentially loving myself. It seemed that whatever I had experienced at that AA meeting was also present in the quiet room. That's as close as I can get to understanding what I was trying to express in that phrase. What happened at the meeting had something to do with receptivity, with being open and being able to hear. That part of it was a gift. From whom I do not know.

Well, Doctor, I'm not much on theodicies, and I can't do much with a young girl going mad as a manifestation of divine grace. I don't know who or what, if anything, is out there and I haven't become religious in any formal sense — I don't belong to a church. So when I said, "God is in the quiet room," I must have meant it in some metaphorical sense. But I did mean it. There was certainly denial in that statement, denial of evil and pain and sorrow, denial of all I hated about the hospital, denial of my rage at the waste that my life had been, but there was something else in it too, something that liberated me to engage in the long, slow, up-and-down struggle for health. In AA we say that sobriety is an adventure; it certainly has been for me.

TAKING ACTION

Herman, Sally, Betty, and David hit bottom in very different ways. Yet all of them made the same discovery — drinking alcohol the way they drank it just wouldn't work for them anymore. Each realized that he or she was powerless over alcohol. All but Herman went through a period of deep despair before they were able to feel hope. Each bottom is unique, yet essentially the same as all other bottoms. Insight is particular and it is universal. Bottoms occur in bars (Herman), at AA meetings (Sally), at home (Betty), and in hospitals (David). They occur at all ages, in all stages of drinking. They are triggered by all sorts of experiences ranging from the quietest inward sense that drinking is spiritually impoverishing to the highest-volume external threats of failing health, job loss, or loss of love.

Since people hit bottom in such different ways, you must be wondering what you need to do to experience your bottom. The first thing you need to do is to decide if you are drinking too much. Problem drinking doesn't necessarily lead to the kind of despair that characterizes bottom. Some kinds of realizing that you are drinking too much are more cognitive — more intellectual judgements than shattering revelations of how totally your life is dominated by alcohol. The first step in dealing with a drinking problem is recognizing it, whether such recognition results from intellectual awareness or from emotional revelation. *What did you decide in the last chapter? Do you drink too much?* If your answer is yes, do you drink too much in the sense of getting drunk on occasion, or in the sense of problem drinking, or in the sense of alcoholic (addictive) drinking? If your drinking too much means drunkenness, the next step is to decide whether or not you are getting your money's worth out of getting smashed. What's the cost/benefit ratio? Is the release, the relief from frustration, the disinhibition, worth the physical and emotional hangover? If the numerator (cost) is greater than the denominator (benefits), that is, if the cost/benefit ratio is greater than one, you have a bum deal. Try to assign some numbers to this ratio — if you come out with more than .5, I would consider trying to find another way of dealing with frustration. Why don't you decide not to get drunk the next few times you're in the mood? If you can't do it, you're not an occasional relief drinker, you're a problem drinker. Consider finding other forms of release, other ways to handle frustration, other ways to let go. Psychotherapy can help you do these things and you can still get drunk now and again if that turns you on.

TAKING A VACATION FROM DRINKING

If you decide that you're a problem drinker, the best thing you can do is to take a drug "holiday." Stop drinking (and drugging) for ninety days. That shouldn't be too hard to do. When we were talking about Betty, I suggested that you stop for a while if you were experiencing emotional distress, but emotional stress isn't the only kind of problem associated with drinking. If you decided that you are having problems of any sort — financial, interpersonal, legal, vocational, physical, emotional, or whatever — with, or because of alcohol, then take my suggestion and go on that alcohol-free holiday. See how you feel at the end of the ninety days. Are you less depressed? Are you less anxious? Are you working better? Have your personal relationships improved? If so, you may want to consider leaving the cork in the bottle and the bottle on the shelf. Maybe the stuff isn't worth it. Or you may want to try drinking again. If you do, drink low-proof stuff and do it in moderation. If you find that you can't do this, then you are not a problem drinker, you are an alcoholic. If you resented stopping when you stopped, you won't feel better — you will have been in a sullen rage the whole time like a baby whose bottle has been taken away. So don't stop unless you really want to — it simply won't work. Problem drinking by definition resolves itself. Problem drinking returns to normal when stress goes down. If you're a problem drinker, you learn from experience. After one DWI (arrest for driving while intoxicated) you don't drink and drive, after losing a job you don't drink at lunch, and so forth. Since both occasional drunkenness and problem drinking are either self-limiting or something else, I won't spend any more time on them. They are states in which voluntary control of how much and how often to drink is still possible. Such drinking is volitional. Relief drinkers and problem drinkers can control their drinking, alcoholic drinkers can not. Admittedly, the distinction is sometimes hard to make and drinkers don't always fall all that clearly into one or the other category. As the statisticians say, trouble with alcohol is a continuous, not a dichotomous, variable. Nevertheless, there does seem to be something like AA's invisible line, the crossing of which cannot be undone. That is why I recommend that those who consider themselves relief drinkers (occasional drunks) and those who consider themselves problem drinkers stop for a while and then resume, if they so choose, to see whether or not they lose control. John Barleycorn himself, so to speak, decides the issue. Many who try this experiment find that drinking is no longer any fun when they resume — instead of being spontaneous and free, drinking is now too self-conscious and constrained. This may happen to you. For those who don't lose control over a period of time or otherwise injure themselves, drinking or not drinking remain possible choices. But what about the kind of drinking too much that isn't self-limiting? What about alcoholism? What can you do about that?

RELINQUISHING DENIAL

The first thing is recognizing it. Peek behind your fear and let a little light come through. Usually the first glimpse behind the veil is a very frightening one. It was for most of the folks who shared their bottoms with us. The ancient Greek philosopher Plato understood alcoholism. In his famous dialogue, *The Republic,* he recounts the "Myth of the Cave." In Plato's myth prisoners are chained to the walls of a cave in such a way that the only illumination comes from behind them and the only things that they can see are the shadows cast on the walls of the cave. They mistake the shadows for the things themselves; illusion for reality. When the prisoners are released from their chains and emerge into the light of the sun which shows them as they really are, they are overwhelmed. The light of the sun is too much for them; they are used to the darkness and shadows of the cave. Overcome by the brilliance of the sun, they run back into the cave and mistake shadows for reality once again. Plato was talking about the human condition when he wrote this, but what a metaphor for what happens when people realize that they are drinking too much. The cave is denial, each prisoner is an alcoholic drinker, the shadows are the drinking, the sun is insight, and the life above ground sobriety. Very many have not been able to stand the sun and have returned to the darkness of the cave of alcohol addiction. That's like almost hitting bottom, panicking (being blinded by the sun), and returning to the bottle. Bottles are a lot like caves, aren't they?

Once you look out of the cave and see the sun, the next thing you need to do is to feel your despair, your hopelessness, your helplessness, your powerlessness over alcohol. Let it sink deep into your pores like a stain penetrating wood until it stains your soul indelibly, then you won't return to the cave. See if you can convince yourself that there is no more solace in the bottle, that on the contrary, there is only agony. Now you know that drinking will no longer bring cessation of pain, let alone pleasure. *You have hit bottom.* Your ego has been deflated by your admission of powerlessness over alcohol, and you have surrendered, admitted that you cannot drink safely or pleasurably any longer. Although you have lost nothing through ego deflation since your inflated ego was empty bravado thinly papering-over your abysmally low self-esteem, you probably don't know this and feel as if you have lost something of great value.

Additionally, the thought that you have *lost control* of your drinking is probably a terrible wound to your self-esteem. To not be able to drink is experienced as a fatal flaw in the self and if you're as perfectionistic as most alcoholics, this is intolerable. You must not be so damaged. You may not want to drink in the worst way, yet be unable to stand the thought of not being able to do so. You are in a dangerous place.

YOU DON'T HAVE TO DO IT ALONE

You need help. The place to find it is AA. You need hope. The place to find it is AA. You need to affiliate with people. The place to find them is AA. You need understanding. The place to find it is AA. I know that I am getting ahead of myself by talking about AA at this point, but I feel so strongly that AA is the best place to be after hitting bottom that I am pointing you that way right now. All of my clinical experience tells me that AA is the way to go. Even if you turn out not to be an AA person and wind up maintaining your sobriety some other way, AA is your best bet for the first year. Try it. Go to a meeting—you can always leave. Only you can get you sober, but *you can't do it alone,* at least not comfortably, and you don't have to. It's too difficult and too dangerous. The idea that you can't do it alone, that you need help, is probably another blow to your self-esteem. The idea of needing help doesn't go with your self-image. Frankly, that's bullshit; we all need help—people are interdependent, need each other, and to deny it is just as futile as denying your alcoholism. Such denial is a manifestation of *pseudo self-suffi-*

ciency. Underneath pseudo self-sufficiency is fear; fear of being swallowed up by other people and/or fear of being hurt or disappointed by them. Generally speaking men have more trouble asking for help than women, but both sexes find this difficult. It goes against the whole American thing about self-reliance. The problem isn't in being dependent, there is no way not to be, but in being dependent in the wrong way, say on alcohol or drugs. Far better to be dependent on — really interdependent *with* — people than on chemicals. One reason this is so hard to accept is that you had the illusion that you had control over your drinking, but you can't control other people however much you would like to, so you are afraid. Well, you have admitted that you don't have control over alcohol any longer, so what do you have to lose by trying something else, say a self-help group like AA? Affiliate with people who understand your problem. You will learn more from the folks who have been there than from anyone else. I would also urge you to get professional help, but more about that in the next chapter.

ONE DAY AT A TIME

The treatment of alcoholism is abstinence from alcohol one day at a time. It is also necessary to abstain from all other mood-changing drugs — pot, uppers, downers, hallucinogens, and tranquilizers. The only exception is medication prescribed by a psychiatrist who knows that you are alcoholic and who has experience in treating alcoholism. There are two things to remember in early sobriety: the first is that you have a disease; the second is that you have to stay away from alcohol only one day at a time. It is only for today. The disease concept means that you don't have to feel guilty about having the disease of alcoholism although you are responsible for treating it. The one-day-at-a-time concept can be modified to an hour or a minute at a time. It works. It works because it reflects reality. We have only today and today is manageable no matter what it brings. It's the way an addiction is treated, a book is written, a home is built, a marriage is sustained. I know. I use the one-day-at-a-time concept to deal with my life, and it works. Before I did, I rarely reached my goals. Now I do. A friend of mine, a brilliant psychoanalyst, told me the way he and his wife dealt with her fatal illness was "one day at a time." For all the elegance, beauty, and power of psychoanalytic theory, it was "one day at a time" that got those people through. Try it. You'll be glad you did.

So now you have tools to help you deal with your sobriety. Sobriety? Yep. If you've followed me this far, you're sober now. The trick is to sustain it. I'll tell you more about how to do that shortly, but first I'd like to tell more about what to expect after you hit your bottom.

LIFE AT AND AFTER YOUR BOTTOM

Sobriety and Others

The effects of your sobriety on others may not be what you'd expect nor what you would wish. It is best to approach sobriety as an adventure into the unknown. Surprising things happen. The surprises are mostly happy ones, but not all are, and in truth, you aren't in a good position to evaluate if things that happen in early sobriety are good or bad for you. AA suggests that you don't make any major decisions, or major changes in your life during your first year of sobriety if you can avoid them. I agree with this. You will change a great deal during the next year and may want very different things then than you do now.

Disappointment over relationships not going the way people want them to after the achievement of sobriety causes so much trouble that I will restate the point: if you get sober, your relationship with him/her may improve and give you great happiness. However, this won't simply happen; all concerned are going to have to work at it, or your relationship may go downhill and fail. *The purpose of sobriety is not the avoidance of divorce.* The strangest things sometimes happen when drinkers quit. I once knew a man, Kevin, who was in the advanced stages of alcoholism. His wife could no longer stand him or his besotten sexual advances. She insisted that he leave her bed. Stung by this rejection, Kevin seethed with resentment. He looked for another bed in which he would be more welcome, but he was too far gone to find one, so he looked for other options. He slept on the living room floor for a while and then had a moment of illumination. Kevin lived in a rural area and kept a few animals. Mobilizing his feeble resources he thought, "She can go hang. I'll sleep with the goat," and he did. He felt accepted and secure with the goat, but his newfound relationship did nothing to arrest his alcoholism. Eventually he collapsed and was hospitalized. During his hospitalization, he hit bottom and stopped drinking. Returning home sober, he found his wife welcomed him back into the marriage bed. He joined AA, came for counseling, and remained sober. After he had been in treatment for quite a few months, he came for a session red-faced and stammering. I had never known him to blush. He said, "Doctor, I don't know how to tell you this, but I've left my wife's bed — I discovered I can't stand her, all she does is criticize and complain — I moved back in with the goat. I don't know if you can understand it, but I'm happy. I like sleeping with the goat; she's warm and loving and having inter-course isn't at the top of my list right now. Besides, the way my wife does it, I'd rather have the goat." As far as I know, Kevin is still married, doesn't drink, and sleeps with the goat. To all appearances he is a happy man. As they say in AA, "Live and let live," so who am I to suggest that this isn't the best of domestic arrangements?

Let us leave Kevin with his goat (and his wife) and return to you. I am going to assume that you have now experienced some form of ego deflation, have hit bottom, and surrendered. If you haven't done these things yet, imagine that you have and follow along in imagination into the days of early sobriety. You are living through or have lived through despair, the dark night of the soul, which is your bottom, and you are, or soon will be, experiencing the exhilaration of the pink cloud. The pink cloud is to be enjoyed for what it is — the thrill of surviving a fatal illness. But it is wise to keep in mind that nothing stays that good forever. The best dinner, the greatest sex, the most outstanding performance comes to an end, but that's no reason not to enjoy them while you have them. The same for the pink cloud. You should also keep in mind that your pink cloud is also a "manic defense" against underlying depression. That is, it is a way of escaping and avoiding a good deal of underlying pain. Manic here does not refer to the serious mental illness called manic–depression. It simply means that your high is in part a protection, a defense against some depressed feelings that are also there but out of your awareness for the moment. That's fine, it's where you are supposed to be in early sobriety. The important thing is that you know that you are on a somewhat artificial high and that you don't entirely trust it. For now, it protects you from having to deal with more than you can handle just yet. In short: enjoy but be wary of the pink cloud.

Perhaps you are oscillating between despair and hope. Although you are certainly in a better space than you were when you were drinking, it may not feel that way. At best, your gains are tenuous. Your task now is to lock them in. How do you do that? The answer is simple but not easy. *Don't drink, and go to meetings.* Don't drink if your ass falls off (and it probably feels like it will at times). Delay, put off that drink. Remember one day, one hour, one minute at a time. "I won't drink now." Time is on your side now. Time has become time to heal and time to grow. If you stopped drinking on your own, it's going to be pretty rough from time to time; if you went through an alcohol rehab it's still going to be pretty rough from time to time. So go to AA meetings and don't drink when your ass falls off—in all likelihood it isn't really falling off, it just feels that way.

Feeling Empty

Earlier, I talked about taking something—alcohol—in from the outside because something was missing inside. Perhaps you had whatever it is you are missing now—a satisfactory, reasonably constant level of self-esteem; the ability to comfort yourself; a secure sense of your identity—before the sauce took it away from you. Perhaps you never had these things, but either way, you're playing with less than a full deck now. That's dangerous. It means that you don't have the very resources you need to maintain sobriety, and without sobriety, there is no way to get those resources. Psychologists use highfalutin terms like internalization and introjection to describe the process of taking things in from the environment — that means the people around us — and making them parts of ourselves. The words don't really explain anything because the process isn't understood — maybe this internalization stuff is only a metaphor — but something like that does seem to happen. What it comes to is this — if you have good experiences with people at the right stages of your life, you take some of that good experience away with you, and you can do things and feel things like experiencing yourself as whole and worthwhile, that you couldn't do before. So now you are able to soothe yourself, maintain your self-esteem, modulate your anxiety, screen out overwhelming stimuli, and be comfortably alone. Now you can do for yourself things that were once done for you by your parents. That is, you acquired these abilities if you were lucky and things went well between you as a baby and toddler and those who cared for you.

If you weren't so lucky, you never acquired the ability to do these things for yourself with anywhere near the reliability that you need to feel secure and safe. So you looked to alcohol to do these things for you. Since you didn't get what you needed from outside yourself — needed from other people — there was no way that they could get inside you, become part of you, so naturally enough you looked outside yourself to the bottle to give it to you. The only problem with doing that is that these capacities, these tools for living as AA calls them, can not be acquired from alcohol; they can only be acquired through relationships with people. Booze can quiet your anxiety, raise your self-esteem, stop you from feeling overwhelmed or from falling to pieces for a while, or at least give the illusion that it does so, but it can never teach you to do these things for yourself. Alcohol induces a sort of mental and emotional diarrhea; the stuff just runs through and you derive no emotional or psychological benefit from it. You can't grow that way.

Heinz Kohut, a psychoanalyst who has written on the development of the self through internalization (1977), compares attempting to build "psychic structure," his term for those tools for living well that should be in our heads and hearts, by drinking to someone with a gastric fistula, a hole in his stomach, trying to satisfy his hunger and nourish himself by eating. No way, Hosea. Nothing sticks, it pours right out. So it is when you internalize martinis instead of loving care — it just doesn't work. If you grew up in an alcoholic home, obviously the conditions necessary for smooth internalization just weren't there, at least not consistently, so you will have trouble with self-esteem, anxiety, taking decent care of yourself, self-cohesion (holding it together), and being creatively alone, even if you yourself are not alcoholic.

Now, you may have not been so unfortunate in your early life and you may have acquired a pretty adequate set of tools for living, but no developmental or psychological battles are won for good and all. You can always go backward and lose what you have gained. So, even if you acquired a good set of skills for keeping your emotional house in order through internalization, identification, and just plain learning, you lost them during your years of addiction to alcohol. Alcoholism impoverishes. It takes away not only your money, your job, your health, but even more importantly, your emotional resources. *Everybody* who reaches bottom, *everybody* who is at the end of an alcoholic career, *everybody* who lives through the addictive process has abysmally low, unstable self-esteem, a tenuous sense of themselves and who they are — if they have any sense of themselves at all — a radically impaired capacity to deal with their feelings, especially anxiety, and not much capacity to maintain a sense of well-being. This is true whether or not you ever had these capacities. Alcohol may not have taken any material things away from you, but *it damaged you emotionally and psychologically.* Prolonged heavy drinking always does that.

The developmental stage at which "psychic structure," AA's tools for living, are normally acquired is called the stage of the development of the cohesive self. It is the stage at which we come together and feel that we are we. Before that, we have feelings and sensations but not much sense of self. Kohut calls the stage before we come together the stage of the fragmented self. There are self-pieces but no center. No sense of having a cohesive self, of feeling centered and together, no sense of being an ongoing enterprise that endures in time and has boundaries in space, no sense of being the initiator of actions. Adults who remain there, or go backward to that point, suffer mental illness. If you are reading this book, you are extremely unlikely to be back at the stage of the fragmented self. When people go back there, we say "they are going to pieces." If you recently stopped drinking, you are most probably one step up the ladder at the stage of the primitive cohesive self. *What you are most afraid of — besides not being able to drink — is fragmenting, falling to pieces.* This is a kind of panic, terror of losing it, meaning yourself. This is terrifying. Your fear is understandable since your sense of yourself is so shaky, but you are highly unlikely to lose yourself in the way you fear. It sure feels like you will, just like it feels like your ass — a part of yourself — is falling off. Talking about your ass falling off is AA's way of talking about the fear of going to pieces, of fragmenting and losing yourself. This kind of panic terror is sometimes experienced as fear of going mad. To go mad is indeed to lose yourself. Let me reassure you, recovery from alcoholism does not lead to madness nor to falling apart. It feels that way because you are no longer anesthetized by the alcohol you were using, so you feel your condition much more acutely. Actually you are more together than you have been in years, but it is going to take a while before it feels that way. Booze deceives. You thought you needed it to hold yourself together when in reality it was tearing you apart.

Why You Feel So Anxious Sober

The kind of anxiety I am calling panic terror of losing the self is so painful that people often turn it into something else — fear of losing things instead of themselves. If you don't convert your panic dread into fear of losing concrete external things, what you feel is sheer terror without an object. You don't know what you fear. That's horrible. If you are experiencing overwhelming anxiety in early sobriety, *it has definite causes* although you don't know what they are. You are anxious because you are afraid that you will lose control and drink; you are anxious because you know that you can't drink; you are anxious because your nervous system is rebounding from years of abuse; but preeminently you are anxious because you are afraid that you will fragment and go to pieces. You won't. Knowing the source of your anxiety doesn't make it go away but does take the terror out of it.

Some of your fears of losing particular things are ways of giving a name to your nameless terror, but some of them are not, they are all-too-real in themselves. You become anxious when you fear loss of love, loss of role, or loss of material things. Your drinking too much may have put your possessions, any or all of them, in jeopardy. Self-esteem comes from within, but getting a few goodies from the outside increases self-esteem and lowers anxiety if you don't feel too guilty about getting them. I once had a patient who understood this very well. He said to me, "Other things being equal, I'd rather be anxious in a Rolls Royce than in the subway." I can identify with that, but it isn't really fear of losing the Rolls that makes you anxious; it's fear of loss of self-esteem, fear of loss of love, and fear of loss of self. The story is told of the man who goes to the doctor and says, "Doctor, my head aches, my bowels are upset, and my feet hurt, and to tell the truth, I myself don't feel so well either." If you are an alcoholic in the early stages of recovery, you are well aware of the headache, the bellyache, and the aching feet, but you aren't so sure about the "I myself." You aren't quite sure if there is an "I myself" or only those not-so-good feelings. In growing up you passed from the stage of the fragmented self, the various aches, to the stage of the primitive cohesive self, the "I myself" of the folk story. This stage is the point in development when psychic structure is built, those tools for living are acquired. And it is precisely those tools, the abilities to soothe yourself, quiet your anxiety, take care of yourself, maintain your self-esteem, and feel centered, cohesive, and good that constitute the core of yourself. Your sense of identity accretes around that core. At this stage of your sobriety your sense of identity is tenuous. You aren't sure who you are or even if you are. Alcohol has brought you back to the insecurities of toddlerhood when you first struggled to achieve an identity.

To make things even more difficult, your self-concept is not clearly differentiated from your concepts of other people. Let me put that differently—you have mental representations of yourself and mental representations of others. In healthy adulthood these representations are distinct and separate, but that wasn't always so. Early in life, self-representations and object-representations— mental images of others—are fused, and it was not clear where you ended and where Mommie began. Psychoanalysts speak of those amalgamated, fused, and confused mental representations as "self-objects." The primitive self is a self-object, it has aspects of you and aspects of others all jumbled up. In early development your concepts of others were part of your concepts of yourself. They were part of you and you were part of them. There is certain richness in this comingling and later on you took aspects of others and incorporated them, made them truly part of you but without any confusion over who is who. For example, when you were being soothed by Father at a very young age, it wasn't clear to you if you were doing the soothing or he was. Later on the ability to soothe became yours although it originally came from him.

Self-objects are both the mental representations and the people we relate to in this way—as part of ourselves. When we grow up, we experience ourselves as more and more separate both in our heads and in our relations with other people. The process of achieving this differentiation is called "separation-individuation." It is the process of becoming you. *Alcohol blurs boundaries,* and you once again become confused about where you stop and the world and the people in it begin. Of course, your sense of who and where you are wasn't totally lost during your drinking; if it was you would not be in contact with reality, your confusion would be too great. But there *is* considerable confusion of this sort in early sobriety and it makes you anxious. Your confusion over your boundaries manifests itself in your *expecting to be able to control other people.* After all, if they are an extension or part of you, they should be under your control just as much as your arm or your leg is. Of course, you don't really have that kind of control over other people and when they don't respond as you wish and expect, your response is rage. This kind of intense rage is dangerous in early sobriety—it can act as a drink signal leading to the "drop dead martini."

So this *regression/fixation,* this going back to or being stuck at the stage of the primitive self in early sobriety, has several very practical implications: (1) it makes you anxious because your sense of self is so insecure that you are afraid of losing it, (2) you are likely to have trouble managing your psychic economy and your emotional life because you don't have some or all of those tools for living securely in your head and heart, and (3) you may be depressed because you feel empty without that psychic structure, those tools within. You tried to fill that emptiness with booze and now that you are no longer doing so, you experience your emptiness more intensely. And (4) you feel anxious because you're not too sure what's you and what's not, where you stop and where the world begins—this kind of confusion is unconscious, outside of your awareness. What you are aware of is intense rage when other people don't respond to you the way you wish—that is, as if they were parts of you. This is complicated psychological theory all right, but it is about real bread-and-butter issues—the difficulties of early sobriety.

There is another aspect to this regression/fixation business that concerns your feelings and how you experience them. There is research evidence that people who use alcohol to excess experience their feelings and sensations more intensely than the average person. This makes feelings hard for them to handle and leads to the use of an anesthetizing, down drug—alcohol—to help manage them. There is a developmental aspect to handling feelings. At the beginning of life and for a long time thereafter, feelings are experienced without much discrimination, without any fine-tuning. They feel good or they feel bad and aren't further sorted out. The feeling good we'll ignore for the moment. What about the feeling bad? Well, healthy adults can usually sort out exactly what kind of feeling bad they are experiencing. They know that they are sad, or tense, or angry, or anxious, or whatever. They can also scale their feelings in terms of intensity so some are mild, some moderate, and some extreme. Then they can either stay with their feelings or do something to change them. Small children can't do that. They don't have labels for the different kinds of bad feelings. They just know that they are terribly upset and can't stand what they are feeling. It all feels awful. Alcoholism takes you back to the stage where bad feelings are massive, undifferentiated, and unmanageable. Any bad feeling makes you anxious, depressed, and panicky, all at the same time. You can't sort it out. This is called "affect (feeling) regression." It can lead to big trouble in early sobriety.

Feelings are biological judgments, evaluations of inner and outer experience as well as guides to action. To be confused about them is to be at a serious disadvantage in life. The way you learned to distinguish and discriminate your feelings was from others. Mommie or Daddy said, "Johnny, you're crying because you're angry," or "Mary, you're feeling blue today." Slowly you learned to do this for yourself. So once again something that becomes part of you, got inside of you, came from the outside — came from other people. Since you've lost at least some of your ability to label your feelings correctly and rate their intensity in the course of your drinking, you need people to do this for you for a while until you relearn, reinternalize this vital component of a healthy psyche. If you never learned to sort out your feelings very well to begin with, this learning will be harder for you, but thoroughly possible. You can get the feedback, the help in labeling and understanding your feelings that you need, from the members of your AA group or from a therapist. This is yet another reason not to do it alone. Not having labels for feelings and not knowing how to sort them out causes anxiety and confusion. It endangers your sobriety. Knowing what's happening inside you changes that. Francis Bacon, the seventeenth-century philosopher who was one of the founders of modern science said, "Knowledge is power." He was referring to knowledge of nature, but it's even more true of self-knowledge.

Developing Trust

There is yet another legacy from childhood that it is hoped you have brought to your adult life. That is the ability to trust. You learned to trust by being treated in a trustworthy way by those who cared for you. If you were fortunate enough to have had good experiences in early childhood, then the world seems like a safe place with good things in it for you. Of course you need mistrust too — the world can be a dangerous place. The trick is to get the right balance with trust predominating over distrust. I once trusted a patient who was a fast operator to pay my fee when he got on his feet. Eventually he did financially, although he was in all sorts of other difficulties. I asked for the sum due. He said, "Why should I pay you? One of my symptoms when I came here was fiscal irresponsibility and you didn't cure that as proved by my owing you money. So I don't owe you anything." Clearly I needed a little more mistrust that time.

Depending on your background and your native endowment, you brought some capacity for trust to your drinking career. After all you trusted alcohol to make you feel good. If your early life didn't provide you enough good things, you probably grew up doubting that there was much good stuff for you in the world and are pretty skeptical and suspicious. You grew more mistrustful in the course of your drinking. In the end, your fermented friends betrayed you, so you have little reason to trust now. You are like the business partners at the annual company picnic. One said to the other, "Oh, my God, we left the safe open." To which his partner replied, "So what are you worried about, we're both here." Besides being betrayed by alcohol, the whole drinking life-style with its conceal-ments, denial, and manipulations has left you distrustful. This is a really serious barrier to recovery. You simply can't recover without trusting somebody or something. What you must do is act as if you trusted me, your AA group, your counselor, or whoever you turn to for help until you have enough good experience to feel genuinely trustful.

ALCOHOL AND LOVE OF SELF

There are two kinds of problems with the self associated with alcoholism. The first has to do with deficits in the self — it lacks tools and is not securely coherent. I have already talked about this kind of problem with the self. The second has to do with a disturbance in how you love yourself. Alcoholics are necessarily overly self-involved. In some sense they love themselves too much; but at the same time they are destroying themselves, so in some sense they must love themselves too little. Can you identify with simultaneously loving yourself too much and not enough? If you are alcoholic you should be able to without much difficulty. The problem is that you love yourself "not wisely, but too well." Love of self is called narcissism. The term comes from the story of Narcissus. In that Greek legend, Narcissus is a beautiful youth who spurns the love of all until he sees his own reflection in the surface of a spring and falls in love with it. He is so infatuated with himself that he remains staring at his reflection until he pines away and dies. He is transformed into a flower, the narcissus. It is fascinating that this flower benumbs, which is the meaning of the Greek root *narke*. The same root is used in the English word narcotic. So Narcissus lends his name to both pathological self-love and to narcotic, that which benumbs. Language itself connects the two. The myth warns us that there is something dangerous about self-love, or at least with self-infatuation. We can love ourselves to death, and this quite literally according to the myth. Narcissus was so hung up on himself that he perished. Yet without self-love we would also perish; it is the force that moves us to take proper care of ourselves, to preserve ourselves, and to maintain our self-esteem. So there are two forms of narcissism, of self-love: one that destroys and one that preserves. The first is called pathological narcissism, sick self-love; and the second is called healthy narcissism, healthy self-love. Sorting them out is one of the hardest of life's tasks. Hillel, the great rabbi of classical antiquity, said, "If I am not for myself, who will be for me? If I am only for myself, what am I? If not now, when?" AA could easily incorporate Hillel's wisdom into its Steps. His sentiments are entirely congruent with the values and ethos of AA, which teaches both the proper form of self-love and the importance of living in the present (if not now, when?). It is for this reason that AA calls itself a selfish Program (if I am not for myself . . .). Here we have another of the paradoxes associated with alcoholism — by being selfish, by being for yourself, you wind up being for others also. In fact, only those who have a healthy love for themselves are capable of healthy love for others. So one of the first tasks of sobriety is to be good to yourself. That may not be as easy as it sounds; you haven't been doing it for a very long time.

Drink Signals

One way that you can be good to yourself is to become aware of drink signals that threaten your sobriety. A drink signal is anything within you or outside you that triggers a desire to drink. A drink signal may be a feeling, say, loneliness, or it may be the stop sign at Front and Main that reminds you that the Feel Good Lounge is in the next block. It may be the heavy-hitting neighbor you used to chug-a-lug with. As AA puts it, drink signals are "people, places, and things" that set you off. Become aware of them, avoid those you can, and be on alert when you're around the ones you can't avoid. If you think it through, you will discover that you can avoid far more of them than you thought you could. Remember, "first things first," and the first thing is staying sober.

I want to go back to the issue of trust because it is so important to your sobriety. I will try to show you that your trust in booze was a pseudotrust and that the only real trusting relationships are with people. You trusted hooch until it turned on you. In fact, you trusted it more than you trusted people. That's one reason you got overinvolved with drinking in the first place. You must have had a problem with trust from the beginning. You drank too much because you believed that you could get whatever you wanted from alcohol. You thought you could control not only your drinking, but alcohol itself. You felt that you could command John Barleycorn to love you and to provide all of your emotional needs. What you were unconsciously attempting was to exercise omnipotent (total) control through controlling the magic in the bottle. This was a delusion if there ever was one, but it was an extremely powerful one. I believe that you related to alcohol as if it were an extension of yourself that would provide you with self-esteem and perfectly mirror your wishes and your fantasies. This is the way small children relate to their parents. The technical way of saying this is that you related to alcohol as a self-object.

I once knew a drinker who was thrilled when the Nobel prize committee announced that it would award six instead of five prizes each year. Now he could win all six. At least that's the way it seemed to him when he read the good news in the bar he had gone to at 8:00 A.M. to stop the shakes. Alcohol, his all-powerful magician, would give the six prizes to him. You no doubt were not so delusional, but nevertheless you counted on John Barleycorn to deliver the goods. Rather than feeling that you could magically control alcohol and get what you wanted from it, you may have experienced alcohol as an all-powerful God who would give you anything if you served him faithfully and merged your identity with his. In either case, you had no need to trust another person who was truly autonomous and not under your control. Can you see how this applies to your drinking? Think about it. One of the hardest but most important tasks of early sobriety is the development of trusting relationships with people you can't control. You never had control over alcohol anyway; that was an illusion, so why not try people?

Get Help

The point of all this is that *you can't do it alone.* To stay sober you have to acquire those tools for living that you lack. You can only get them from people. Since all the good things you want for yourself originally come from good experiences with other people, you need other people to do the things you can't do yet for yourself. It's another one of those paradoxes of alcoholism; you can only become independent by being dependent. You don't like that idea and are probably thinking, "Damn it, that means I'm a dependent weakling. I'd just as soon go back to drinking." Take it easy. We're all dependent — interdependent with each other that is. Right now you need lots of help. Can you accept it? It's there. It's there in the rooms of AA. It's there in counselors' and therapists' offices. It's there for

the asking if only you can get by your damn pride. It's false pride—
it can kill you and it will surely readdict you. Throw it out the
window and get help. It's true that only you can do it, but you can't
do it alone. Nobody really does. Build in all the support that you
can—self-help, professional help, friends and family if you are
fortunate enough to still have decent relations with them. Then you
will have a safety net, a support system that will provide you with
the security you need to stay sober and to grow.

"Grow?" Yes. You can't stay sober the way you are—if you
could you wouldn't be a drunk. But right now all you have to do is
to stay sober. Just like you can't grow behind alcoholism, you can't
help growing behind sobriety. Later on, you can work on yourself in
other ways, but right now just don't drink or use other drugs even
if your ass falls off.

CHAPTER 5

Getting Help: Counseling, Therapy, and Self-help Groups

I ended the last chapter with the admonition, "You can't do it alone." I know that goes against your grain, nevertheless it is true. At the very least, you would be cheating yourself by doing it alone because your desire to do it alone is part of your problem. It had a lot to do with your drinking too much. In sobriety, a healthy kind of needing people comes to replace an unhealthy need for alcohol. Once you accept that you need help from people, that you can't do it alone, the next question is what kind of people do you need and where can you find them? Actually you need help from two kinds of people: *professionals and peers.* Your best bet for a smooth, sustained recovery from problem drinking or alcoholism is a combination of professional help from a psychotherapist or an alcoholism counselor and peer help from a self-help program such as Alcoholics Anonymous. Finding professional help is not always easy. There are too many different kinds of professionals doing too many different things and it is hard to find out who is good at what and for what. There is also a lot of bad treatment out there and you don't want any of that.

Getting help from peers is less difficult, but it has its pitfalls too. I am going to try to help you find what you need with the least possible trouble. Nevertheless, you may find yourself in the wrong place. Don't give up; it sometimes takes some trial and error to find the right fit between your needs and the person or facility that can meet them. Let's first look at professional help and how to get it.

KINDS OF PROFESSIONAL HELP

There are a whole roster of professionals who have something of value to offer you: physicians, social workers, psychologists, psychiatrists, nutritionists, and alcoholism counselors. Some of them are private practitioners, some of them work for public agencies, and some of them are affiliated with private hospitals, clinics, rehabilitation units, and aftercare facilities. I will try to make clear what each of them does and what they can and cannot do for you. Since your first stop should be at a medical doctor, I will start there.

Medical Help

You know alcohol in high doses repeatedly self-administered is poisonous. If you have been consuming large quantities of alcohol for any length of time, you have poisoned yourself, to a greater or lesser degree; therefore, it really makes sense to have a physical examination. Such an examination does two things: (1) it gives your physician a chance to determine if you need medical assistance to detoxify, and (2) it will either reassure you that everything is all right or give you an opportunity to take remedial measures to rectify any damage alcohol has done. Going to the doctor may frighten you; nevertheless, you need to go. Medical assistance is the first kind of help you should get.

If you have been drinking much you may be worried about your health and rightfully so. Even if you weren't before reading this book, which I doubt, you are now. Your worry may have been unconscious and you may have drunk to anesthetize your unconscious worry about the damage your drinking was doing to your health. If that sounds crazy, it is; but that doesn't mean that you didn't do exactly that. Health worries easily become foci for guilt— guilt about drinking. Just like worry, guilt can be conscious, unconscious, or both. Conscious worry or guilt is the tip of the iceberg. One tenth is above water—conscious; nine tenths is below the water—unconscious. So assume that you are worried as hell and that worry can lead you straight back to the bottle. Do something to alleviate your worry. See a physician. If there is nothing wrong, you will find that out; if there is something wrong, you can do something about it. In either case you won't wind up drinking to numb your conscious and unconscious fears about your health.

Finding the Right Physician

Getting good medical help for a drinking problem used to be damn near impossible. Physicians weren't trained to treat drinking problems and most had no interest in doing so. Lack of knowledge combined with lack of interest was overlaid with the physician's personal prejudices regarding drinking. Some dismissed evidence of alcoholism short of terminal cirrhosis: "Ten martinis a day won't hurt you; all salesmen drink a lot." Other physicians condemned excessive drinking, "He's a bum—I'll give him a quick check and get rid of him." In either case, treatment was abysmal. This wasn't the doctors' fault; the medical schools ignored the third most serious medical problem in America, so it is not surprising that untrained professionals simply reacted with their personal feelings about drinking. This has changed for the better, but there are still plenty of physicians out there who don't know the shakes from a cocktail shaker and who are totally useless when it comes to helping people who drink too much. Religion, politics, sex, and alcohol engender powerful feelings in everybody. Physicians are no exception, and unless they are trained to recognize and take into account their own feelings about drinking, they will not be objective and you will not get good treatment. So any physician will not do; it is vital that you go to one who is knowledgeable about alcoholism.

There are four broad critera for *finding the right physician:*

1. Determine if your present physician (if you have one) is suitable.
2. Call your medical society for a referral to an alcohol specialist.
3. Ask a recovering friend for a referral.
4. Ask at an AA meeting who people in the group go to for medical care.

Don't forget to interview the candidate(s) before engaging him or her.

"How do I do that?" you ask. *Speak up!* If you have a doctor, ask flat out, "Are you knowledgeable about alcoholism? Are you comfortable with it? If you're not, please refer me to someone who is." If you draw a blank or don't have a physician to start with, there are other things you can do. There are now specialists in alcohol and addiction problems. You can call your local medical society and ask for the names of several. You will find a specialist in the field especially helpful, but a physician doesn't have to be an alcohol specialist to serve you well. An internist or general practitioner who treats drinkers is fine. If you know a recovering alcoholic, you can ask him or her to recommend a physician. That will probably get you good care. If there is an employee assistance program (EAP) at your job, you can ask there for a referral.

There are some basic questions you should *ask of your physician.*

1. Do you have training in the diagnosis and treatment of alcoholism? If so, what kind and how extensive?
2. Do you regard alcoholism as a disease?
3. How do you feel about people who drink too much?
4. How do you feel about people who don't drink at all?

Don't engage anybody who won't respond to your questions. You want somebody with training, experience, and nonjudgmental attitudes.

A serious problem you may encounter with a physician

untrained in alcoholism is that of having inappropriate minor tranquilizers (benzodiazepines) prescribed for you. This is another reason you need someone who knows what he or she is doing. *Don't* let a physician prescribe Valium, Librium, Xanax, Ativan, or other minor tranquilizers for your "nerves." These drugs *are* properly prescribed for detoxification from alcohol. In that case you will be given a limited number of pills to be taken at decreasing doses over three to seven days. If a physician suggests you use minor tranquilizers for any other purpose, fire him or her. Don't forget, you are the customer. You are buying a service; if the service isn't good, move on. The minor tranquilizers are antianxiety drugs. There are better ways of dealing with anxiety. These drugs are addictive; they build tolerance and are all too similar to alcohol. They are not a permissible way for you to deal with anxiety. They will lead you right back to alcohol. Antidepressant medication is another story. It is not addictive or habituating and you won't get hooked on it. Most likely you are depressed because you drink. It is highly probable that your depression will lift with sobriety. If it doesn't, you will need to be evaluated by a psychiatrist who is expert on drinking problems. More of this later. For now, get thee to a physician.

It may seem too obvious to need saying, but you can't get adequate medical treatment unless you are honest with your physician. Tell him or her in as much detail as possible about your drinking — how much you drank, how frequently, and for how long. Be sure to mention when you had your last drink and describe in detail your other drug use, if any.

Detoxification

Once you establish a relationship with an alcohol-competent doctor, the two of you will settle down and get your sobriety off to a good start. First, your physician will evaluate your need for detoxification. Do you need any medical assistance to stop drinking? If so, what sort of assistance? Tranquilizers to be taken at home for a few days? A short stay in a hospital or detoxification facility? Withdrawal from alcohol can be *dangerous* as well as unpleasant.

Most people prefer to withdraw at home either with medication or without it. In most cases this is perfectly safe, but if a competent physician, and you shouldn't be seeing any other kind, tells you that you should be an inpatient, don't argue. It is easier, safer, and a hell of a lot more comfortable.

"I've stopped drinking lots of times so what's the big deal?" you ask. Probably it isn't. But if it is, it is an extraordinarily big deal and nothing to tangle with. Is it possible you are afraid to stop drinking because it feels so bad when you do? Are you fooling yourself in thinking that withdrawal isn't a problem for you: If you have been drinking heavily daily for long, it very well may be. In that case, let a physician decide how you should stop. Most of you simply stopped drinking and had no physical problems, most of you tapered off over a few days without great difficulty; but some of you will need medicine to withdraw safely and reasonably comfortably, and a few of you will need three to seven days in an inpatient detoxification facility.

Your Physical

Once the medical side of getting off the sauce has been decided — and this won't even be an issue for you if you haven't been drinking for a week or more before your examination — the next order of business is a complete physical. This should include complete laboratory work including blood levels of vital nutrients since vitamin and mineral deficiencies are so common in heavy drinkers. Liver enzymes also have their tale to tell. After the examination and the test results are in, your physician can treat any alcohol-related problem you may have and can give you shots of vitamin B_1, vitamin B_{12}, and whatever other vitamins or minerals you may be lacking. Most alcohol specialists think shots of B_{12} are a good idea in early sobriety.

The treatment for most physical problems associated with excessive drinking is abstinence and good nutrition. If additional measures are indicated, your physician will explain them and start you on the road to physical health.

Antabuse®

The last issue you should discuss with your physician is the use of Antabuse. Antabuse (disulfiram) blocks the conversion of acetaldehyde, produced by the first step in the metabolism of alcohol, into acetate. This results in a buildup of acetaldehyde in your bloodstream. Acetaldehyde is highly toxic — it makes you sick as hell. If you take Antabuse you can't drink without becoming dreadfully ill. If you don't drink, Antabuse has no effect. To resume drinking without feeling like you want to die, you have to stop taking Antabuse and wait four or five days. By then you probably won't want to drink. If you are having trouble with "cravings," Antabuse may be a good idea. People who use it usually stay on it six months to a year.

Antabuse is a kind of internal/external control, something not you but inside you, that gives you control over the impulse to take a drink. This internal/external control constitutes another of the paradoxes of alcoholism. The thought of having something inside you that guarantees that you will remain abstinent, at least for a few days, may feel as if a loving parent were setting limits for you and that may make you feel safe, loved, and secure. Or, it may feel like a punitive, prohibitive parent is inside you squashing your freedom. If you react that way, you will feel angry, depressed, and controlled. Most Antabuse takers have both sets of feelings. Since either, or both, can be unconscious, what they usually experience is confusion and conflict.

Simply taking Antabuse is not a good idea. If you use it, you need to explore and express your feelings about taking it with a trained person. Since slips can be planned, the effectiveness of Antabuse has been questioned and recent studies found no significant difference in recovery rates between Antabuse takers and others; however, that is an average and *some* drinkers are definitely helped by Antabuse. You could be one of them. If you don't want to drink, but find that you are unable to stop for any length of time, speak to your (alcoholwise) physician about trying it, but remember taking Antabuse in itself is not an effective treatment for problem drinking or alcoholism.

Nutritional Help

If you have been drinking heavily for any length of time *you have nutritional deficiencies.* You don't think so because you have always been careful to eat as well as drink. It is good that you have done so; you would be in much worse shape if you had not. Nevertheless, alcohol impedes the absorption of vitamins, minerals, and amino acids. Further, that hard-working factory, your liver, is stressed by alcohol and has not been able to do all the metabolic work it needed to do to make vitamins and other essential nutrients available to your body. And to tell the truth, it is highly unlikely that you really have been eating well. It is far more likely that you fooled yourself here as elsewhere — after all, fooling yourself is part and parcel of overdrinking. Now that you are sober, it is wise, indeed vital, to treat yourself well in the food department. If your physician is into nutrition follow his or her advice. If not, consult a nutritionist. Some are quacks, but others are excellent. As long as you have no liver damage, a high-protein, high-carbohydrate diet supplemented by a good multivitamin and periodic B_{12} shots should do the trick. If you have liver difficulties, you will have to restrict your protein intake — follow medical advice on that one. Start taking multivitamins, and make sure your multivitamin is also a mineral supplement. Heavy drinkers tend to be deficient in zinc, magnesium, and vitamin B_1 (thiamine). When your physician takes blood, make sure he orders vitamin and mineral levels so appropriate remediation can be instituted for specific deficiencies.

The amino acid L-tryptophan is a precursor of the neurotransmitter serotonin. It is used by the body to make serotonin. Levels of serotonin are often deficient in alcoholics. Therefore, some recovering alcoholics used to take L-tryptophan. It was believed to be a nonaddictive antianxiety and antidepressant agent and was widely available in health food stores. Tryptophan has turned out to be dangerously toxic. Don't use it.

A word about sugar and caffeine. There is a correlation between hypoglycemia, low blood sugar, and alcoholism. Drinking lowers your blood sugar level. In fact, very heavy drinking can depress blood sugar level so low that coma or death results. Some authorities believe that recovering alcoholics continue to be subject to hypoglycemia. The treatment for hypoglycemia is abstinence from sugar. Of course, sugar can't be totally eliminated from your diet, but foods that are essentially nothing but sugar can be avoided. Alcohol and sugar share a final common pathway when they are metabolized. The last part of the process of metabolizing each of them is identical. Long-term, it is best to avoid excess sugar, especially the artificial, highly processed sugar in junk foods. There are sugar hangovers and sugar anxiety states, and there is a rebound low-sugar state following heavy sugar consumption. This is especially marked in hypoglycemics. All this is true. But for now, unless you have a problem with sugar, forget it and pig out whenever you wish. As they say in AA, "first things first," and the first thing is to take care of your alcohol problem.

Not all authorities in the field agree with me, but I think doing one thing at the time makes sense. Trying to become a health saint in one step is just setting yourself up for failure. So take care of the booze and consider doing something about the sugar, if that's a problem for you, later on. If you suspect hypoglycemia, ask your physician for a fasting five-hour glucose tolerance test. Barring a positive finding for hypoglycemia, I recommend substituting sweets for alcohol in early sobriety—it is not a bad response to a drink signal. It is pretty difficult to drink a beer on top of a milkshake. Nauseating thought, isn't it?

I feel the same way about caffeine. Heavy coffee drinking is not good; it makes you jumpy and anxious. But, again, first things first and, if coffee is a good substitute for the hootch, use it. Later on, you can think about cutting down. If caffeine jumpiness makes you want to reach for a drink, then you have to deal with your coffee, cola, and tea drinking now, but if you're comfortable with it, then relax. The same with smoking—tobacco that is. Smoking will kill you, but a few more months on the weed won't make much difference, so *don't stop drinking and smoking simultaneously.* The most likely result of that is continuing to do both. If you're a heavy drinker, you are a creature of extremes. As long as you are giving up alcohol, you may very well also want to eat perfectly, drink nothing containing caffeine, not smoke, and be canonized this week. Forget it, just don't drink today and the rest of it will sort itself out down the pike.

Nutrition is plagued by fads and fanaticism. It is difficult to get adequate help in this area. Most physicians are poorly trained and disinterested in nutrition, whereas most nutritionists are true believers with little respect for scientific method and less knowledge of science. I'm editorializing here, but that's my experience. So try to find a physician with a "wellness" orientation — they exist — ask around. An AA meeting is a good place to get a referral. Or find a nutritionist who knows what he or she is doing and who treats the subject as a science and not as a religion. The truth is, you don't need a great deal of professional help, although you do need some, to improve your nutritional status. The basic idea is simple. Eat well, take a vitamin-mineral supplement, get B_{12} shots, make sure your blood level of essential nutrients is adequate, and most important — *don't drink.* It is alcohol that causes the overwhelming majority of your nutritional problems — if you stop drinking, the rest will take care of itself.

Psychotherapy — The "Talking Cure"

One of Freud's mentors, Joseph Breuer, treated a memorable woman named Berta Papenheim, who suffered from "hysterical" symptoms. She suffered from paralysis, sensory impairments, and other ills that had no physical cause. On the contrary, they were caused by emotional conflict. Breuer tried various medical treatments, but none of them worked. Then he tried just sitting and talking with her and an amazing thing happened. As Berta talked to him, she would remember traumatic, intensely painful, highly conflictual incidents that she had forgotten. When she remembered these repressed memories and reexperienced them with strong feelings, the symptoms related to the trauma disappeared. Berta called this the "talking cure." Breuer and Freud wrote up her case in their famous book *Studies in Hysteria* (1895). They called her Anna O., and under that name, this brilliant woman became the first modern psychotherapy patient. Many forms of the talking cure, from psychoanalysis to behavior therapy, have been developed since Berta's treatment. We tend to undervalue mere talk. This is nonsense. The ability to communicate is the essence of being human and human communication is largely verbal—talking and listening. So is poetry, so is courtship, so is education, so is virtually every field of human endeavor. Talking cures are powerful.

Psyche is the Greek word for mind or spirit. Like the German *Geist,* it is broader than the English mind, soul, or spirit. It encompasses all three. So psychotherapy is the treatment of the mind or spirit. This work is done by professionals with very different types of training: psychiatrists, psychologists, social workers, alcoholism counselors, and mental health counselors.

Psychotherapy and psychotherapist are generic terms. They do not specify the exact nature of the treatment, the profession of the person performing it, nor the format (individual, group, etc.) in which it is administered. The consumer—in this case you—must choose a member of a mental health profession who subscribes to a particular theory and who works in a particular way in one or more modalities (see Chart 5-1). It is a question of picking one from column A, one from column B, and one from column C and putting them on the same plate. All this sounds quite confusing, but it need not be. I am going to take you through professions, styles, and modalities one by one and give you clear clues on how to choose a psychotherapist.

The distinction between counseling and psychotherapy is hazy. The connotation of "therapy" is more medical. In general, "therapists" have more status than "counselors." Counselors tend to work shorter-term and in a more focused manner. But that's not always true. The distinction between counselor and therapist is pretty meaningless—it is a territorial dispute of more interest to competing professionals than to consumers. Not all counselors are alcoholism

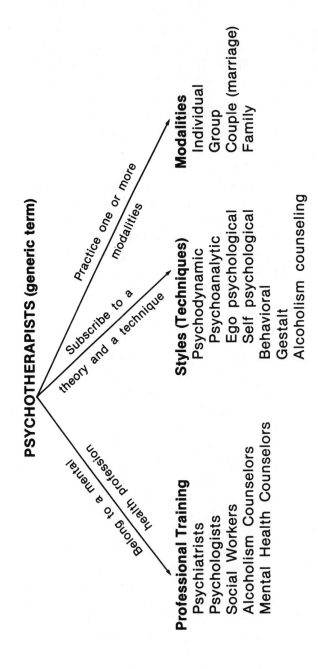

PSYCHOTHERAPISTS (generic term)

Belong to a mental health profession

Subscribe to a theory and a technique

Practice one or more modalities

Professional Training
Psychiatrists
Psychologists
Social Workers
Alcoholism Counselors
Mental Health Counselors

Styles (Techniques)
Psychodynamic
Psychoanalytic
Ego psychological
Self psychological
Behavioral
Gestalt
Alcoholism counseling

Modalities
Individual
Group
Couple (marriage)
Family

Chart 5–1

174

counselors. In fact, most are not. There are certified mental health counselors, marriage counselors, rehabilitation counselors, and vocational counselors. What's important to you is that your counselor or therapist understand *ethanolism*. Never heard of ethanolism? Don't worry, I just made it up. Given the negative connotation of alcoholism, it may be the coming word — after all, the graveyard became the cemetery, which is rapidly becoming the memorial park. Perhaps it is no accident that the analogy that came to my mind for a less offensive word for pathological drinking concerned death.

Selecting A Therapist

Get a Referral:

1. From a recovering drinker who is having (has had) a successful therapeutic experience (AA meetings are a good source of referrals)
   or
2. From a nonproblem drinker who is having (has had) a successful therapeutic experience

To a Person with:

Education	Experience
PH.D. or D.Psych. in psychology or M.S.W. (Master of Social Work) M.A. or PH.D. in counseling or M.D. + psychiatric residency or C.A.C. (Credentialed Alcoholism Counselor) + at least an M.A.	Experience in treating both active and recovering problem drinkers

PLUS or including training in alcoholism

Tell that Person:

1. About yourself and your drinking.

Ask that Person:

1. What is your professional training?
2. What is your theoretical orientation and therapeutic approach?
3. Do you have special training in problem drinking and alcoholism?
4. What experience do you have in working with problem drinkers and alcoholics?
5. What is your approach to alcohol problems?
6. How do you work with active drinkers? With recovering drinkers?
7. How do you feel about people with drinking problems?
8. Do you think that you can help me?
9. What is your contract? Fee? Policy on missed appointments? Etc.?

Engage that Person:

1. If the individual has knowledge of and experience in alcoholism *and* you feel that the two of you have some rapport.

Knowledge of alcoholism and the ability to relate are what count.

Mental Health Professions and Professionals

Knowledge and training are extremely important, but which degree your therapist has is relatively unimportant. A psychotherapist may be trained in medicine, social work, counseling of various sorts, or psychology. Academic background is far less important than the ability to enter into a relationship with you, to communicate with you, and to help you. Good psychotherapists aren't defensive. They will tell you their training, experience, and areas of expertise. If they feel they can't help you, they will refer you. Stay away from anyone who isn't open in this way. However, be aware that you may be looking for flaws in a prospective therapist so you can avoid getting help and continue to drink. Fault-finding can be defensive rather than sensibly self-protective. In interviewing a therapist, neither blindly credulous nor overly skeptical be. A psychotherapist should be frank about fee, the nature of the treatment, its likely duration, and such things as your financial responsibilities for missed appointments. The "contract" should be clear and up front. Any professional who gives you the runaround on any of this isn't for you. Pick somebody *you can talk to,* but remember that any relationship takes time to build, and trust must be earned. First impressions are often good guides to conduct, but you have a right to change your mind. In any psychotherapeutic relationship strong feelings are aroused and there will be times you hate your therapist. Some of your reactions will be defensive, or in the service of your denial. They are to be expected. However, if they can't be talked through, that's a bad sign. Good therapists are clear, relevant, and honest. They keep their personal lives out of your treatment unless they are asking you to identify with their personal recovery, and they are sensitive to your feelings but not afraid to confront you. If that's not happening, something is wrong. Don't switch therapists without talking through your feelings and sorting out what's coming from you and what's a response to the therapist's inadequacies. But don't be afraid to move on if after talking it over you still don't feel safe with that person.

Good therapeutic relationships—those that facilitate your making constructive changes in your life—are good matches. A therapist may be terrific for somebody else, but not for you, and the professional who really helps you may be utterly wrong for your friend. So look for a relationship that clicks. Don't worship initials after people's names, but take them into account. The best way to find a good therapist is by word of mouth. If you know a recovering person who is having a good therapeutic experience, ask him or her for a referral. Even if that particular professional person is not right for you, you will be in the right therapeutic milieu and you will be referred to someone with suitable training who will be right for you.

Although it is unlikely that a psychiatrist will be your psycho-therapist, I am going to start guiding you to a therapist by talking about psychiatrists and what they do. I am starting with them because you are probably more familiar with psychiatry than with the other "helping" professions. Most people think of psychiatry when they think about "having their heads examined."

Psychiatrists

Psychiatrists are physicians who have additional training in treating mental illness. They have completed a psychiatric residency of three years after their medical internship. Being physicians, they are attuned to things of the body and are likely to view mental illness and emotional disturbance as organic in nature, as diseases of the nervous system. They are prone to treat these diseases physically, usually by prescribing medicine. Although most of them pay lip service to psychotherapy, many psychiatrists don't really think much of it. Very few of them are good at it. What psychiatrists do is extremely valuable. Many emotional difficulties are indeed helped by medication. Drinking too much rarely is. I have already discussed the use of Antabuse, which can be prescribed by a psychiatrist or by an internist. Antianxiety drugs—the minor tranquilizers and the barbiturates—are contraindicated except during withdrawal and are to be avoided at all costs. The major tranquilizers, or neuroleptics, such as Thorazine, Stelazine, and Haldol are not used in treating problem drinking. They *are* helpful if you are a dual-diagnosis person. That is, if you have a psychiatric illness in addition to alcoholism. Some people do. If that is the case, then you have been drinking in a mistaken attempt to medicate your psychiatric illness. You have been using the wrong medicine. A psychiatrist can treat your psychiatric problem and you won't need to drink to try to feel better. But you will still need help for your drinking problem. The odds are high that you are not a dual-diag-nosis person, but, if you are, you must remember that you have two problems and must treat them *both*.

There are medications—often highly effective—for treating depression. If you remain depressed after several months of not drinking, seeing a psychiatrist for a medication evaluation is wise. Antidepressants are not habit-forming, addictive, or kick-inducing. Depression that is secondary to alcoholism responds to psychotherapy—if you're not drinking. If it does not, then you should consider antidepressant medication. Be sure to continue your psychotherapy while you are on medication. If you have tried to get sober but keep slipping, it is possible that primary depression (one not caused by drinking) is your problem. In that case, antidepressant medication can help you achieve stable sobriety.

Not all psychiatrists understand alcohol problems. Make sure yours does. Some psychiatrists take a year-long substance-abuse fellowship after their residency. If you can find one who did, you are in luck. Others may know very little about alcoholism; inquire and get a referral if your guy or gal does not have the requisite knowledge and experience. You need a psychiatrist who knows alcoholism to determine the relationship between your drinking and your depression or other emotional difficulties—to determine what's causing what and to decide whether or not medication is indicated. If a competent psychiatrist who is hip to booze thinks you should try antidepressants, do it. When they work, they really work and you may feel enormously better.

You may have extreme highs as well as extreme lows—mania as well as depression. The treatment for manic–depression is a drug called Lithium Carbonate. However, the cycle of getting high followed by a physical-emotional hangover is very like the manic-depressive cycle and I wouldn't recommend that you go on lithium before you are sober for a good while unless there is a very definite indication for it. A psychiatrist who understands alcoholism can distinguish between manic–depressive disorder and alcoholism mimicking it. If you're like the vast majority of problem drinkers, your mood swings will level out in sobriety. If they do not and psychotherapeutic help does not relieve them, then you have a "chemical imbalance" and need pharmacological treatment. Lithium is not an addictive drug and does not interfere with recovery from alcoholism; on the contrary, it facilitates recovery when it is properly prescribed.

There are psychiatrists who are excellent psychotherapists, but they are in short supply. They also tend to be expensive. Therefore, I do not recommend that you go to a psychiatrist as a first step in getting help with your drinking problem. A nonmedical therapist is a better bet. Of course, if you happen to link up with a psychiatrist with whom you have a good relationship, stay right where you are. The person is more important than the degree. If you don't feel better after a few months of sobriety, then a psychiatric evaluation is in order. I don't think that psychopharmacology without psychotherapy is a good idea. If you need medication and your psychiatrist does not do psychotherapy or does not do it well, you should see a nonmedical therapist who is in contact with your psychiatrist so the two of them can coordinate their efforts in your behalf. If your problem is alcohol, the odds are excellent that you don't and won't need a psychiatrist, although your psychotherapist might happen to be a psychiatrist. I know I have been rough on psychiatry, so I am a little ashamed to note that some of my best friends are psychiatrists.

Psychologists

That brings me to the psychologists. In its literal meaning, psychology is the science of mind, although most contemporary psychologists would define it as the science of behavior. Psychologists are highly trained; the ones that you will consult either have masters degrees or doctorates. The traditional degree in psychology was the Ph.D., but younger psychologists often have a D.Psych. (Doctor of Psychology). It doesn't matter which set of initials follow your psychologist's name. Not being medical, psychologists do not prescribe medicine. What they do is help people change their behavior. Mostly they do that by promoting self-awareness. Psychologists also do evaluations of various kinds. *Not all psychologists are trained in helping people.* Some are much more academically oriented. The kind of psychologist you need is a *clinical psychologist,* one who is trained in working therapeutically. Doctoral-level clinical psychologists study four years in graduate school and then do a year-long internship. People with doctorates in clinical psychology are smart and know a lot. However, the Ph.D. is given for research more than for clinical ability, so a master's-level psychologist with clinical training may do just as well. The ability to relate well to you and knowledge of your disease are what count.

Some psychologists administer tests. A psychological test battery can be helpful in delineating your problems and highlighting your assets. If a test battery is suggested, take it — you will learn some valuable things about yourself and the information gleaned from the test battery will enable your therapist to help you more effectively. Expect to be anxious while taking a psychological test battery. It's natural to be afraid the results will show you to be totally insane. They won't. What they will do is give a balanced picture of your personality, your strengths and your weaknesses, and your largely unconscious psychological defense mechanisms.

Psychologists differ in their orientations. Ask your psychologist what his or her theoretical and clinical orientation is. It makes a difference. Psychologists, and other mental health professionals, do different things depending on their point of view about treatment and how the mind works. *Dynamically (analytically) oriented* psychologists are interested in making you aware of your defenses, your modes of relating, your excess freight from the past, and other things outside of your awareness. They are into making the unconscious conscious. This is not helpful while you are drinking. Dynamic (psychoanalytical) psychotherapy can be highly growth-promoting once you have achieved stable sobriety, but I don't work that way with patients during the first months of their sobriety. During early sobriety, you need somebody who is directive, supportive, and focused on helping you avoid slips (drinking episodes). That person may be a dynamically oriented psychologist who is alcoholwise and who knows what to do when. Analyzing dreams, unless they are about Brandy Alexanders for breakfast, isn't what should be being done during those first difficult weeks and months of hard-won sobriety. *Ask your psychologist how he or she works with drinkers. Ask how he or she works with clients who are newly sober.* If you get a blank stare or a refusal to answer, or an evasive answer, go elsewhere.

Other psychologists are *behaviorally* oriented. That means that they are more interested in changing behavior than they are in increasing awareness. They use a variety of highly specific techniques to help their clients reduce anxiety, increase assertiveness, and overcome irrational fears (phobias). Behaviorists, as they are known, can be extremely helpful if you have highly focused psychological symptoms, but unless they are booze mavens, I would stay away from the strict behaviorists during your first year of sobriety. Most of your highly focused symptoms, like fear of falling in front of the subway, will simply disappear with sobriety. If you have residual symptoms, such as fear of heights, after you have been sober for a year, then a behaviorally oriented psychologist may be just the ticket.

Yet other psychologists are what are called *cognitive behavior therapists.* Cognitive behavior therapists are interested in changing their clients' thoughts, attitudes, and beliefs, for example, the belief that drinking alcohol will alleviate your depression. Many cognitive psychologists are trained in, and interested in, treating addictions including alcohol addiction. They can do a lot to help you achieve and maintain sobriety. If you can find a psychologist with this orientation who knows alcoholism and the two of you relate well, you are highly likely to be helped. If the thought that you are going to be helped to stop drinking and stay stopped doesn't scare you too much, stay right where you are — you are in the right place. Later on, if you think additional therapy would be of value, move on to a dynamically oriented therapist. If you have solid sobriety, you may not want any treatment after six months or a year, and that's fine.

Psychologists are good choices as therapists, but only if they are clinically trained. The ideal person would be a Ph.D. or D.Psych. with a lot of experience treating alcoholics, who is dynamically oriented, but who works cognitively-behaviorally during early sobriety.

Social Workers

Although there are social workers who have no academic training beyond their bachelors' degrees, fully professional social workers have two years of graduate study in a school of social work and have received a Masters of Social Work (MSW) degree. Unless a social worker has an MSW, he or she is not likely to be a good choice for your therapist. There are exceptions. If you really hit it off with a social worker who lacks graduate training, stay with him or her, but don't go out of your way to find a bachelor's-level social worker for a therapist. Social work school is highly treatment-oriented. Social work per se has no theory or body of knowledge of its own, rather it draws on the social sciences for its theoretical base and applies that base to working with people. Social work is a practical field. Many social workers would not agree with my comments, but social work simply doesn't have the academic rigor of psychology or of psychiatry. Some social workers are no great shakes intellectually, while others are extremely bright. Again, the person is more important than the field of study. There are a goodly number of MSWs who are also trained alcoholism counselors (see below). Social workers who are also alcoholism counselors are excellent choices as therapists. I recommend the combination.

Some social workers go for additional training at a psychoanalytic training "institute." Social workers with such additional training are a good bet, but only if they are hip to alcoholism. Ask your social worker if he or she has graduated from an advanced training institute. If they have, it is likely that they are very bright and know what they are doing. The majority of psychotherapy is done by social workers. They vary enormously in their skills, knowledge, style, and theoretical orientation. If you can find a social worker who has attended a training institute and who is also an alcoholism counselor, you are in splendid hands. Unless you have very strong reason to do otherwise, stay where you are.

Alcoholism Counselors

Alcoholism counseling is a field that has exploded during the past few years. There are good reasons that it has. Drinking too much is one of America's, indeed the world's, greatest health problems. It is a problem long ignored that has finally come out of the closet. TV, press, radio, industry, education, and government have drawn attention to the problem and one response to that attention has been the development of a new profession, alcoholism counseling. More and more states have a certification process and license or certify alcoholism counselors. In New York State, alcoholism counselors obtain the C.A.C., which stands for Credentialed Alcoholism Counselor. Check to find out if your state certifies alcoholism or substance abuse counselors. The exact title varies from state to state. I don't recommend your going to an uncredentialed alcoholism counselor. Most C.A.C.s work for public or private agencies or for alcoholic rehabilitation programs, but some are in private practice. The educational requirements for Certified Alcoholism Counselor are minimal. In most states you don't even need a high school diploma. That may shock you, but such is the case. What alcoholism counselors do have is alcohol-specific training. They know about alcohol, alcoholism, and recovery from alcoholism. The majority of them are recovering persons themselves, and to some degree function as peer counselors. Alcoholism counselors can be highly effective. They know what they know, and they know it well. Generally, they do short-term, directive counseling aimed at breaking down denial and helping people get sober. Some mental health professionals are also Certified Alcoholism Counselors. Such people have much more training than people with only a C.A.C. or its equivalent. I myself would not go to an alcoholism counselor who did not also have at least a master's degree in either social work, psychology, or counseling. A highly trained therapist who doesn't have training in, and understanding of, alcoholism is likely to do you more harm than good, while an undertrained alcoholism counselor is limited but is unlikely to make things worse. If your choice is between the highly degreed who don't have alcohol-specific training and the un-degreed who do, you are better off with the relatively uneducated alcohol specialist. But you can do better than that. Your best bet is a master's-level, or higher, trained psychotherapist who is also knowledgeable about alcoholism. Such a person will have some such letters as M.S.W., C.A.C. after his or her name. There are, of course, psychotherapists who don't have alcoholism credentials but who do understand the subject. They are also to be recommended.

Certified Mental Health Counselors/Rehabilitation Counselors

Mental health counseling is another relatively new profession. Such counselors are master's- or doctoral-level professionals. If they have training and experience in alcoholism, they are also excellent choices as therapists, as are rehabilitation counselors.

Marriage and Family Counselors

Marriage and family counselors are generally social workers who specialize in family work, although persons with other professional training also work in this field. In my experience marriage and family counseling is not effective while you are still drinking. Nor would I recommend it in early sobriety. Although it is true that alcoholism is a family disease, you have enough to do in concentrating on yourself during the first months of your sobriety. Later on, marriage and family counseling can be very helpful—indeed necessary—for a comfortable sobriety.

In encouraging you to get the best possible treatment and to find the most effective therapist you can, I don't want to suggest that being overly critical or too picky in choosing a psychotherapist is a good idea. It isn't. Don't become a shopper going from therapist to therapist without ever sitting down and doing some work. Getting help is scary; it threatens your drinking. So be an informed consumer, but don't let your fear drive you away from a potential helper. There isn't a uniquely perfect therapist whom you must find. On the contrary, there are many professionals who know alcoholism with whom you can establish a facilitating relationship. Find one and stay with him or her until your head clears up.

Styles of Psychotherapy

The difficulty in choosing a therapist comes not only from members of disparate professions practicing psychotherapy; it also

comes from members of each of those professions doing psychotherapy in very different ways. They do different things, not
because they went to different kinds of professional schools, but
because they have different beliefs about how to help people. You
know the cast of characters — social workers, alcoholism counselors,
other types of counselors, psychologists, and psychiatrists — what
you don't know is the various roles that these characters play. The
roles are psychoanalyst, ego psychologist, self psychologist, gestalt
therapist, and behavior therapist. Let me tell you about them.

Psychoanalysis

Psychoanalysis is both a theory about our minds and how they
work *and* a treatment for emotional illness. In it, the patient lies on
a couch three to five times a week and says whatever comes into his
or her mind while the analyst listens, tries to understand, and offers
"interpretations" — comments on the meaning of the patient's disclo-
sures. Psychoanalysts used to be psychiatrists who underwent
additional training in a psychoanalytic institute. Today a psychoanalyst may be a psychologist or social worker with advanced
training. Psychoanalysis is one of the great attempts of the human
mind to understand itself; it is *not,* however, an effective treatment
for problem drinking or alcoholism. Don't go to a psychoanalyst to
be analyzed. It is contraindicated; it makes things worse, not better.
I once treated a man who had fourteen years of psychoanalysis, but
whose alcoholism had not been dealt with. He was not doing well.
His alcohol abuse had been treated as a symptom of his neurosis
rather than as a disease in its own right. There are analysts who
understand alcoholism and treat it before doing anything else. In
that case, their advanced training is an asset, but an analyst's office
is unlikely to be the place for you right now. Analysis is a powerful
and helpful experience after you have achieved stable sobriety — but
not now. There is a famous study of Menninger Clinic analytic
patients which showed that the patients who didn't improve or got
worse were substance abusers. So stay off the couch until you get on
your feet.

Ego Psychology

Psychoanalysis has several variants. One of them is called *ego psychology*. An ego psychologist is not necessarily a psychologist, but is a psychotherapist, who may be a counselor, a social worker, a psychologist, or a psychiatrist by training, who focuses on the part of the mind Freud called the ego. The ego is the part of your mind that tries to reach a reasonable compromise between your needs, your wishes, your conscience, and the demands of society. It is sort of like an executive who doesn't have too much power, so he often feels threatened. The ego uses various psychological defenses to ward off anxiety. Psychological defenses have their uses; they reduce pain. But they can also cause a lot of trouble, especially if they are too rigid. Ego psychologists are interested in the way the ego develops, how it works, and how it defends itself. Their goal in treatment is to strengthen the ego. If a therapist tells you he or she is an ego psychologist, that's fine. The emphasis in treatment will be on making you aware of your maladaptive defenses — drinking too much is certainly maladaptive in that way — but again too analytic a treatment is wrong for now. Tell your ego psychologist about your drinking problem, and if he or she is more interested in helping you understand your drinking than in helping you stop drinking you are in the wrong place. Ego psychologists have much to offer you if they are also trained in alcoholism.

Self Psychology

There is a school of psychoanalysis called *self psychology*. Self psychology is not a form of self-help; it is theory about the mind that emphasizes the self, how it develops, what can go wrong with that development, and what can be done to strengthen the self. People's sense of self is weakened by alcoholic drinking. What self they have left suffers, is scarred, and their self-esteem is inevitably near zero. Alcoholism is a disease of the self — a form of poisoning of the self by the self, so not surprisingly the insights of self psychology are useful in the treatment of alcoholism. Self psychology was developed by Heinz Kohut, whose thoughts about addiction being an attempt to fill an inner emptiness make sense to me. A psychotherapist of whatever professional background who is trained in both self psychology and the treatment of alcoholism is an ideal person to go to for help. It is a good idea to ask your therapist if he or she has read Kohut and if he or she uses self psychological techniques in his or her work. If they look blank, that is a minus in evaluating them; if they respond positively, score some points in their favor. However, rapport is more important than your therapist's theoretical orientation and you may find just the right therapist for you who has never heard of Kohut and who isn't too sure who Freud is either, but who understands you and ethanol. Freud, by the way, is a Newfoundland dog who more or less dominates my home. I'm not sure what he thinks of his namesake.

Psychodynamic Psychotherapy

Psychodynamic (psychoanalytic) psychotherapy is not psychoanalysis. It is once- or twice-a-week face-to-face therapy that looks at unconscious motivation as well as what is on the surface. It isn't as anxiety-provoking as psychoanalysis, but it works in roughly the same way. Psychodynamic psychotherapists who are also trained in alcoholism pace treatment so that alcohol-related issues are dealt with first, and that's the kind of treatment you want.

Behavior Therapy

I have already had occasion to discuss behavior therapy, but I want to tell you more about it. Behavior therapists use a branch of psychology called *learning theory* to help people unlearn harmful behaviors and learn more adaptive behaviors. There are traditional behavior therapists who focus on relieving symptoms and on changing behavior, and there are cognitive behavior therapists who focus on changing thoughts and beliefs. Behavior therapy techniques such as relaxation training are very helpful in early sobriety. Even if you once new how to relax, you have been tense for so long that you forgot how you did it. A behavior therapist can help you learn (or relearn) how to relax. Relaxing is better than relapsing. Many people who become problem drinkers are tension- and anxiety-prone to begin with and that's one reason why they are attracted to a sedative drug like alcohol. So it makes a great deal of sense to acquire a new technique for quelling your anxiety.

Traditional behavior therapy also uses *assertiveness training* as a way of helping people feel better. Heavy drinkers are often defiant, oppositional, given to angry outbursts and to being difficult — any identification here? — but they are rarely firmly, persistently, and effectively assertive. Part of being sane is knowing how to be sane. An enormous amount of drinking too much is a futile attempt to relax or to be assertive. You may think that you don't have a problem with assertiveness, but if you have been drinking very much for very long I'll bet that you do. You may have once been assertive and lost that skill as your drinking robbed you of your self-confidence, or you may never have had it. In either case, assertiveness training is a form of therapy that can be extremely helpful to you early in your sobriety. It is usually done in a group — a sort of class — which runs six to ten sessions. Relaxation training and assertiveness training may be done by a counselor, a social worker, or a psychologist, but behavioral psychologists are usually the best trained in these techniques. You may feel that this stuff is for the kindergarten and far beneath you, especially if you are among the highly educated. That's just more denial. Traditional behavior therapy is basic, but that is its great strength. If you have an opportunity to participate in relaxation and/or assertiveness training, do it.

The other kind of behavior therapy is *cognitive behavior theory* — the kind that tries to alter self-defeating thoughts and modify counterproductive attitudes. AA says, "alcoholism is a disease of the attitudes," and there is a lot of truth in that. Cognitive behavior therapy is essentially didactic and educational — it instructs. It is a kind of retraining in thinking more productively. There is a character in Molière's play *The Bourgeois Gentleman* who discovers that he has been speaking prose all his life. I have been doing cognitive behavior therapy with you throughout this book but I haven't called it that. My teaching about alcohol, alcoholism, and how they have affected you and your attitudes is cognitive behavior therapy. This is the kind of talking cure you need now — you don't need to specifically seek out a cognitive therapist, any therapist who understands alcoholism uses cognitive behavioral techniques in the early stages of therapy with problem drinkers.

There is another behavior therapy technique that is specific to the treatment of problem drinking — *adversive conditioning*. Adversive conditioning is based on the *learning theory* principle that pairing (bringing in close proximity) punishment and a behavior reduces the frequency of the behavior. Learning theory teaches that people tend to repeat pleasurable experiences and not repeat painful experiences. If the frequency of a behavior is increased, it is said to be reenforced; if the frequency of a behavior is decreased, it is said to be punished. Drinking alcohol gives immediate pleasure — tension reduction, disinhibition, and release from reality constraints — all of which reenforce drinking behavior. Punishments associated with drinking — hangovers, divorce, job loss, and liver disease — occur long after the pleasure that comes from drinking. So punishment and drinking are not linked in your mind. This lead behavior therapists to try moving punishment — or as they put it, the adverse consequences — forward so it occurs immediately after drinking. According to this theory, drinking should "extinguish" as a behavior after being paired with punishment.

Adversive conditioning works like this. You are put in a free-drinking situation — provided with an attractive open bar — and told to drink whatever you wish. When you drink, however, you become violently ill because you have been given a drug that causes incredibly intense nausea. Then you retch for an hour. This is repeated three or four times per session. These "treatment sessions" go on for several weeks. Pain and drinking are so firmly linked in your mind that, in theory, your drinking will diminish to zero.

If you aren't into vomiting, you can find therapists who use electric shock as a punisher. Shocking those whose behavior is shocking is less popular than it used to be. Punk therapy is "in" in adversive-conditioning circles.

Obviously you have to be highly motivated to subject yourself to adversive conditioning. It is always *voluntary* so don't worry about being subjected to adversive conditioning without your consent. Usually adversive therapy is done in settings that also offer alcohol education and group therapy. It is a method reputed to be quick and effective, but research evidence shows that the "cure" doesn't last. I once knew a man who underwent adversive conditioning. He told me that he so enjoyed the idea of the doctor giving him drinks that the pain was inconsequential. Needless to say, he continued to drink. He was a reporter who specialized in reporting multiple axe murders and similarly edifying events. He had a rather jaundiced view of life, which must have had something to do with his choice of treatment and its failure.

I strongly disrecommend adversive conditioning unless you are at death's door and nothing else has helped you. You will not hear anything about this treatment unless you seek it out. Don't.

Gestalt Therapy

Gestalt therapy focuses on here-and-now interactions between therapist and client. Gestalt is the German word for form. Gestalt therapists believe that completing the gestalt — getting closure on an issue or an emotional conflict — is curative. Gestalt psychology is a theory about perception, about how people experience the world. Gestalt therapy claims this theory as its spiritual ancestor, but in practice there isn't much connection. Gestalt therapy is the child of a one-time analyst named Fritz Perls. Perls was highly flamboyant — a showman.

Gestalt therapists emphasize intensity of feeling; they attempt to arouse strong emotion and help their clients express and discharge these powerful feelings. They use a variety of techniques to do this.

One of them is the empty chair in which you imagine, for example, your hated/feared father sitting and tell him what you think about him. Gestalt therapists are very confrontive; they go after defenses strongly and directly. A practitioner of gestalt therapy may be a counselor, a social worker, a psychologist, or a psychiatrist who usually has advanced training from a gestalt institute. Almost all therapists have learned something from the gestalt school, particularly about confronting defenses — denial for example — and integrate it into their way of doing therapy.

Speaking of denial, I just had a thought about yet another aspect of alcoholic denial. It is another of those paradoxes that characterize drinking too much, namely, that alcoholics overuse and misuse denial when it comes to their use of alcohol because they are deficient in their ability to use denial adaptively — positively. Denial — as do all psychological defense mechanisms — has a positive side, a valid use. Denial allows you to postpone immediate awareness of traumatic events and only later to gradually allow the horrible truth to penetrate so that you are not overwhelmed. That way, painful realities can be come to terms with in manageable doses. If you can't deny some things sometimes, life is extremely painful. So painful that you turn to alcohol to blot out painful thoughts as a sort of artificial defense mechanism. Ironically, that leads to the unhealthy denial of a life-threatening behavior, alcoholic drinking. One of your tasks in sobriety is going to be building healthy defenses so you don't need chemical ones.

Gestalt therapy arouses extremely intense feelings, which are difficult to manage during early sobriety. Therefore, I do not recommend going to a gestalt therapist for the treatment of problem drinking unless he or she is an alcohol specialist as well. Gestalt stuff is great for getting feelings out if there is enough support and security surrounding it — that is why gestalt-type techniques are used so much in inpatient alcohol rehab units (see below). That's different than letting it all hang out for 45 minutes and walking out into a street lined with bars — just the place to get something to calm you down. Leave the gestalt stuff alone until you have substantial sobriety behind you.

Treatment Modalities

You can be treated individually, with your mate, with your family, or in a group. Each is valuable and each is a different experience. At some point in your recovery, you may want or need to participate in any or all of these treatment experiences. So far I have been telling you about individual therapy, so let me tell you something about the other modalities.

Group Therapy

Many people in the alcoholism field believe that group therapy is the best treatment for problem drinking. I disagree. I think you need individual attention to put some balm on the wounds you suffered during the last years of your drinking, and there are things that are easier to talk about one-to-one. The reason group is said to be best for drinkers is that "it takes one to know one" — that it is hard to bullshit another drinker about your drinking. That's true enough and groups are very effective in breaking down denial. Another advantage of group therapy is the opportunity for identification with peers. Therapy groups are typically composed of six to eight members and a leader, although there are larger groups and some groups have co-leaders. The group setting affords you an opportunity to get immediate feedback on how you relate to others. Group therapy is less costly than individual therapy and that too contributes to its popularity.

With all these advantages to group, you must wonder why I recommend individual therapy. The reason I do is because I believe you need and deserve an exclusive relationship that offers an intensity and directness of focus on you, which is not available in group. I want to make it clear that I think groups can be wonderful. If you have an opportunity to participate in a group *in addition* to individual therapy, do it. You will learn a great deal. There are relatively few privately run groups. Most are found in clinics, hospitals, and alcohol rehabs, and not all therapists are trained as group leaders. If a therapist wants you to enter a group, find out if he or she has advanced training in group therapy. If not, do not join. Some groups are awful. They become forums for members to dump their aggression on each other while the leader gets his or her jollies watching. This is rationalized as letting it all hang out. This is nonsense. You have been hurt enough; you don't need to be a member of an S&M gang. Besides, you don't have to pay to be insulted; you can easily find plenty of folks who will do it for nothing. On the other hand, a group in which the members just make nice and don't confront each other when confrontation is called for is useless. So you don't want brutality and you don't want Nelly nice. Look for a group leader who has an advanced certificate in psychodynamic group therapy and who is trained to work with alcohol problems in a group setting. There are counselors, social workers, psychologists, and a few psychiatrists with such training. They are what you want. If you still actively drink, you don't want to be in an all-purpose outpatient group. Their focus is too diffuse for your purposes and you won't get enough help with your drinking problem. You want to be in a group focused on dealing with alcohol. They are hard to find outside of a clinic setting. That's another reason to start with individual therapy.

Rehabs also sponsor *aftercare* (early sobriety) groups. These groups focus on alerting members to "drink signals"—people, places, and things that induce cravings for alcohol. I have not been impressed by their success rate. The idea is a fine one, but for whatever reason it generally doesn't work. The best aftercare group is AA.

Finally, there are "stage-three groups" for recovering alcoholics with stable sobriety of some duration. I don't think they are a good idea either. Group experience after you have stable sobriety can be an excellent vehicle for personal growth. However, I advise joining a psychodynamically oriented group whose members have diverse problems. Of course, you can and should talk about your drinking, as well as other problems, in such a group. Right now you are a long way from stable sobriety so this seems pretty irrelevant, but the time will come when you will be looking for ways to enhance your sobriety and group therapy may be just the thing.

Couple Therapy

Couple therapy involves you and your mate meeting with a therapist who points out communication barriers, power relationships, projections and displacements onto your partner, and helps each participant express his or her feelings. The relationship is said to be the "patient" and the whole focus is on what goes on between the two of you. The couple doesn't have to be a married one, any two people in a relationship can go for help.

Couple therapy doesn't work when one partner is drinking and the other wants him/her to stop. There is too much game-playing. If you stop drinking for him or her, you will pick up a drink the first time you get angry at whomever you stopped for. On the other hand, you can always find a reason to get angry at him or her to have an excuse for drinking.

Drinking too much corrodes and distorts relationships. I don't recommend couple therapy for active drinkers, but I *do* recommend it three to six months after you stop drinking if there are tensions between you and your mate. You are both going through a tremendous readjustment and may need help to negotiate it.

Family Therapy

Family therapy is conducted in various ways depending on the theoretical orientation of the therapist. Essentially, it tries to make manifest the latent power relationships, "payoffs," and communications within a family. It is a cross between couple and group therapy with the family being the group. All the things I said about couple therapy apply to family treatment. Unless you participate in family therapy as part of an alcohol rehab program, I recommend leaving it alone for a while. Later, it can be enormously helpful in facilitating expression of feelings, including those about drinking, between family members.

Most experts believe that family therapy is the treatment of choice for teenage substance abusers. Couple and family therapists are most often social workers by training, but mental health professionals from all disciplines practice it.

SELF-HELP PROGRAMS

Alcoholics Anonymous

AA is a unique organization. The first of the self-help programs, it has changed millions of lives, and served as a model for numerous other self-help groups. It was started in the thirties by Bill Wilson, an alcoholic stockbroker, and Bob Smith, an alcoholic physician. Bill wasn't in any shape to sell stocks so he couldn't have caused you any difficulty, but Bob Smith was a practicing Akron, Ohio, surgeon specializing in proctology. If you had hemorrhoids in Akron in 1935, you were in trouble. Bill W., as he is known in AA, had a "peak experience," an intensely emotional affirmation of the worthwhileness of life, while he was a patient in Knickerbocker Hospital. Knickerbocker was a well-known New York drying-out tank. Bill was shaken to his core by his experience in Knickerbocker. He went through a profound emotional reorganization and left a different person. The religiously inclined interpret Bill's emotional revelation as a "conversion experience"; the more secularly inclined interpret it as a reaction to his insight that his despair was caused by his drinking and need not continue. In any case, Bill's peak experience gave him hope and served as his bottom.

Bill entered Knickerbocker after talking to his drinking buddy, Ebby Thacker. Ebby showed up at Bill's place, of all damn things, sober. Bill poured another drink. As he drank it, Ebby told Bill of joining the Oxford Group. The Oxford Group was an upper-class revival movement that had its origins at Oxford University. It aimed at converting the leading men in a community hoping that their example would spread down the ranks. Ebby told Bill that he had been sober since joining and recommended that Bill also join. Wilson did so when he left Knickerbocker. He stayed sober, but he wasn't comfortable. He found the Oxford movement too dogmatic. On a business trip to Akron, Bill found himself tormented by a desire to drink. However, he had the insight that he wouldn't act on his desire if he could find another alcoholic to help in the way Ebby had helped him. Bill found Bob Smith, who was too shaky to perform a scheduled operation. Bill fed Bob a beer on his way to surgery—it stopped Bob's shakes. As they drove, Bill told Bob his story. In that act of sharing both the torments of drinking and the joys of recovery, AA was born. Neither man ever drank again. They had discovered that there is something special about two people with the same problem sharing their "experience, strength, and hope." It is curative. Bill soon discovered that open sharing and identification helps problem drinkers regardless of their personalities or circumstances. It still does. It changes the way they feel about themselves, it changes their drinking, and it changes their lives. It can do the same for you.

To get to an AA meeting:

1. Look in the phone book or ask the operator the number for Alcoholics Anonymous.
2. You will be given the number of your local AA Intergroup— coordinating office. Call it.
3. An AA member will answer and tell you the time, place, and type of AA meetings near you. He or she will also answer questions and share personal experiences if you wish.
4. Go to a "closed" AA meeting and listen. That's all there is to it. If you wish, the recovering alcoholic on the Intergroup phone will arrange for AA members to meet you and take you to a meeting.
5. If you don't like the group where you first attend, it's okay to shop around and try other meetings—but remember, part of your reaction is a defensive response to a threat to your drinking.

Returning to New York, Bill left the Oxford Group, organized meetings for alcoholics, and founded AA. The Oxford Movement recommended a series of steps for spiritual growth to its members. Bill modified them into AA's Twelve Steps of Recovery. AA grew rapidly and today is a worldwide organization with a vast membership. It works very well for who it works for, which is not every person with a drinking problem. Nevertheless, it is your *best single bet* for achieving comfortable, nay enjoyable, sobriety.

What's an AA meeting like? Well, there are two main types: the open meeting and the closed meeting. Open meetings are open to anybody — all are welcome. I send my students to them. At an open meeting, the chairperson reads the AA preamble and introduces the speaker(s), who "qualify"; that is, tell their stories. AA qualifications consist of a "drunk-a-log" — an account of the speaker's experience with alcohol, and an account of what sobriety has been like for the speaker. After the qualifications, the chairperson closes the meeting with the AA Serenity Prayer: *"God grant me the serenity to accept the things I cannot change, courage to change the things I can, and wisdom to know the difference."* There is no discussion and the "audience" doesn't participate, so there is *absolutely* no pressure of any kind on those who attend open AA meetings. At most meetings, you get coffee and cookies. At some point, the basket is passed, and you can put no more than a dollar in it if you wish, but you don't have to.

Closed meetings are restricted to "those who have a desire to stop drinking." At a closed meeting there is usually one speaker whose qualification is followed by discussion. Sometimes there is a show of hands and sometimes they go around the room. But you don't have to say anything; you can just say, "I pass" and nobody will press you. AA is nonconfrontational. I strongly urge you to go to an AA meeting whether or not the AA Program turns out to be for you. It is certainly a fascinating experience. The openness and honesty manifested at most AA meetings touches people at a deep level regardless of whether or not they have a drinking problem. Of course, like any group of people, AA has its losers — members who are obnoxious, unlikable, or downright mean. As they say in AA "principles before personalities," so don't let a speaker you dislike or a member who rubs you the wrong way discourage you or turn you off. As I said in an earlier chapter, the trick is to identify, not compare. Being overly critical and feeling different from the others at the meeting are in the service of denial. They are your disease telling you that you don't have it. You don't have to like everything about AA to benefit from it.

AA meetings reflect their communities. If you go to a meeting in a Vermont village, it will be somewhat different than a meeting in Greenwich Village, yet it will be the same. If you are concerned with anonymity, go to an AA meeting outside your community, but go someplace where you are likely to feel comfortable. In my experience, AA has an excellent record in keeping its members' membership private and in preserving their anonymity. You may see some familiar faces — that's nothing to worry about, they're there for the same reason you are.

A word about AA "spirituality" as embodied in the Twelve Steps. Some folks love that aspect of AA from the beginning, others are intensely uncomfortable with it. My advice is to ignore it. What's important for you at this stage in AA is the group support, the unconditional positive regard and acceptance of you and your disease, the possibilities for identification, the reduction of guilt that comes with sharing your experience of the ravages of alcoholism, and the deep emotional response so many people have to "finding a home" in AA. It is surrender — acceptance at a deep level that booze has you beat and that you need help — that is liberating. AA is the place most drinkers surrender and experience emotional release from their compulsion to drink. That may happen to you. Once it does, people stay in AA for the reenforcement and fellowship and to make sure that denial doesn't return and lead them back to alcohol and all its miseries. You'll probably stay for the same reasons.

AA talks about a Higher Power. Depending on your background and beliefs, that may be welcome or it may be abhorrent. In my view, your reaction isn't too important as long as it doesn't prevent you from getting the help for your drinking problem that you need. Fervent believers sometimes go on drinking and skeptics often get sober. Neither belief nor nonbelief are necessary to benefit from AA. The purpose of introducing a Higher Power is to get the focus off of you, to give you some reference point outside of yourself. That way you won't get in your own way and trip yourself up. Egotism and grandiosity are dangerous; they can easily lead you back to the bottle because they help you convince yourself you are more powerful than your disease. You aren't. There is an AA slogan to the effect that, "Only two people can get me in trouble, the 'Great

I Am' and 'Poor Me.' " The purpose of AA's Higher Power is to keep the Great I Am in check. Reactive grandiosity — bluster and all that — is an inevitable reaction to, and a defense against, your underlying feelings of guilt, worthlessness, and your abysmally low self-esteem. You may not be aware that you feel that way about yourself, but you do. The Great I Am is the flip side of self-hatred. The Higher Power idea gives you perspective and the idea that you don't have to, indeed can't, do it all or do it alone. Your Higher Power doesn't have to be theistic — a god or God — your AA Group will do fine as a Higher Power, as will anything that conveys the idea that there is more in the universe than you alone.

AA's Higher Power is a good guy. Loving, forgiving, and accepting. If you grew up believing in a harsh, punitive God who will send you to Hell, you may have internalized him and now condemn yourself in much the same way. AA's Higher Power helps get that fierce voice of a punishing God out of your head and that's all to the good. Guilt only leads to pouring another drink. An AA Group can serve quite well as a loving, forgiving, accepting Higher Power whose only interest in you is to promote growth. Again, don't worry about the ideology or the theology — I don't think that's the important thing about AA — just go and let the people there help you get started in sobriety. Literally hundreds of thousands of agnostics and atheists have gotten sober in AA. AA is gentle and you don't have to believe anything you don't want to believe to affiliate and benefit from it.

People do different things with AA and their involvement with it varies over the long term. Some remain intensely involved for many years, others diminish their participation as time goes on. But you don't have to worry about that right now. Just take AA, like the rest of your life, "one day at a time," and you will do splendidly. I strongly believe that AA is the best route to sobriety and that staying close to the Program, as its members call it, is strongly indicated during your first year of recovery. After that, many folks thin out their attendance, but maintain some involvement with AA. That, too, strikes me as wise. After all, alcoholism is a chronic, relapsing disease, and, like any other chronic condition, you need to continue to treat it. But again, that's not your immediate problem.

You can find AA in your phone book, or call information and ask for the Alcoholics Anonymous Intergroup number. AA Intergroups are central offices that keep track of what is going on in their areas. They are quite helpful. If you call your local Intergroup, an AA member will answer and tell you all about the meetings in your area and answer any questions you may have. He or she will also mail you a Meeting Book listing the time, place, and type of all the meetings in your part of the world. If you wish, AA will send several of their members to your home to tell you their stories and to take you to a meeting. Odds are you will prefer to go on your own, but if you would like some company and support, don't hesitate to ask for it.

Other Self-Help Groups

There are many other Twelve-Step programs modeled on AA. They use the same principles of sharing, identification, group support, community, and self-examination as AA and work in similar ways. Al-Anon is for people (spouses, parents, friends) whose lives have been intimately affected by their relationship with an alcoholic. ACOA is for adult children of alcoholics who may or may not be alcoholic themselves. Alateen is for adolescent children of alcoholics. The purposes of NA (Narcotics Anonymous), CA (Cocaine Anonymous), and GA (Gamblers Anonymous) are self-evident. Incest Survivors is also a Twelve-Step program. There are Sobriety Without God groups and AA meetings aimed at agnostics, gays, men, women, cops, physicians, and what have you. These specialized AA meetings are listed in AA meeting books. In the beginning, go to nonspecialized AA meetings—the universality of the Program is one of its great strengths.

At some point in your recovery you may find attendance at one or more of these other programs helpful. But I believe in doing one thing at a time, and I recommend that you restrict your self-help-group involvement to AA for now.

Structured Programs

Structured programs provide more help than therapy and AA are able to do, even in combination. If you want to stop drinking and cannot, you might consider availing yourself of them. The structured programs I want to tell you about are detoxification facilities, alcohol rehabilitation units, structured day programs, and halfway houses.

Detoxification Facilities

If your physician advises you to go inpatient to detoxify, do it. A good detoxification facility provides support and alcohol education as well as medical assistance. It is a safe place to be. It is awfully tempting to drink if you're feeling shaky a day or two after your last drink. If you are in a detoxification facility, there is no temptation. Inpatient detoxification facilities are sometimes units in general hospitals, sometimes they're autonomous, but most often they are attached to alcohol rehabilitation programs. Any AA Intergroup can direct you to a high-quality detox. Detox units are equipped to avert the more serious consequences of withdrawal from alcohol and to shore up your self-esteem at a time when it is perilously low. They are staffed by nurses, alcoholism counselors, and social workers as well as by physicians.

Rehabilitation Programs

The idea of being an inpatient in a rehabilitation program no doubt terrifies you. It probably angers you, too. Quite possibly, you are thinking something like this, "You [meaning me, the damn author of this book] really roped me in. 'Just keep an open mind and you will learn a lot about alcohol and yourself,' is what you told me. Now you're suggesting I lock myself up in the booby hatch. You can go to hell." I quite understand your feelings. I don't blame you for wanting to tell me off. But as long as you have gone as far as you have, why not read a bit more and find out about alcohol rehabilitation programs?

Well to start with, they're posh, for the most part. The kind I have in mind are privately run, highly profitable, very comfortable twenty-eight-day inpatient programs that help some people sometimes. These programs run twenty-eight days because that's what most insurance policies pay. Alcoholic rehabs are not psychiatric hospitals, although they are sometimes located within psychiatric hospitals as special units. Unless there is some special reason not to do so I recommend choosing a freestanding — not hospital-affiliated — rehab, if you go to one. That keeps the whole idea of hospitalization out of it. I think that's all to the good — for your self-esteem and to avoid the stigma that, unhappily, still attaches to a psychiatric hospitalization.

"Whoa! I'm not going to one of those places anyway so what are you talking about?" I believe that the vast majority of readers of this book will do just fine with therapy and participation in AA, but don't close the door on anything that might be of use to you. Rehabs have advantages: (1) they buy time in which to heal and in which to gain internal controls — you can't drink while you are there — that can be very useful if you're having a hard time getting started in recovery; (2) they are an investment in yourself, a chance to go on a retreat during which you can devote a month to exploration of yourself, to increasing your self-knowledge, and to personal growth. It can be a very good investment. If you have been drinking very heavily, very long, going through a rehab may be the best way to start on the route to sobriety.

What goes on in a rehab? Well, they are all AA-oriented, so you will be exposed to a lot of AA — meetings within the unit and meetings in the community. That's good. You will be in a daily group, have individual counseling, get a complete physical, take part in recreational and occupational therapy, attend lectures on alcohol and alcoholism. Perhaps most importantly, you will be part of a class going through "basic training" together, which builds a lot of esprit de corps and gives you the strength to endure the pain that is part and parcel of gaining insight into yourself.

Finally, your family will be invited to participate in the rehabilitation process. This is both for their sake and yours. They have been distressed by your disease and it has profoundly affected them, so they too need an opportunity to experience and express their feelings, and to learn about alcoholism—its effects on the drinker and its effects on those who love the drinker. You will probably feel threatened by the involvement of others in your treatment. Don't worry. Rehabs are good at maintaining confidentiality and yours will be respected. Family therapy sessions give all of you a chance to hash things out in the presence of an objective professional skilled at facilitating communication. Family therapy sessions can be very painful, as guilt, rage, sorrow, and love contend in the hearts and on the lips of the participants. Well conducted, they can be extremely helpful to you, giving you and your loved ones an opportunity to clear the air and either start to reconstruct things, or, if that isn't in the cards, to separate without needlessly wounding each other. Early sobriety isn't the time to decide if your marriage or relationship is worth saving; it is the time to learn to communicate better and to express feelings. That's what family therapy in an alcohol rehab is all about.

When it works, going through a rehab is a wonderful experience. Nevertheless, I don't recommend it as a first step unless you have to be detoxified in a hospital. If you do, then you are sick enough to need some time off, so go from detoxification directly into rehab. Otherwise, try therapy and AA first. If you "slip around," that is, can't stay sober, then go into a rehab. One reason to go to a therapist first is that he or she will know about rehabs in your area. Rehabs, like everything else, change with time. Staffs change and so do administrations. Therapists stay current on programs and know how to facilitate your admission if that seems to be the way to go. If you go to a therapist knowledgeable about alcohol who advises you to go through a rehab program—do it. Therapists don't make such recommendations frivolously. If your therapist thinks your going into a rehab is the best thing to do, ask why. You will be given an explanation and that will help allay your apprehension. Nevertheless, expect to be scared—that's natural—

just let yourself feel whatever you're feeling. Then walk through your fear and invest some time in yourself—you won't regret it.

Structured Day Programs

Insurance companies are starting to balk at paying for traditional twenty-eight-day rehabs. They are very expensive. Structured day programs provide much of what a rehab does on an "after-school" basis. Essentially, they are four-night-a-week group-therapy and alcohol-education programs. They are relatively new and not yet widely available.

Halfway Houses

These are semistructured long-term residential programs available in most communities for people who have really been hurt by their drinking and are not yet able to "make it," i.e., stay sober, at home. Rehabs sometimes recommend a stay in one for patients who are very shaky. Few problem drinkers need halfway houses, but they have saved many lives and made even more lives worth living.

Employee Assistance Programs (EAPs)

EAPs are assessment and referral resources within workplaces. They can help you find a physician or a therapist, or refer you to a detox, a rehab, or a day program. Most large organizations have such programs, as do an increasing number of smaller ones. Their quality and respect for confidentiality varies widely. When they are good, they are very good and can be enormously helpful to you. Nevertheless, I don't recommend going to an EAP for help *unless* you have heard good things about the one in your organization.

To sum up, get three kinds of help: *medical, psychological,* and *peer.* Do that by seeing a physician who understands alcohol problems, by seeing a counselor or therapist who understands alcohol problems, and by joining the folks in AA, who understand alcohol problems because they are recovering from them. If your physician or therapist suggest hospitalization for detoxification or going into a rehab, do it. Otherwise, see how you do with therapy and AA. If you are having trouble then you can reevaluate and consider entering an inpatient treatment program.

CHAPTER 6

Co-dependency

Co-dependency has become a buzzword these days. If you say good morning to your spouse you're co-dependent — oriented to your mate instead of yourself — and that's bad. This is unfortunate because the term "co-dependent," as originally used, illuminated and brought to people's attention a very important and previously little-noted phenomenon — the addictive quality that characterized relationships with alcoholics. Language is like that; it loses its edge and precision as meanings generalize. I am sure that a new word will be coined to denote relating to an alcoholic in a compulsive way, but for now, there isn't any so I will use co-dependency to mean being locked into a relationship with an alcoholic in such a way that you feel trapped and powerless.

Co-dependents are usually marital partners of alcoholics, although they can be friends, lovers, parents, children, or even employers. Just as alcoholism has been falsely regarded as mostly a male problem, co-dependency has been falsely regarded as mostly a female problem. Co-dependents come in all sizes, colors and genders. A co-dependent, as I define it, is a person who cannot detach from a love/hate bond to an alcoholic or other substance abuser and who is being hurt by his or her attachment. Co-dependency frequently entails enabling—doing things to sustain and support the drinker's drinking—but it doesn't have to.

FACILITATING HITTING BOTTOM

People's bottoms, these days, tend to be higher than they used to be. We know more about alcoholism and are better able to recognize its signs and symptoms earlier in the progression of the disease. There is less reason to go to the last stop on the elevator. This is true for the drinker and it is also true for those involved with alcoholics. You don't have to go down with your alcoholic loved one. You can either help him or her stop or "detach with love." If you see the signs of addiction to alcohol (or to other drugs) in your child, parent, lover, friend, or spouse, the first thing you must do is to *stop enabling.* Alcoholism has been described as a "family disease." It is. It affects not only the drinker; it affects *everybody* involved. The drinker, the people caught up in his or her web, and the web itself are called the "system." Alcoholic family systems are said to be "dysfunctional." That means that they don't work the way they should. They sure don't. One way they don't work is that everybody in them sees things through amber-colored glasses. That means that everyone in your family is in denial. Alcoholism engenders such powerful feelings of shame and humiliation that nobody wants to acknowledge its presence. Your denial may be overt denial, or it may be more subtle, taking the form of denial of your feelings. Another form denial can take is denial of your investment in "your alcoholic's" drinking. "Investment in his drinking? I *hate* it!" Yes, you hate it, yet you may be vastly enjoying the power and control that has fallen into your hands as your alcoholic has become less and less functional. You probably aren't aware that you are, and are even less aware that you would resent relinquishing that power and control as you might have to if he got sober. Is it possible that there are some goodies for you in the status quo? Might you be unconsciously keeping things the way they are in spite of your protests to the contrary? Is it possible that, like Satan in Milton's *Paradise Lost*, you would "Rather reign in hell/ Than serve in Heaven"? Think about it. It is not necessarily, or even likely, that you wished things to turn out the way they have, yet you may have come to like some things about living with a drunk. I know that sounds crazy, yet it happens all the time.

There is another reason people stay in relationships with alcoholics, namely, that they are reenacting their relationship with an alcoholic parent. They usually have absolutely no idea that they are doing this. I don't know why this is so and neither does anybody else, although there are many theories about why people repeat, indeed precisely reenact, painful early experiences. The reasons why are in doubt, the fact that it happens is not. People are deeply conservative in the sense that they hold onto the familiar and seek it out. People who were beaten as children seek out and find somebody to beat them, physically or emotionally, as adults. Freud (1920) called this the "repetition compulsion," and that's as good a name for it as any. You repeat because the known is, or at least seems, safer than the unknown; you repeat in the unconscious hope that the repetition will be less painful, less traumatic than the original; you repeat in the expectation of gaining mastery over past pain; you repeat in order to turn the passive into the active, to do rather than be done to; you repeat because you have been conditioned by the past; you repeat because you are afraid of the new. This is exactly what happens in alcoholic families. The players repeat the past and replay the present like a stuck record. Each member of an alcoholic family system is meeting some need by participating in it. Alcoholics often become less functional and less interested in the family as their disease progresses. As this happens, the decision-making power passes to the other family members, usually the spouse, but not necessarily so. Alcoholics can be belligerent and aggressive, but they are rarely effectively assertive. That means that someone gains power as the alcoholic declines. Human beings don't relinquish power gladly or easily. Family members sometime enable to main-

tain power. This is sometimes a child who is more or less forced to
assume adult responsibilities at far too early an age. The child may
come to like this and may grow up with an abnormal need to
control. Children who play this role in alcoholic families are called
"parentified children." It is not a happy role. If you are the one who
has gained power you probably like it, in spite of the fact that you
resent the responsibility that goes with it. In that case, you are not
in denial about your spouse's or children's or lover's alcoholism.
What you are in denial of is your role in enabling them. The first
thing to do is to become aware of it. Without awareness, no change
is possible. It is harder to become aware of unconscious motivation
than to see overt acts like drinking, so look very carefully at your
relationship with your alcoholic. Are you enabling him or her? Are
you covering up, making excuses, financially supporting the habit,
emotionally supporting the habit? You are? Stop doing it, today.
Don't enable one day at a time. It takes real courage to see yourself
clearly, and it is difficult. If you are involved with somebody who is
drinking alcoholically, you need professional help. It is also wise to
attend meetings of the self-help group Al-Anon. Al-Anon is for the
families and friends of alcoholics. Al-Anon was founded by Lois
Wilson, wife of Bill, and is an excellent place to get help if your life
is entangled with an alcoholic's. It uses the same Twelve Steps of
growth as AA and is, therefore, known as a Twelve-Step Program.

Once you break through denial and clearly see your loved one's
addictive drinking, recognize your piece of the action, and stop
enabling, you have three choices. You can stay in the situation and
"Detach with love," as Al-Anon puts it. You can leave. Or, you can
confront the alcoholic. Essentially, what you need to do is to say,
without rancor and without anger, that you can no longer tolerate
his or her drinking. "Because I love you and can't stand to watch you
destroy yourself, I will leave you, fire you, not sleep with you, or
whatever, if you don't go for treatment." This is called an "Intervention." Confronting someone who has been disrupting and
disturbing you and your family without anger is easier said than
done. Active alcoholics provoke enormous rage. So, of course, you
are enraged and need to know it, but an intervention is not the place

to express it. Your alcoholic will just get defensive and feel justified. Anger can be a trap and become a sort of addiction in its own right. Yet another reason people sometimes stay with and continue to enable an alcoholic is that they need an outlet for their anger and their alcoholic serves that purpose very well; they are folks who have become addicted to the violent upheavals in their alcoholic systems. It may be the case that the excitement makes them feel alive. This is particularly likely to be the case with people who feel dead, consciously or unconsciously, inside. Do you identify with any of this? Do you need your alcoholic as a target for your rage or need the fights as a way of feeling more alive?

Of course, you may be angry at yourself, perhaps because of guilt, again probably unconscious, and need to punish yourself. This is called masochism and living with an active alcoholic provides ample opportunity for gratification of masochistic needs. Many and various forces enter into the maintenance of an alcoholic system and keep you in there enabling and hating yourself for doing it. I want to be very careful here not to blame the victim. Sometimes people stay and enable not for emotional reasons, but because they don't know what to do, or think that they have no options. This brings us back to interventions.

The purpose of an intervention is to raise a particular alcoholic's bottom and get him or her to go for treatment. Treatment in this case means entering a rehabilitation program. There are people who conduct interventions, that is, arrange a confrontation between the alcoholic and the family, clergyman, boss, friends, and whomever else cares enough to participate.

Remember that you too are powerless over alcohol. That realization is your bottom. You can only decide and say what you will do, not what your drinker will do or not do. After that, there is nothing to do but let go and go about living your life. "But Dr. Levin, weren't you just telling me that I could raise my alcoholic's bottom? How do you reconcile advising that I admit my powerlessness with your suggestion I take action?" Well, by now you should be used to the paradoxical nature of things alcoholic. This is merely another instance of it. Just as the alcoholic finally becomes able to arrest his disease when he admits his powerlessness over alcohol, you will be able to act effectively—which doesn't necessarily mean that he or she will stop—only when you too face your powerlessness over alcohol. You too have been made sick by alcohol and, in a very real sense, you also have a disease. It is called the disease of co-dependency. Hitting bottom, in the sense of realizing your powerlessness over alcohol, is a kind of ego deflation for you too, but it is one that frees you. You will no longer be caught up in the "addiction game."

Just as active alcoholics "know," yet don't know, that they are alcoholics, so too do active co-dependents "know," yet don't know, that they are co-dependent. As long as you are involved in the alcoholic maelstrom, as long as you are a member of an alcoholic family system, you can't see it, at least not with any degree of clarity. You already know a lot about the effects of alcohol on the mind, body, and spirit of those who drink it. You are about to learn about the effects of alcohol on the minds, emotions, and spirits of people like you who love/hate those drinkers. It is going to be difficult for you to apply that knowledge to yourself. Your feelings are too conflicted and they are too powerful.

You feel ashamed, you feel angry, you feel frustrated, you feel depressed, you feel helpless, you feel empty, you feel confused, you feel sad, you feel numb—you simultaneously feel too much and nothing at all. You feel all these feelings because you are co-dependent and don't know it. People become co-dependent for all sorts of reasons: ignorance, inertia, lack of resources, a need to be punished or to suffer, a need for power and control, and the unconscious reenactment of a relationship with an alcoholic parent. You are co-dependent for one or more of these reasons.

The first step in dealing with co-dependency is to become aware of it. To help you do this, I am asking you to try to identify with a number of codependents as they think aloud about their lives and their relationship with a drinker. There is probably something about each of them that you can relate to and there is at least one in whom you will recognize yourself. Until now, you have focused on your alcoholic. I am going to ask you to switch your focus from him or her to yourself. You can't change another person, but you can change yourself. As soon as you focus on yourself, you become less helpless. You are now dealing with something that you do have potential control over.

You may not be sure if your loved/hated one is drinking too much. What's too much is a value judgment. You have the *right* to choose or not choose to affiliate with somebody whose drinking bothers you. That doesn't mean you can alter that person's behavior, but it does mean that you can state what is acceptable to you and decide what *you* are going to do if the other person doesn't want to, or can't, drink in a way that doesn't make you unhappy. It is possible that you are involved with a person whose drinking is socially acceptable and far from alcoholic, yet unacceptable to you. You don't have to be with that person. That may seem obvious, but it isn't to many people who don't feel free enough to act on their gut feelings. You may be one of them.

Because denial is present in all members of an alcoholic family system, I am going to give you some objective signs of alcoholism. Drinking too much in nonalcoholic ways is harder to define; essentially, it means drinking in a way you don't want to be involved with. Back to alcoholism: read the following signs. Think about your loved one's drinking behavior and see if three or more of these signs characterize that behavior. Put the list away and repeat your evaluation in a few weeks. If you still come up with over three signs, you are involved with an alcoholic and must decide what you want to do about it.

Signs of Alcoholism:

1. Drinker doesn't remember what happened when he or she was drinking (blackouts).
2. Radical personality change when drinking.
3. Monday-morning absence from work.
4. Fighting and abusive behavior when drinking.
5. Health problems related to drinking.

6. Depression that doesn't remit with treatment.
7. Defensiveness about drinking that sounds crazy because what the drinker maintains is so clearly contrary to fact.
8. Trouble on the job, especially otherwise unexplained faltering performance.
9. Otherwise unexplained decrement in functioning in any important life sphere.
10. Passing out, usually rationalized as "relaxing" after dinner.
11. Violence when drinking.
12. Restlessness and agitation when alcohol isn't available.
13. Morning drinking.
14. The shakes or other symptoms of withdrawal.
15. Neglect of personal hygiene.
16. Daily drinking of more than socially expected proportions.
17. Frequent drunkenness.
18. Otherwise unexplained moodiness and emotional withdrawal.
19. Increasing suspiciousness and seclusiveness.
20. Increasing self-centeredness in a person who was not previously self-centered often manifesting itself in making drinking more important than anything else.

Now that you have an objective criterion to evaluate your loved one's drinking, turn the focus back to yourself and think about your relationship and why you're in it as you read the following monologues.

LILIAN, A DOORMAT

Lilian is married to an alcoholic, although she doesn't know it. She thinks that she is the cause of the difficulties in her marriage. She never blames her husband Henry or his drinking for their unhappiness.

Why is Henry so mean to me? I must be doing something wrong. He's always yelling at me. The priest said that I should be grateful he has another woman, it will make him appreciate me all the more, but it doesn't seem to be working that way. I don't think the priest understands, but he's a priest so he must be right. I try to please Henry; a woman is supposed to please a man. I did everything for my father and always obeyed him. Henry drinks an awful lot, but I don't want to nag him. He's a hard worker and a good provider.

He wants me to put my mouth there. I try to be a good wife, but I can't do that. When he's drunk, he tells me about her and the things she does for him. That hurts me so much.

I hate it when he tells me to shut up in front of other people. He says I'm stupid. I feel so humiliated. I wish Henry wouldn't drink so much. He never humiliates me when he isn't drinking. I want to be a loving wife and please him. Men drink after work. Henry works so hard. Just like he says, he's entitled to a drink when he comes home, but I can't help wishing he would stop after the first six-pack.

Lilian may seem an anachronism, a throwback to an earlier time. Surely such women don't exist anymore. After all, it's the nineties and women's lib has been with us for twenty years. I'm afraid that just isn't so. I meet Lilians frequently. They come for therapy because they're depressed. Doormats usually are. Lilian may be a little extreme, but ask yourself—is there anything about her way of relating to her husband that you can identify with? Are you overly compliant, willing to please at any cost, avoidant of recognizing the intensity and depth of your mate's aggression against you? Were you submissive as a child and submissive now?

Lilian is married to an abusive drunk. He degrades her, ridicules her, and screams at her, but only when he drinks. Lilian knows this, yet won't admit that Henry's drinking is the problem. She is in denial. Are you in denial of your spouse's obvious alcoholism? Obvious to everybody else, that is.

Lilian and Henry are playing a game. A deadly one. He insists on oral sex, which he knows she abhors, then uses her refusal to have an excuse to drink. Lilian tells herself that Henry has a right to drink because "he works hard" and "she isn't a good (i.e., sexually compliant) wife." Their game protects both of them from having to face Henry's alcoholism. Such "deals" are endemic in alcoholic families—they don't have to be sexual. Is there a similar tradeoff in your relationship?

Henry torments Lilian by telling her about his girlfriend, but her real rival is alcohol. Henry doesn't care about other women; he cares about drinking and uses infidelity to divert her attention from the real problem and to hurt her. Part of Lilian likes to be hurt so she takes it. Are you being diverted from the real issue too?

Lilian is sitting on volcanic rage. Are you sitting on a volcano? Lilian wants to kill Henry just as she wanted to kill her tyrannical father. She stuffs her rage and turns it into its opposite, so Lilian is all sweetness and light. Instead of cutting Henry's throat, she is submissive and fawning. She'll do anything for Henry—except *that*. Are you sweet? If you are, don't trust it.

Lilian has multiple reasons for "not knowing" about Henry's drinking problem: she is afraid to rock a boat that, however storm-tossed, is afloat; she thinks that pleasing men is a woman's duty; she needs to avoid fanning her rage; and last, but definitely not least, Lilian's feelings of shame at being married to an alcoholic keeps her head in the sand. Don't underestimate the power of shame to keep you from facing your loved one's alcoholism. Are you ashamed of your loved one's drinking? Does that shame prevent you from doing anything about it?

TOM, AN ADORING FATHER

Tom is having trouble with his son, Joe. He wonders why Joe isn't doing better in life, but he isn't ready to consider the possibility of alcoholism.

I gave him a job. He can't really do it, but I never say anything. Joe's so nervous all the time, if it wasn't for his mother and me, I don't know what would happen to him. I know he takes money from the business, but he never asks us for money. Thank God he's still living at home with us — who knows what kind of trouble he'd be in if he didn't. His mother worries about his drinking. She doesn't understand. All young fellows drink a lot. I did; besides, Joe's so nervous he needs a belt now and again. I always straightened things out when Joe got into jams at school, and his mother did everything for him, so I don't know why he's so nervous. Good sense of humor, though. Some of our best times together are tossing a few down after work. I suppose he goes on drinking after I go home, but so what? That's what kids do. He's just having a slow start — he'll be a fine fellow in a few years. Good thing I play bridge with that judge or I would never have been able to get him off when that bastard of a cop insisted on running him in — the kid only had a few. They're hysterical about drinking and driving now. Give him a little time and that boy will settle down and turn my business into an empire.

Joe is 35. His parents have been enabling him at least since he flunked out of his third college. Joe's father is clearly letting Joe live out something for him. Part of him enjoys Joe's drinking and Joe's failure to grow up. Joe's antisocial escapades give his father some sort of vicarious pleasure. Tom was a heavy hitter in his youth. Now he experiences life as all-too staid. Joe provides the excitement in his life.

Tom's identification with his son prevents him from seeing Joe realistically. Tom assumes that Joe will settle down and become a successful businessman just like he did. But, that isn't going to happen because Joe is an alcoholic.

There is another aspect to his father's enabling of Joe. Tom is unwilling to let Joe go. Tom doesn't want Joe to grow up and do normal adult things like leaving home. Tom doesn't know this and believes the opposite to be true. Tom's own drinking, which has changed from problem drinking to life-style drinking, also influences his behavior toward his son. Heavy drinking is natural to him. Tom may also fear his son as a competitor and need to keep him helpless—in effect castrated. If so, Tom is certainly not aware of it.

Tom is an enabling parent writ large. It is easy for you to see what he is doing. But it isn't so easy for you to see your own behavior if you are a player in a similar drama. Not all parental enabling of alcoholic children is as transparent as Tom's. Consider if you may be enabling your child in more subtle ways. Ask yourself how your own drinking influences your relationship with the person whose drinking concerns you. That person need not be your child. You may be quite surprised with what you come up with. More than one co-dependent has discovered that his or her drinking is a problem in its own right.

There may be a darker aspect of Joe's father's behavior. He may be acting out unconscious hostility toward his son and trying to destroy him as a viable person by supporting his drinking. Enabling is not infrequently driven by hostility. That's an ugly possibility, the mere thought of which might upset you. Yet your enabling and overprotection is killing your loved one. Is there a hostile side to your enabling of your child or your spouse or your parent or your lover? The very suggestion seems outrageous, but difficult as it is, you need to look at the possibility that hostility motivates your enabling. Unconscious motivation is so difficult to ferret out that it is best done with the help of a therapist.

Some parents have a hard time letting their children grow up. Joe's parents are certainly among them. Growing up includes having to deal with the consequences of your actions. Overprotective parents don't give their children the opportunity to learn from their mistakes, so they repeat those mistakes. Are you an overprotective parent rationalizing infantilizing Junior as "helping him out"? Having an alcoholic child is excruciatingly painful. If you have an alcoholic child, guilt, rage, shame, sorrow, disgust, and fear vie with one another for domination of your emotional life. You may not be aware of these feelings, yet they are there distorting your thinking and causing you pain. If you suspect that your child is alcoholic, get professional help. You are too close to the situation to see it clearly.

I wonder about the mother's role in Joe's drinking. She seems to be a passive lady who wrings her hands and moans that Joe is ruining himself by drinking too much. But she doesn't do anything about it. She is less in denial than her husband, but her needs are being met in some way by the status quo — or she wouldn't acquiesce to what's going on between Joe and his father. Perhaps she needs to blame her husband or perhaps she is afraid of too much closeness and needs Joe as a buffer between Tom and her. Do you identify with any of this? Do you feel helpless as you watch somebody in your family enable an alcoholic relative? If you do, see if you can figure out why you go along. Ask yourself, "What am I getting out of things as they are?" "What's my 'payoff'?" I know this way of thinking seems strange to you. But try to set aside your abhorrence and look at what you gain by enabling.

Joe's mother is part of the family *homeostasis*. Homeostasis is an important concept. It helps make sense of co-dependency and the behavior of alcoholic families. Homeostasis is a concept borrowed from physiology, where it refers to the body's self-regulatory mechanisms for maintaining constant optimal levels of physiological states such as temperature and blood sugar concentration through the use of feedback loops. It is the body's attempt to keep things the same. For example, when your blood sugar level falls, your liver releases sugar into your bloodstream to bring your level of blood sugar back up. Conversely, when your blood sugar level goes too high, your liver takes some of it out of circulation. Your body has many such self-regulating mechanisms. Families work the same way. A family is a system that tries to maintain homeostasis. It resists change and responds to it by attempting to reestablish the old balance. This means that families have a built-in bias toward stability over growth, even if its stable state is unhealthy. Of course, it is the people in your family who, consciously or unconsciously, strive to maintain the status quo, but your family as a whole behaves as if it is an organism seeking stability. Your family's alcoholic's drinking may be an important element in its stability. The emotions engendered by your drinker's drinking, the power relations resulting from it, and the distribution of responsibility necessitated by it all meet needs, conscious and unconscious, of each and every member of your family. Because needs are being met and because people like things to stay the same however much they deny it, your family resists change just as your body resists changes in its physiological status. Alcoholic families are notoriously resistant to change and a member of your family becoming sober would be a drastic change. No wonder you have so much unconscious ambivalence about your loved ones becoming sober.

JIMMY, A FURIOUS HUSBAND

Jimmy is enraged at his wife. He can't stand Helen's drinking. Nothing in his life is as upsetting to him as coming home and seeing Helen sipping at a drink.

> That bitch is drinking again. Screw her. I'll break her neck. If there is one thing I can't stand, it's to come home and see my wife with a glass in her hand. It's disgusting to see women drink. Only whores do that. Helen only drinks to annoy me. My mother listened to my father. She gave him respect. I'd like some of that. When dad said something, everybody jumped. I sure did. It was the strap if I didn't. Great guy though. He was right when he insisted I take Latin in high school and join the army even though I didn't want to. Learned a lot in the service. Funny guy, dad—Latin, sports, the military. But what a man. Mother drank for God's sake. A cocktail at a party, but not every day. Damn Helen. She can't do this to me.

I won't take it. No way. I'm the one who should have the drink at the end of the day. You drink like a man, not like a woman. That time I came home drunk, my father taught me how to drink like a man. He made me drink a whole bottle without puking or staggering or anything. I was sick for a week, but boy did I learn to drink like a man. My mind's wondering, what's all this have to do with Helen drinking like a whore? I can't wait to get my hands on her; she'll stop all right.

Jimmy's wife isn't alcoholic. Helen is a life-style drinker. Jim and Helen are in a power struggle. He doesn't want her to drink; she wants to drink. Although Helen enjoys her evening cocktail, her drinking is almost a matter of principle. As she puts it, "There's no way that bastard is going to tell me what to do." Jim and Helen's issue is *control*. Helen is a daily drinker, but she doesn't drink much. Two old-fashioneds a night. Occasionally a third. It is her way of relaxing at the end of the day, and it is a common practice in her social circle. She doesn't drink anymore on the weekends, and she doesn't get drunk. Drinking isn't all that important to her and she might even give it up if Jim didn't make an issue out of it. Helen could get in trouble with alcohol, daily drinking doesn't have much to recommend it, but, so far, it isn't a problem for her. Of course, Jimmy doesn't have to be married to a drinker if he doesn't wish to be. But that isn't his real issue. He often has a drink in the evening and would even enjoy Helen's having a drink with him. It is her defiance and her drinking without him that drives Jim up the wall. He is "turning a passive experience into an active one" as the psychoanalysts say. That is, he is treating Helen exactly the way his father treated him. He doesn't know this and thinks he wants to be treated by his wife the way his mother treated his father. He does want that, but he wants other things even more. Jim was totally controlled by his father, now he wants the same kind of control over his wife. Helen resents and resists this. Alcohol is the currency of their power struggle.

Can you identify with any of this? Are you trying to control another person's drinking because you need to control? If you were raised by an overcontrolling parent, you may need to control your spouse in exactly the same way you were controlled. It is unlikely you are aware of what you are doing or why you are doing it. Again, therapy is the best place to gain insight into your need to control.

Jim is an angry man. He is enraged about his entire upbringing, particularly by the way his father treated him, but he is in *denial about his anger.* Instead of recognizing and dealing with it, he displaces his rage toward his father onto a safer target—his wife. If Helen stopped drinking Jim would find something else about her to be angry with.

Often in a situation like Jim and Helen's, where a spouse is in a fury over the husband's or wife's nonalcoholic drinking, the complaining partner finds the drinking intolerable because he or she had an alcoholic parent and reacts strongly to any use of alcohol. If you grew up in an alcoholic home, watching your mate drink stirs up painful feelings and deep-seated fears. The powerful rage you once felt toward your alcoholic parent, you now feel with all its original intensity toward your drinking spouse. Alcoholism in the family leaves scars. If you found mother sloppy drunk when you came home from school with your friends, your wife's casual drinking may be very upsetting. Did you grow up in an alcoholic family? If you did, you may be reacting out of deep-seated fear to your current loved one's drinking and that fear may be inappropriate.

Of course, your fear may not be inappropriate. It is entirely possible that your loved one does have a problem with alcohol, but that your real interest in his or her drinking is in control. What you want is to control your spouse, rather than to help him or her recover. How important is exercising control to you? Do you identify with Jimmy's compulsion to control Helen's drinking? Motivation is never pure and you may both want to control *and* want to help. Ask yourself, is your issue telling the other person what to do, or is your issue drinking that is unhealthy and disruptive of your relationship with that person? Once you can answer that, you will be in a position to do something constructive.

Jim and Helen are stuck. They are in a power struggle neither understands. Unless they get help, they are headed for the divorce court and divorce won't solve a problem that Jim doesn't even know he has. He will go on trying to control people and venting his anger on them, and they will, in turn, react with anger, defiance, or rejection.

CLAIRE ANN, AN ABUSED WIFE

Claire Ann is also stuck. But she is stuck in a different way. She is married to Ted, whose drinking is out of control. Claire Ann is desperate but she sees no way out. Her thoughts are pain-wracked.

> He never hit me before. God, it hurt. My nose bled. My face doesn't hurt anymore, but the pain inside won't go away. We've been married ten years and nothing like this ever happened before. Ted always had an awful temper, yelling and swearing and pushing but never hitting. . . . I wish my father were alive. He would beat the shit out of Ted if he knew. I really want that—just once—then maybe he'd stop drinking. Dad stopped when I was 6. Mom said Dad was a real crazy when he drank, but I don't remember that. I just remember how much I loved him. I never really got over it when they called and said he died on the job. Just dropped dead as he was climbing into his truck. I was only 12. There wasn't much money after that and Mom got more and more nasty. Looking

back on it, she must have been depressed—six kids, just like me, and no money and no husband. I didn't understand. I thought I hated her. Then Ted came along. I married him because he wore a white shirt and a tie. He was the only boy I knew who wore a white shirt. I really loved him in the beginning. My God, lovemaking was wonderful. For about six months. His muscles were so hard and I thought his roughness was strength. I felt safe. Ted didn't talk a lot—but I didn't care much about that. We had our own place—it was so exciting—I was only 16. Buying curtains and knickknacks and not having to listen to mother bitch and moan. I was free and happy, but it didn't last long. Once I got pregnant Ted was different. It was like the lights went out. My life was over. Ted was home less and less and he started drinking. The white shirt never came out of the drawer and his blue shirts smelled of sweat and beer. I guess all construction workers drink a lot, but not like him. That was ten years ago and things never got better and now I have a swollen nose. I'm still bleeding inside—in my soul. I can't stop crying. I want to get out—how the hell do I get out with six kids? Where do I go? The social worker at the agency said I was staying because I wanted to stay—that Ted was my father or some bullshit like that. Ted isn't one bit like my father. Why didn't she tell me what to *do* instead of telling me what I was feeling? I didn't need that shit. She said, "I'm here to help you explore your inner world." What's she think she is, a gynecologist or something? I don't know what to do—where to go. I don't have a cent; Ted even took the checkbook. Somebody please help me.

Claire Ann is trapped. She is living with an alcoholic who has become physically abusive toward her. If Ted keeps on drinking, the physical abuse will reoccur. It always does. Ted's abusive behavior is likely to get worse. Claire Ann and her children are in danger. There is *no* hope that things will get better, so long as Ted is drinking. It is a virtual certainty that things are going to go downhill and that life is going to become rougher for Claire Ann. If Ted continues to drink, his job performance will deteriorate and the economic security that keeps Claire Ann with him will disappear. If you are living with a person who is violent and/or physically abusive when drinking, *leave* him or her. I know that is easier said than done, but it can be done. Child abuse (physical and sexual) and spouse abuse are highly correlated with alcoholism. The odds are high that abusive spouses and parents are heavy drinkers. Most family violence occurs under the influence. Has there been violence in your family or in your relationship? "Yes," you say, "but he didn't mean it, it was the booze." Don't minimize such incidents. Of course it was the booze, that's the point. He's still drinking, right? Do you identify with Claire Ann's terror, rage, and feelings of helplessness? If you do, your denial is likely to be powerful. It is humiliating to admit that you have been a victim of violence. It is easier to dismiss it— "He only pushes me; he doesn't really hit me." . . . "I guess I deserved it; I shouldn't have screamed at him when he lost his job." . . . "She didn't mean to cut me with the knife; she was crazy that night." Physical abuse has a way of escalating, leading to serious injury and even death. Don't minimize it.

Claire Ann is working-class. "Surely," you say, "family violence doesn't occur in middle-class life, let alone upper-class life." Let me assure you that it does. Your Bowery can be Park Avenue. Indeed, I have treated spouses and children of alcoholics who lived on Park Avenue, and believe me, their fifteen-room apartments were skid row. "Oh well," you say, "the decadent rich are capable of anything, but I belong to a solid middle-class family. We go to church, work hard, send the children to good schools and help them with their homework." All that may be true, yet there may be alcoholism in your home and that alcoholism may have lead to violence. I see *battered middle-class co-dependents* frequently. Almost always they are in denial when they first come to me and conceal and dismiss the most appalling happenings out of shame and out of fear of their own rage. Are you minimizing or denying the violence in your family?

However terrible life in middle- or upper-class alcoholic

homes, it is different from life in a working-class alcoholic home on
the margin of financial deprivation like Claire Ann's. She and her
children live on the edge of poverty, and fear of poverty keeps her
with Ted. You may be in the same situation. *You don't have to stay with
a physically abusive alcoholic,* although you think that you do. There are
things you can do that you haven't thought of . . . yet. You are
acting in a crazy way by letting yourself be abused, not because you
are crazy, but because you are ignorant — you lack knowledge of the
options open to you. You can go to a shelter for abused women.
They exist in most communities — call information or your Department of Social Services. You can go on welfare. You are eligible for
many social service benefits you may not be aware exist. Day care
may make your working possible. You may be eligible for vocational training or educational benefits to upgrade your skills so you
can support your family. You can obtain free, or at very low cost,
psychotherapy from a social agency in your community to help you
recover from the trauma of being with an abusive alcoholic. Claire
Ann thinks she has no options, that she is trapped; she isn't. Her
choices are narrow and difficult, but they exist. You aren't trapped
either; although you think you are.

Claire Ann is a victim. Her social worker wants to blame her
for being victimized. Fortunately, she is healthy enough to refuse to
accept the blame. The responsibility for her husband's disease is not
hers. I hate blaming the victim. It's ugly and there's a lot of it
around. Children who are incest victims aren't responsible for being
sexually abused; the blacks who were enslaved weren't responsible
for the destruction of their family structures; and the Jews of
Europe weren't responsible for the Holocaust, although supposedly
rational people attribute just such responsibility and blame to them
all the time. The same thing happens to the victims of alcoholism.
They are often blamed for the pain they have endured. The concept
of co-dependency is basically a liberating one. It has helped millions
of people see how their unconscious needs kept them in destructive
and unhappy situations. Used thoughtlessly and uncritically, however, it has done much mischief. Claire Ann's social worker is using
the concept of co-dependency mindlessly. It doesn't apply to Claire

Ann's situation. What Claire Ann needs is concrete advice about what she can do to leave Ted. She needs to be informed about what services she is eligible for and what social agencies will work with her to assist her in protecting herself and her children. She needs legal advice on how to get an order of protection against Ted. She needs to be directed to Al-Anon. *If you are in a similar situation, you need the same sorts of help.*

If you are a middle-class mother without independent financial resources, married to an abusive alcoholic, your situation isn't too different from Claire Ann's, and you need similar kinds of help. It is *always* better to suffer an economic loss, a drop in your standard of living, than to continue to be abused. You can reverse your economic loss much easier than you can undo the psychological scars that accrue in an alcoholic home. Don't count on it and don't do it for that reason, but your leaving may be the occasion of your spouse's hitting bottom. Sometimes the shock of a long-suffering partner's walking out forces the drinker to abandon denial.

I have the feeling that Claire Ann will do okay. She has a lot of strength; it shows in her sense of humor about the social worker and in her reaching out for help. What she needs is somebody to give her hope and to show her an open door someplace; once she sees it, she will have the courage to walk through it. However, Claire Ann does need more than what social workers call "concrete services." She would benefit enormously from supportive psychotherapy that aimed at increasing her self-esteem, alleviating her feelings of helplessness, and putting her in contact with her rage. Claire Ann is like an accident victim — she has what psychologists call "post-traumatic stress disorder." She has been physically and emotionally battered. She has lost her self-confidence and her sense of possibility. She sees no open door. Effective psychotherapists see doors that you can't see because your pain blinds you and they help you see them also. If you identify with Claire Ann, find a therapist who can help you get out and who can help you deal with your feelings of worthlessness, helplessness, and hopelessness. *Taking action* is the key to feeling better. Get that order of protection, attach his salary, change the lock, go to the shelter, move in with friends —

do whatever you have to do to end the abusive situation. And get supportive help—at Al-Anon, at a consciousness-raising group, from a therapist. If you are co-dependent in the way Claire Ann is, the way you feel is *caused* by living with an alcoholic; you aren't living with an alcoholic because you feel the way you do. It is like depression caused by alcoholism. The drinker thinks he or she drinks because of depression, while the depression is caused by the drinking. Similarly, you aren't co-dependent because of your emotional difficulties; your emotional difficulties are caused by your co-dependency. When you get out of your co-dependent situation, a great deal of your depression, anxiety, low self-esteem, feelings of worthlessness, feelings of helplessness, and feelings of hopelessness will disappear. Of course, you will have much work left to do on yourself, but you will be in a far better position to do it.

Claire Ann, like all of us, has her share of conscious and unconscious emotional conflicts and her marriage to Ted certainly has unconscious determinants. She didn't marry him *only* because he wore a white shirt and was a ticket out of an intolerable home situation. There was something about him that satisfied some deep need within her and she certainly stayed with him for emotional as well as practical reasons. That's true for you also. Those emotional reasons are out of Claire Ann's awareness—unconscious. For example, she feels guilty because she hated her mother and "abandoned" her to struggle with five kids when she married Ted. Ted's abuse of her fulfills her need to be punished for that hatred. Psychotherapy would make Claire Ann aware of this, but psychological insight isn't what Claire Ann needs right now. Psychodynamic issues aren't relevant to Claire Ann's situation. She needs to take action now and analyze her motives later. Her social worker wasn't so much wrong, as way off in her timing. "First things first," as they say in AA.

Try to identify with Claire Ann's feelings, even if you never have been hit by your alcoholic. You may find that you too feel trapped and see no way out. The dynamic reasons for your being in the situation you are in aren't immediately relevant. Learning more about them won't help you change things until you see a way out. You may also have post-traumatic stress disorder—that needs treatment. Years of degradation leave scars. The important thing is to realize that you aren't trapped and that your feeling that you are results from tunnel vision and from having been beaten down for so long. You *do* have options and you need to act on them.

PERRY, STILL TRYING TO SAVE HIS FATHER

Perry has lived with Stanley for many years. They are lovers. They were once happy, but they are not happy now. Stanley's drinking has gotten to the point where Perry cringes when he sees Stanley reaching for the bottle. Perry is thinking of leaving, although he is not ready to do so. Perry is struggling with conflicting emotions.

Why do I stay? He's going to lose his job if he keeps this up. We never have any fun anymore. I'm afraid of AIDS if I start cruising again. I haven't done that for ten years. It was so exciting to be young in New York. I loved the hunt. New faces, new people, wild sex—the bars, the making contact, the going home with a stranger. I drank a lot then, everyone did. Ten years of partying was enough. If you don't stop, you become ridiculous. I didn't want to be a kid forever. I thought of marrying and almost did, but then I met Stanley and it was love. Me falling in love; that was amazing. A mathematician in love is an odd thing. Reason and passion had been my life—abstract reason during the day, passion at night. I couldn't bring them together. One-night stands, then more equations and more lovers. I don't want to go back to that. It was a stage. I'm glad I had it. It isn't only AIDS; I don't want to live that way anymore. Am I still in love with Stanley? Yes, damn it, and he's hell-bent on killing himself. Drunk every night. God knows what he does in the bars. Why in God's name do I still love him? We never go to the opera any more. Our sex life is awful.

We fight all the time. Yet I stay. Fear? Of AIDS? Of loneliness? Of emptiness? I guess so. But that's not it. I still love him, plain and simple. It sure doesn't "prove," but as Pascal said, "the heart has its reasons that reason knows not." My analyst says that Stanley is just like my father: impulsive, self-destructive, alcoholic. I hate to admit it, but Stanley is alcoholic. He even has veins in his nose. Looks like hell. He's still handsome, though. Distinguished-looking. Nobody would take him for gay; I like that. I don't think I stay because he's like Dad. It's more that he complements me. Impulsive while I'm controlled; extroverted while I'm introverted; worldly wise while I have academic smarts.

Our temperamental differences aren't all good. Stanley still likes the bar scene; I'm through with it. I love our home, our paintings, our music, our peaceful evenings. Who am I kidding? There aren't any peaceful evenings any more. The truth is that I'm living with a falling-down drunk, who doesn't function. He's losing everything—his looks, his success, his sanity. The truth is, there is nothing in it for me now. Yet I stay. Why? Damned if I know. I could get my own place and find somebody else. But damn it, I love him. I don't want to see him destroy himself. It's so ugly to watch a human being—a decent, bright, caring—at least he used to be— human being—kill himself. It's like watching Dad die again. Another decent man who killed himself. Dad didn't wait for alcohol to do it; he put a bullet through his head. I'll never forget Mom's face after she found him. I don't like to think about that. Usually don't. I guess it's the analysis that makes me think of these things. Maybe the analyst is right and I am staying to save Dad once removed. It won't work, though. Stanley is getting just as depressed as Dad. He'll kill himself too. Then I'd be free. What am I thinking? Do I want him dead? No! Of course not; it's just that I can't stand the slow destruction, the

constant decline. Stanley, please stop. I can't stand this
and I can't leave you.

Do you identify with Perry? Are you living with an alcoholic
you love in spite of everything and in spite of yourself? Are you
puzzled why you stay? What on earth keeps you bound to a
near-corpse waiting for the end? You don't know. Don't let Perry's
homosexuality be a barrier to your identifying with him. It is his
feelings, not his sexual preference, that counts. Of course, if you are
gay, you feel additional kinship with Perry, but "the heart has its
reasons" for the straight as well as the gay. Perry, unlike Claire Ann,
is a "psychodynamic co-dependent." His analyst is right; he is
choosing to remain with a rapidly declining alcoholic in the hope of
saving him because he was unable to save his father. Freud spoke of
the "compulsion to repeat." He considered this drive to relive
emotionally powerful experiences as basic to human nature. I think
he was right and that the more traumatic the experience, the
stronger the unconscious drive to repeat it. People do this because
they secretly hope that the outcome will be different, and they do so
in the hope of mastering the trauma, of dealing with feelings that
were overwhelming the first time. Their secret hope is a secret from
themselves and they don't know they are reliving traumatic early
experience.

When you are caught up in the compulsion to repeat, you act
instead of remembering. You repeat not only in the hope that things
will be different, but in the hope that you will finally come to terms
with searing pain and put it behind you. In reliving traumatic
events, you turn a passive experience into an active one and that
feels good. You are doing it rather than having it done to you.
Paradoxically, you inflict pain on yourself in order to overcome
pain. Reexperiencing the pain is the price you pay for gaining
control by doing rather than being done to. Don't underestimate the
power of this unconscious process. It drives a good deal of human
behavior, including yours. Are you staying in a relationship with an
alcoholic because you were in a relationship not of your choosing
with a parent who was alcoholic? Are you trying to save that parent?

Kill that parent? Have an opportunity to express your anger to that parent? Mourn that parent? Feel powerful rather than helpless? Feel in control rather than controlled? All by reliving your relationship with your alcoholic parent with your alcoholic spouse or lover.

The problem with the compulsion to repeat is precisely that it is a compulsion. You do it even though you don't want to do it. Co-dependency, like alcoholism, is a losing game. In the end, you have no power, no ability to control, no opportunity to change the outcome. You wind up reliving the trauma instead of mastering it. You get hurt again. This may be precisely your situation. If you were raised by alcoholics, and you are now living with an alcoholic, although you think you don't want to, consider very carefully if you identify with Perry and his reasons, conscious and unconscious, for staying with Stanley. Insight into your unconscious motivation will help you take action. Claire Ann doesn't primarily need insight into her psychological reasons for staying with Ted; Perry does need insight into his reasons for staying with Stanley. If you are a psychodynamic co-dependent, you need insight too. Perry has intellectual insight but that isn't enough; he needs emotional insight—the emotional conviction that he is staying in a nothing relationship because he has never gotten over his father's death from alcoholism. True, his father committed suicide, but that suicide was the direct consequence of his father's alcoholism. A large percentage of suicides are. You too need emotional conviction as well as intellectual insight to change.

Perry isn't aware of it, but he is enabling Stanley. It is possible that his enabling will result in Stanley's suicide, but there is also a risk that Stanley will commit suicide if Perry leaves him. Perry knows that somewhere and that is another reason he stays.

Do you identify with Perry? "Yes, I do," you say, "but, Dr. Levin, your theory is crazy. My mate wasn't alcoholic when we met, so how could I have known that things would turn out like they have?" Perry met Stanley in a bar. Did you meet your mate in a bar? Perry was drinking heavily when he met Stanley. Were you drinking heavily when you entered your relationship? It is amazing how people find what they "need." They can smell it. Although it never occurred to you that your alcoholic was alcoholic when you linked up with him or her, your unconscious smelled the resemblance to your alcoholic parent and found you a mate who would allow you to live out your unconscious compulsion to repeat. Fantastic? Maybe, but that's the way people work. If you are a co-dependent in the style of Perry, that's the way you worked when you got into your relationship with your alcoholic.

"Okay," you say, "you're right, but what difference does it make? I love her and can't leave." Yes, love is love and I agree that love can't be explained by the compulsion to repeat or by other psychological hypotheses. Love is indeed mysterious—not fully accounted for by scientific explanations. Yet you can somewhat understand why you love and why you love who you love. If you are staying with your alcoholic because you love him or her, remember that staying with an active alcoholic, albeit out of love, is enabling that alcoholic. Your love may be a love that disables and a love that kills. "But I can't help it," you say. "Besides, what can I do?" Well, you can confront your loved one's alcoholism and stage an intervention. I will tell you how to do that shortly. If you know your loved one is alcoholic and you can neither leave nor confront, you are in trouble and need professional help *now*.

One reason, and a central one, that Perry can't make a move either to confront or to leave Stanley is that he has never mourned his father. Failure to mourn is catastrophic. It can keep you depressed for a lifetime. It can lead to your turning to alcohol or drugs, and it can involve you in self-destructive unconscious reenactments like Perry's with Stanley. You can't mourn behind an addiction, including addiction to an alcoholic. Your co-dependency is in lieu of mourning. Perry was unable to mourn his father at the time of his death and he can't grieve his loss because he has Stanley as an unconscious substitute and in that sense his father isn't dead for him. Although he needs to feel his grief and his rage and his helplessness, he does not and he remains stuck and unable to get on with his life. Are you stuck in a co-dependent situation because you have failed to mourn an alcoholic parent? Are you unable to mourn that parent because you are in a co-dependent situation? Do you see the vicious circle you are caught in and the need to break out?

I tell my psychotherapy students that they are in training to be professional mourners. I am exaggerating to make a point, a valid point. I believe that after sobriety is achieved or co-dependency relinquished, the most important things that happen in successful psychotherapy are mourning, getting in touch with your aggression, and getting that aggression out front working for you rather than against you. The energy tied up in unresolved mourning becomes available for pursuing life goals once your mourning is done. If you are co-dependent, it is extremely likely that you have some mourning to do.

Meaningful mourning requires emotional intensity. It is depth of feeling that frees you from the past. The necessity for emotional intensity brings to mind the story of the man who visits the cemetery but finds that he feels very little as he stands by his lost loved one's grave. In his distress, he becomes aware of a mourner at the adjoining grave who is weeping fiercely and bitterly. The weeping mourner keeps crying out, "How could you die? How could you do it to me? Oh, how could you die?" Our visitor to the cemetery felt envious. As his neighbor's weeping and wailing continued, he turned and said, "Excuse me sir, but I can't help but see how deeply you are affected by your loss. Who did you lose? Whose loss causes you such grief?" The weeping continued. "Is it your mother?" the visitor to the cemetery asked. "No," replied the weeper. "Your father?" "No." "Your wife?" "No." "Your child?" "No." "Your friend?" "No." "For God's sake, whose loss is so painful?" "How could you do it to me? How could you die?" continued the lamenter. "Sir, please won't you tell me whose death causes you such grief?" The heartbroken mourner responded, "It's my wife's first husband." You need to feel your losses as intensely as the man who lamented his wife's first husband's death so you can work them through and get unstuck and get on with your life. Your alcoholic parent doesn't have to be dead for you to mourn the desolation of your childhood and the impoverishment of your parent's life.

JACK, AN ALCOHOLIC CO-DEPENDENT

Jack can put them away himself, but compared to Sally his drinking is a drop in the bucket, or should I say, a shot glass in a fifth. Jack isn't concerned with his own drinking, but he's sure concerned about Sally's drinking. He is humiliated by his wife's sloppiness and by her public drunkenness. Jack is frustrated, enraged, and wildly upset. Jack is given to unspoken outbursts.

> That bitch. Drunk again. Puked in the car. Good thing the kids were home with the sitter. Why can't Sally drink like a man? Belt down a few, relax, have some fun, and go home halfway straight. Shit, I had to stop at 10 because there was no way I was going to let her drive. All I need is to have my wife taken off in cuffs. In this town my business would drop in half. They're a bunch of sanctimonious, self-righteous hypocrites. The whole town was down on John Tower. They all drink, though. Saturday night at the country club, the bar sure isn't empty. Everybody but Sally knows how to drink. Shit. Puking in the car — teenagers do that. Everybody knows she was soused again. I'm becoming a laughingstock. Sally blames it on me. Says it's all because I did the maid in the back bedroom. How the hell was I supposed to know she would come home from her mother's two days early? I've been basically faithful. A few meaningless things in fifteen years. Why the hell did she hire a sexy kid as a live-in maid and go away for a week? What did she expect? I was half in the bag and didn't know what I was doing. Besides Sally isn't much fun that way since she started drinking so heavy.
>
> Maybe I should spank her the next time she gets drunk — that would really shake her up. Naw. That's a silly idea. Damn, I really would like to slap her just once, but that's not me. I scream at her. Tell her I'm going to

divorce her. I've even poured her bottles down the drain. Nothing helps. Now she's hiding her bottles — that's real alky stuff. Why can't she have a martini or two before dinner like me? I should never have suggested wine with dinner would be classy. It's too much for her after cocktails. She loses control. I know when to stop — never have more than a brandy or two after dinner. Boy, that stuff's expensive. Of course, I only buy the best. No sense wasting it on her. I know she drinks during the day. Doc Rosen gave her those pills, but they don't help one bit. She drinks more than ever. Valium I think they were. Maybe she's crazy; I could have her put away — naw, the whole town would find out. After their curiosity was satisfied, they'd never come in the store. If she goes to that PTA meeting soused, I'll kill her. Okay, I'll sit down with Sally and tell her no drinking during the day; I'll stop the wine with dinner; I'll tell her she has to stop after the second martini; and I'll tell her she can damn well stay home Saturday night if she doesn't know when to stop. Yeh. That'll do it. Jack, you solved that one; you deserve a reward. I think I'll have a snifter of that two-hundred-dollar-a-bottle Napoleon Brandy. Ah, smells wonderful. Why can't Sally drink like a gentleman and really enjoy it like me?

Sally is an alcoholic. Jack is an alcoholic also. The only difference is that Sally's disease has progressed to the point where it is obvious to everybody. Sally is hurting enough that she is reachable. If Jack wasn't so invested in his own drinking, he could confront her and insist she go for treatment — enter a rehabilitation unit. At this point, Sally would not put up much resistance. However, that confrontation is not going to happen, because Jack likes to drink too much to do anything to upset the apple cart. For all his bluster, he doesn't want Sally to stop drinking. He just wants her to "drink like a man." That's not possible. Sally is neither a man nor a social drinker. She is an alcoholic woman in bad trouble. Sally no longer functions as a housewife or a mother. She embarrasses herself and her husband by her public behavior and she is seriously endangering her health — mental and physical. Sally is ready to throw in the towel, to surrender, but she doesn't know how to do it in a face-saving way. She knows that she can't do that in the way that he wants her to. So she goes on drinking alcoholically. Jack and Sally's relationship may seem ridiculous, but set-ups like theirs, where the hidden agenda isn't far below the surface, are common.

Are you ambivalent about your loved one's drinking? Do you want him or her to cut down, but not to stop, to drink like a gentleman or a lady, and not be an embarrassment to you? Does your loved one's not being able to drink at all seem as great an embarrassment as his drinking too much? Do you wish your damned fool of a mate could drink "normally"? Unfortunately, neither Sally nor your loved one can safely drink anything at all because they are alcoholic. Your loved one's potential abstinence from alcohol is threatening for a variety of reasons: it is socially unacceptable to you; you are afraid of change; it forces you to admit that your loved one has a degrading malady; and, most saliently, it is threatening because, at some level, you, like Jack, know that your loved one giving up alcohol means that your drinking will have to be different. How do you feel about changing your drinking habits? You don't have to be alcoholic to be invested, consciously or unconsciously, in your loved one's drinking. You can be a serious social drinker, not an alcoholic, yet feel almost as threatened as if you were. Drinking is important to you. You like the rituals attending it, the sociability that goes with it, and, yes, you like the effect of alcohol on your tense body and mind at the end of the workday. Having a mate or companion who can't drink would be a pain, however much his or her overdrinking upsets you. It's kind of selfish to feel that way and you know that, so you feel a little ashamed that you feel the way you do, but "Hell, why can't he/she drink normally like me?" Well she/he can't and that's all there is to it. As you know by now, alcoholism has nothing to do with volitional efforts to "drink normally." On the contrary, the inability to drink normally is the essence of the disease. Your hope that your loved one will gain control, cut down, or slow up is in the service of your denial. It is not to be. Don't underrate your ambivalence — underrate how mixed your feelings about your loved ones not drinking are. You are aware that you have some mixed feelings, that's the conscious part. It's like an iceberg — you see the one tenth above the water, but not the nine tenths below the water. So figure you are ten times as ambivalent about your loved one's not drinking as you think you are.

There is another reason you avoid confronting your loved one's alcoholism and possibly having him or her stop drinking — your partner drinks so much more than you do that you have constant confirmation that you don't drink all that much. After all, your alcoholic downs X times the amount you do so there can't be anything wrong with your drinking.

An awful lot of co-dependents have drinking problems themselves. Are you one of them? Looking for help for your loved one may be a covert way of looking for help for yourself. I know you feel outraged by my suggestions that you too drink too much. Nevertheless, consider it. Drinking problems come in a variety of forms — you may not be alcoholic, yet you may be drinking too much. If so, you may want to cut down your consumption and limit your mental preoccupation with drinking. You may even conclude that you too are alcoholic. In either case, your loved one's going into treatment, or joining AA, or just stopping would certainly change your relationship and have an impact on your life-style. Change is always threatening, always resisted. However, things just aren't working out as they are so you have to do something.

There is a barrier to identifying with Jack. Namely, he is a self-centered son of a bitch who seems to care more about his business and his reputation than about his wife. You may share Jack's feelings about business, reputation, and wife, but if you do, you aren't likely to admit it. Most likely you're a nicer person than Jack. But don't be too hard on poor Jack, he may not be so bad after all. A great deal of his self-centeredness comes from his alcoholism. It is manifestation of the narcissistic regression that is part and parcel of alcoholism—you don't drink alcoholically without becoming self-centered. Sally's drinking is partly a response to not feeling loved. Jack and Sally are locked in a vicious cycle, or worse, a downward spiral, of his not caring because she is a drunk; and of her being a drunk, in part, because she feels unloved. Do you recognize your situation in Jack and Sally's?

Jack *buys into* Sally's alcoholism. Buying in is the essence of co-dependency. There are many reasons people, people like you, buy in.

Protecting their own drinking; economic security, or the illusion of it; unconscious reenactment of childhood relationships with alcoholic parents; power and control, or the illusion of it; and avoidance of painful feelings of guilt, shame, rage, and hurt are common reasons people buy in. Are you buying into your loved one's alcoholism for any of these reasons? Are you buying in for a reason personal to you that I have not mentioned?

I once treated a man who had stopped drinking and drugging about a year before he came to me. He was hurt and puzzled by his girlfriend's withdrawal from him in sobriety. She was an artist who had a studio at the beach, which she would not let him visit and who, in general, gave him little time or attention. As we examined their relationship, it became clear that they had had an unspoken deal—he could go off drinking or drugging leaving her to pursue her art as long as he didn't make too many demands on her time during his sober interludes. They both got what they wanted—he could drink and withdraw into himself and she could paint and withdraw into herself. She bought into his drinking because it allowed her to have a relationship that didn't make great demands on her extremely limited capacity for intimacy. Their arrangement worked for a long time, until his drinking got to a point where he could no longer function. She demanded that he quit drinking. He did, but then all hell broke loose. With sobriety, he wanted more of her than she could or would give. The only way the relationship could endure was if he returned to drinking. When my patient realized this, he broke off and is still sober.

Jack isn't "taking his own inventory." Instead, he is "taking Sally's inventory," as they say in AA. Focusing on somebody else is a classic way of avoiding looking at yourself. As a co-dependent, it is vital that you take your own inventory — that you look at yourself as well as, indeed before, looking at your loved one. Taking your inventory, of course, includes looking at your own drinking, but it refers to much more than that. It refers to learning more about yourself so that you don't go on running on automatic with little or no awareness of what you are doing.

HEATHCLIFF, A SHOCKED SON

Heathcliff is worried about his mother. She is 87 and has just been admitted to the hospital. Heath is walking around her apartment in a daze. He is in shock. He has just found out something he never suspected.

> I can't believe it. A blood alcohol level of 0.6, enough to be legally intoxicated. My mother? Mother never drank. Maybe she'd take a drink when she and Dad had people in or at a wedding. But my mother drinking, I can't believe it. Yet, that's what the doctor said. Drunk, and I thought that she had a stroke. What's this under the bed? Empty bottles. Oh my God, six empty whiskey bottles. I bought her a bottle of good whiskey two years ago so she would have something to serve when people came in. It's still in the kitchen, half-full, so she must have been trying to fool me. Hiding her drinking! Oh God, Mom a secret lush. It's kind of funny, though. Have to give the old girl credit, becoming a souse at 85. Not many people could do that. Most people are dead at 85, not my Mom. Dead drunk maybe, but not dead. It has been painful to watch

her decline the past two years. Up to then she was a ball of fire. Shopped for herself, took care of her apartment, went to the theater and the movies. Always did love the movies, but I wish she hadn't named me Heathcliff. I guess she was taken with Lawrence Olivier.

It took her a while to get over Dad's death. But once she did, she did fine. She hasn't been herself for the past two years. More like my daughter than my mother. I guess that happens when people age. But now I know why — it isn't senility, it's alcohol. Mother! How could you do it? How can I face the kids and tell them that Granny is in the hospital because she was blasted? I turned red when the doctor told me. Will she have to go to AA? My mother in AA? I am so ashamed. I won't tell anybody. I'll get her a companion and tell her to watch Mother's drinking. I'll get somebody who needs a green card and doesn't have much English so nobody will know.

Heathcliff is very uptight. He is so afraid that somebody, anybody, will know that *his* mother is a drunk that he was unable to see what was happening right in front of his eyes, although there was ample evidence if he had cared to look. He assumed that his mother's decline was due to age and he dismissed the fact that his mother's breath always smelled of alcohol when he visited. He rationalized that she had lots of friends who came in to share a glass of sherry with her, when he knew damn well that most of her friends were dead. Most likely, Mom started drinking after her husband died to anesthetize the pain of that loss and to numb the blows to her self-esteem inflicted by aging.

Heathcliff lives in a world where people drink, but drink in a limited way on clearly defined social occasions. The whole idea of drunkenness, let alone alcoholism, is foreign to him; it is "ego-alien" as psychoanalysts put it. Having a parent who drinks excessively is not part of his conception of himself or his world. Although Heath didn't want to see that his mother was drinking because he was ashamed of it, it is also true that alcoholism was so far from his experience that he was genuinely naive. It never occurred to him that his mother's problem was alcohol.

Do you identify with Heathcliff? Have you overlooked a loved one's drinking partly to avoid feeling shame, but mostly because alcoholism is so foreign to your experience that you never even considered it? If you have, your problem is not so much emotional denial as ignorance. Who would ever think that your aged mother would suddenly develop alcoholism, especially when there has never been a case in your family? Well, alcoholism is an equal opportunity disease. It is no respecter of age, gender, ethnicity, religious belief or lack thereof, education, or socioeconomic status. Persons of one background rather than another may be, and are, more likely to develop alcoholism, but it hits all kinds, colors, and ages of people. Late-onset alcoholism causes a lot of unnecessary death. The elderly have fewer physical resources and relatively low doses of alcohol do them great harm. The moral of Heathcliff's story is that if somebody you love suddenly declines intellectually, emotionally, or in their overall ability to function, don't overlook the possibility that they are drinking, and that their drinking is the cause of their decline. Watching parents age is painful in any case; watching late-onset alcoholism devastate a parent is dreadful. Late-onset alcoholism can be successfully treated. As in treating any alcoholism, the key is overcoming denial—yours and your aged parent's.

Parental alcoholism in the not-very-old is equally difficult to deal with. Often the best that can be done is to "detach with love," as they put it in Al-Anon. I know it sounds crazy, but, paradoxically, detaching with love gives you a much better chance of helping mother, father, sister, brother, wife, or husband to recover. Because you are no longer playing the alcoholic game you can be objective and do what needs to be done or, if nothing can be done, you can get on with your life as best you can.

SHELIA, A CONTROLLER

Shelia is at the peak of her professional career. She is head of the science department at the high school. She runs it well and she runs it with an iron hand. She is also one of the best teachers in the school. Shelia is a super-mom guiding her two teenaged children through the pitfalls of adolescence with uncanny prescience. She is an unhappy woman, however, or at least she says so all the time. Sam, her husband, hasn't drawn a sober breath for years. Shelia has a few feelings about her marriage to Sam. She is about to share them with you.

My sister is married to God and I am married to *him.* She sure has a better deal. I thought it was sad when she joined the convent. If I had only known, I would be there too. I am sure that God does not drink. Sam does. St. Paul said it was better to marry than to burn. Clearly it is better not to marry at all. If I did choose to marry because I mistakenly thought I needed to satisfy my natural needs, why did I have to marry Sam? Why him? He can't even keep the checkbook straight. I have to write all the checks and take care of all the bills. A man should take care of money matters, but I have to do it all. If I give him too much money, he drinks. He is always complaining that his allowance is too low. Too low indeed. He drinks every cent of it. The last time he was in the hospital, I found out that Sam was taking money from the business, or what's left of it, and drinking that. If he goes off his Antabuse again, I will move to have him committed. Sam still thinks that he has rights as a father. Over my dead body. He only corrupts their innocent souls. I and I alone guide and discipline the children until he takes the pledge and lives up to it. I am God's representative in this home. I say that with all humility. If

I didn't have to take charge, I wouldn't, but as long as I
do things will be done as the Lord would want it.
Drunkenness is ungodly. It is the sin of gluttony. Sam is
a glutton. Sam is a fool. Sam is an incompetent. It is a
good thing that I earn good money for I have no idea how
long it—I suppose I should say he—can continue in the
business. If he drinks on top of his Antabuse again, it
may be the end. So be it, if that is God's will. It would be
a release for all of us. Sam would have a chance for
salvation if he was in purgatory. He has none here. I am
being punished for marrying for sensual fulfillment.
Thank God there is no more of that. Sam can't be allowed
to do anything. I even have to run the business, although
I know very little about it. Fortunately, I am highly
intelligent. He was good at making money and I will
make sure that we keep what we have. I don't believe that
he will be good at making money or at anything else
again. God in his wisdom has given me the penance of
running this house and I will carry my cross. When Sam's
liver gives out, which cannot be very much longer, the
children and I will be well provided for. Thank God I had
the foresight to make Sam take out more life insurance
before his liver enzymes gave him away. Perhaps he will
do better when he leaves the hospital this time, but I do
not think so. I will do my duty and do what I must as long
as the Lord gives me strength.

Shelia is a controller. She loves running the show. Although
she takes Sam to doctors and puts him in the hospital, she has no
wish for him to recover. She doesn't know that and honestly believes
that she wants Sam to get sober. Shelia enjoys complaining about
the burdens put on her almost as much as she enjoys running things.
If Sam actually stopped drinking, all hell would break loose in their
home. Shelia will never willingly give the checkbook back to Sam.
Nor will she allow him to function as a father. Clearly Sam is very

sick, in the last stages of alcoholism, and his chances of recovery are poor. But, it could happen. If it does, Sam and Shelia will almost certainly separate and probably divorce. Shelia is the need to control in a co-dependent writ large. She is an extreme case, but a real one.

I have met quite a few Shelias. Can you see part of yourself in Shelia? You need not identify with Shelia's demeaning Sam nor with her sadism to see your own power drive in her. Can you identify with the wish for your alcoholic to remain helpless so you can run things? Is it possible that part, even a small part, of your relationship with your alcoholic is similarly motivated? Think about it.

There is a hasidic story about a guilt-ridden rich man who goes to the Rebbe for advice. The rich man wants to fast and practice all sorts of austerities. He asks the Rebbe for guideposts for living an ascetic life. The Rebbe replies, "Na, na, no austerities. I want you to eat cakes and drink sweet wine." "What?" says the rich man. "Why don't you want me to fast?" "If you fast the poor will go hungry too. You will be so certain of your piety that you will see no reason to give to charity. On the other hand, if you eat well and give yourself other pleasures, you will feel generous and contribute handsomely to charity. So the poor will get to eat also." The Rebbe was no fool. He understood the "martyr game" very well. He would have made an excellent therapist for Shelia. She plays the martyr with a vengeance. Martyrs, of course, are entitled to compensation for their suffering. Shelia's compensations are moral superiority and control. You, too, may be playing the martyr game. If you are, I suggest that you eat cakes and enjoy them. I am not so sure about the sweet wine.

Clearly Shelia always had a strong need to run things. Perhaps you have been forced to do so by your alcoholic's progressive abrogation of responsibility and progressive loss of the ability to function adequately in the tasks of daily living. It wasn't always that way and you once enjoyed the mutuality of marriage. But no more. That is no longer possible, and lo and behold, something you honestly didn't want, that was forced on you, now feels damn good.

It is pretty nice to make the decisions, to spend the money, to decide what the kids can and cannot do. When you really think about it, you realize how much you like things as they are — at least you would if he or she wasn't drinking. The status quo minus the drinking would be pretty good. Of course, it isn't black and white. Part of you does want your alcoholic to function better, to take responsibility, to recover. You have made a virtue out of necessity and come to accept with some alacrity that necessity. If your alcoholic gets sober, you will be surprised at your reaction. You won't entirely like it and you and your family will need professional help in redefining roles and accepting these role changes.

Shelia isn't a very attractive person. But she does things we all do — hide behind belief systems to justify grinding our particular axes; deny that we get pleasure from things we enjoy but are not comfortable with; wish some people dead; and enjoy being morally superior to those around us. You have some of this stuff. What aspects of Shelia do you identify with? How do they contribute to your co-dependency?

GETTING PROFESSIONAL HELP FOR YOUR CO-DEPENDENCY AND YOUR LOVED ONE'S ALCOHOLISM

Everything that I said in Chapter 5 about getting help for a drinking problem of your own applies to getting help for an alcoholic you love and to getting help for yourself as a co-dependent. It might be a good idea for you to reread Chapter 5.

You feel so overwhelmed and confused that you have no idea where to begin. Start by getting help for *yourself.* You have been and still are involved with a person with a chronic disease. If you were involved with a person with terminal cancer, you would have no trouble admitting that you were under tremendous strain and that it was taking a heavy toll on you. It is no different with alcoholism. You have been hurt, you have suffered, you feel sad, angry, hopeless, helpless, enraged, ashamed, humiliated, vulnerable, and generally at the end of your rope. There are two reasons for getting help: one, you need it; and two, you will be better able to help your alcoholic if you do. AA and Al-Anon say that they are "selfish programs," and in some ways they are. That is all to the good. You are confused about who you are and you don't know how to love yourself in a healthy way. You need help in finding out who you are and in learning how to love yourself. That help is available from professionals and from your peers in the self-help movement.

I have already said quite a bit about professional help. All of it applies to you. You have just as much trouble with alcohol as a person who drinks compulsively. Therefore, you should see a *professional with special training in alcoholism.* It doesn't matter too much whether that professional is an alcoholism counselor, a social worker, a psychologist, or a psychiatrist. What does matter is that you have a good relationship with your therapist and that your therapist has knowledge of alcoholism and co-dependency. Inquire into the therapist's background, training, and experience. Inquire explicitly into his or her knowledge of alcoholism. Remember, you are buying a service and have every right to pick someone whose training and experience meet your needs and with whom you feel rapport.

Let me say flat out that if you have been living with or are deeply emotionally involved with an alcoholic *you need psychotherapy.* No ifs, ands, or buts about it. You may not think so. You may think that only your alcoholic needs therapy, but you are wrong. I have never met a person who was deeply involved with an alcoholic who was not profoundly damaged by that relationship and who didn't need help to recover from the ravages of alcoholism. Alcoholism wounds all it touches, not just the drinker. Further, let me urge you to get individual psychotherapy, at least at the beginning. When one member of a family is ill, the attention of the family goes to the ill one, and the other family members suffer neglect, neglect of all sorts, but especially of their emotional needs. You have been so neglected. You need some individual attention and the place to get that is in individual psychotherapy. Couple therapy and family therapy are great stuff but they focus on relationship and family, respectively, not on the individual. You may need couple and/or family therapy as well, but you need one-to-one first. It will give you a chance to clarify your thoughts and feelings without the interference of your alcoholic's denial or your response to it. You need to work in a static-free environment for a while. Of course, family dynamics and interactions have to be explored but they should not be your first priority in therapy. You have been focusing on someone else for far too long. Now is the time to turn your energies inward and focus on yourself. I know this sounds strange since you are looking for help in getting your alcoholic sober. Nevertheless, it is what you need to do. You need the support that a good therapeutic relationship will give you. With the aid of that support, you will be able to look at yourself and see how and why you are buying in, if you are, and you will be able to see what unconscious patterns and drives are being enacted in your relationship with your alcoholic. But that comes later. First things first. And the first thing is to have a opportunity to experience and express your feelings about your situation and all it has done to you. After you detach, with or without love, you will be able to act.

Al-Anon is the Twelve-Step Program for friends and relatives of alcoholics. It was founded by Lois Wilson, wife of AA's Bill Wilson, and has a similar format, ethos, and ambience. It uses the same twelve steps of spiritual growth, the same sponsorship system, and the same philosophy of healing through sharing. It is a good place for you to be. Al-Anon is in your phone book, or you can get their number from information. The person who answers your call will tell you about the meetings in your area. Go to one. You will find friends there. Al-Anon is a good place to get a referral to a counselor or therapist if you don't have one. In my judgment, Al-Anon isn't as successful as AA in the sense that it seems to work for fewer co-dependents than AA works for alcoholics. I suspect that the common bond isn't as strong between co-dependents as it is between alcoholics. Be that as it may, Al-Anon is a good program. Definitely give it a chance. You will learn a lot about alcoholism, about co-dependency, and about yourself.

There is another self-help group I highly recommend. It is Adult Children of Alcoholics (ACOA). If you are a child of an alcoholic, or if alcoholism importantly touched your childhood, go to an ACOA meeting. ACOA meetings tend to be angrier than Al-Anon meetings and I think that's good. I have seen many people helped by ACOA. Many of my patients attend it. If you are such a child of an alcoholic, I suggest you join an ACOA group and get active in it. It will not only help you come to terms with the trauma of growing up in an alcoholic home; it will help you deal with your current co-dependency. ACOA is a newer organization than Al-Anon and has fewer meetings. But the odds are high that you can find a meeting at a reasonable distance from your home. ACOA, like Al-Anon, is in the phone book or you can start at Al-Anon and ask them which ACOA meetings they recommend. Many people belong to both.

Sponsors can be very helpful. I suggest that you get an Al-Anon or ACOA sponsor. A sponsor in any of the twelve-step programs is a more experienced member who acts as a mentor to a newcomer. It is wise to be selective in choosing a sponsor as long as you don't become so choosy that you reject all candidates. Be careful you don't link up with an overcontrolling sponsor. Try to pick someone who is open about him/herself and who is willing to share his/her experience with you. If the relationship goes sour, bail out, but keep going to meetings.

Finally, I recommend that you go for some couple or family counseling. Don't go into couple or family counseling until you have a few months of individual therapy and a few months in Al-Anon and/or ACOA. Couple or family therapy with an active alcoholic has little to recommend it unless it is aimed at breaking down denial in all concerned. I have not found it helpful, except in rare instances, while one of the partners is drinking. There is too much defensive anger and evasion on the part of the drinker, and too much game-playing by the nondrinker for marital counseling to do much good. If your loved one is still drinking, I recommend that you go for family counseling *only* if the purpose is clearly arresting the alcoholism. Otherwise, every kind of irrelevant side issue will be used to avoid the real issue, which is untreated alcoholism. It is all bullshit.

I feel very differently about couple and family counseling once sobriety has been achieved. I believe it is vital then. The adjustment to a loved one's newly won sobriety always brings all sorts of surprises for all concerned and there are all those old wounds to be dealt with, anger to be expressed, and healing to be accomplished. So, by all means, go for family or couple therapy, but do it *after* your drinker has stopped drinking.

Now you are in individual therapy, you are attending Al-Anon or ACOA, and you have tried family counseling aimed at arresting active alcoholism, but your loved one is still drinking. What do you do? Let go. Detach with or without love. Admit that you are as powerless over alcoholism as the alcoholic. Then take action.

Taking Action

There are three actions you can take. You can break off your relationship with your alcoholic. Letting go and detaching are mental and emotional operations—they happen inside you. They are attitudinal changes that precede, or best precede, action. Breaking off means severing your physical relationship with your alcoholic, not living with him or her, and not seeing him or her. It is ending it. That may not be what you want to do, but it may be your only viable option. On the other hand, breaking up and off may not be possible or desirable. Another option is to continue living with him or her, while emotionally severing your relationship by emotionally detaching and going about living your own life. Wives with small children who don't want to break up their homes sometimes do this. So do parents with teenaged or young adult children who are in trouble with drugs and alcohol. Emotional detachment can save your sanity and give you a modicum of peace of mind, but it may entail enabling, at least to the extent of providing a home for the drinker. Your last, and often best, option is to conduct an intervention. An intervention is a planned confrontation of an alcoholic with his or her alcoholism with the goal of the alcoholic going for treatment in an alcoholic rehabilitation center.

CONDUCTING AN INTERVENTION

Most rehabilitation units conduct interventions. They have staff members who are expert at directing interventions. Today, alcohol rehab programs advertise in newspapers, magazines, and on radio and TV. It is not hard to find one. You can call and ask for the service of an interventionist. Alcohol rehab units are also listed in your telephone book. The only trouble with doing it that way is that you lose control. Many alcoholism counselors also conduct interventions. If you want help in staging an intervention ask your counselor or therapist for it. Your therapist will refer you to an interventionist if he or she does not do this kind of work. Or you can conduct your own intervention. If you do so, think it through very carefully. Plan before you act. What you must do is this:

1. Decide what action you want your alcoholic to take. Asking him or her to join AA and go to ninety meetings in ninety days, while not drinking, is the minimum you can ask for. But I would ask for this plus seeing a therapist who is alcoholwise as my minimum. More traditionally, what is asked for is entering treatment in a rehab unit. That generally means a twenty-eight-day commitment on the part of the alcoholic.

2. Arrange all the practical details such as making an appointment with the therapist or obtaining a bed in a rehab in advance. Rehabs will not take patients without cash on the barrel or preapproval by an insurance company. You have to arrange for approval by your insurance company *before* the intervention.

3. Decide who should take part in the intervention. Try to include people who have clout with the drinker. Children, parents, friends, spouse, physician, clergyman, and sometimes employer are commonly participants in interventions. Watch yourself. You may open some doors you can't close and let a genii out of the bottle. Sometimes by the time an intervention is called for, the employer is

all too aware of the drinking problem, but this is not necessarily so. Alcoholics often function better occupationally than interpersonally. If time off from work is going to be required, figure out how that is going to be handled. A lie that keeps the roof over your head is better than compulsive honesty.

4. Have each person involved think out and write down exactly what they are going to say. Generally, each speaker at the "event" must *both* express concern and state what he or she will do if the alcoholic refuses to stop drinking and go to AA and therapy, or as is more usual, go into a rehab. Some interventions are conducted without such therapeutic leverage. I don't think they work. All persons in the intervention must mean what they say and be prepared to carry out whatever action they say they will. Each person should say something like, "We are all here and I am here because we all, and I in particular, love you and don't want you to die of the fatal disease of alcoholism. Therefore, we have gathered here to persuade you to stop drinking and go to AA or to enter such and such a rehabilitation unit. We want you to do that today. Everything has been arranged. One of us will go with you; there is a bed waiting for you; and you have time off from work. If you don't go to rehab, I cannot continue to enable your killing yourself. Therefore, I will not talk to you . . . stay with you . . . live with you . . . sleep with you . . . employ you . . . give you money, or whatever, unless you go for treatment." Then the next person speaks. The alcoholic is given a chance to respond at the end of the confrontation, but the only response that the intervention group will accept is an agreement to follow the steps decided upon before the intervention.

5. Think through your own part in the intervention. Be very clear about what you are prepared to do if the alcoholic won't follow the intervention group's recommendations. Be sure that you are willing to do what you say you will do, for example, walk out. If you don't mean what you are planning to say, don't do an intervention. It will only make things far worse.

6. Conduct a rehearsal, or better, a series of rehearsals. An intervention is not a place to express or act out anger, however

understandable or justified that anger may be. Therefore, you must drop any potential participant who can't control his or her anger. Be very sure that your own anger isn't too strong for you to conduct an intervention.

7. Find a time and place where you can bring together the alcoholic and the intervention team and do your intervention. The actual confrontation is known as "the event." You may hold the event in your home, in a therapist's office, in a physician's office, or in a clergyman's study. It doesn't really matter where you hold it. What does matter is doing it right. Think out and rehearse every aspect of your intervention before the event.

Interventions change things in an irreversible way. They can fail and lead to immediate disruption of a family. Be aware of your risks and your potential gains and only then decide whether or not you want to proceed. Good luck.

I am not a great believer in interventions by themselves. When they work they are phenomenal and really change things; when they don't, they can cause a lot of harm. I believe that the *attitudinal change in you* is the most important thing. Only when you are ready to risk your relationship rather than continuing as a co-dependent is it time to intervene. Then it is definitely worth a shot since you have nothing to lose and everything to gain, and you may save a life and improve the quality of many lives by intervening. Just remember, work on yourself first, then make your move on your alcoholic.

CHAPTER 7

Recovery

WHAT TO EXPECT

Now you are sober or you are no longer a co-dependent. In one or the other of these ways, you are no longer enslaved by alcohol. You are wondering what sobriety will be like. That's a little like wondering what life will be like. During your drinking life, you were not fully alive. You were anesthetized and barely conscious. No longer. You have come alive again, and, like the toddler first exploring the world, you are having a love affair with it. But there is danger as well as wonder out there and in there, in the world and within you. In a very real sense, it is all new and you are starting life again. To borrow a far overused but here-appropriate phrase, you have been reborn, and, like all newborns, you don't know what to expect. It is all so new. Frightening and wonderful, all at the same time. Sobriety, like life, is going to be an adventure. If you can enter into it in the spirit of adventure, sobriety will indeed be "beyond your wildest dreams." Since it is beyond your wildest dreams, you have no idea what it will be like. The joys of sobriety are joys you have not envisioned. The things you did dream of may well no longer be of interest to you. You are in some very real way a new person, yet still the same old you. Integrating the you that you know into your new self is going to be one of the most exciting tasks you will undertake in the adventure of sobriety. Adventures entail hardships as well as excitement. This is true of sobriety. Sobriety is going to be beyond your wildest dreams because you are going to experience things — within yourself and in the world — that you quite literally never thought existed, not even in your dreams. Your horizons have been too restricted. They no longer need be. This is yet another of the paradoxes of alcoholism. Alcohol allowed you to dream of glory, to realize your most grandiose fantasies — only in your head to be sure — but realize them nevertheless. Fantasy can feel awfully real. Yet you are going to find that your alcohol-mediated daydreams were impoverished — you dreamt too small and you dreamt too narrowly. All that grandiosity was empty display, and, even if you had received that Nobel Prize the same year you were MVP in the NL, it wouldn't have made you happy for very long. The dreams of sobriety aren't like that. They may seem more low-key, more small-time, but they aren't because they satisfy and nurture, enliven and enrich. Their satisfaction is enduring. What are beyond your wildest dreams are largely things of the spirit, emotional and relational goods, but sobriety certainly isn't going to make it any harder to advance your career and do better in the world.

There is nothing wrong with wanting material rewards in sobriety. I once knew a man whose goal was to be the richest man in AA. I don't know if he made it, but he seemed to be having fun trying to get there. Status, power, career advancement, and financial security are certainly things worth going after in sobriety and you may get them — after all, you are playing with a full deck for the first time in years. But what is beyond your wildest dreams is not material. Rather, it is such things, or should I say such states of mind, as freedom from fear, self-esteem, serenity, the ability to mourn, not being chronically depressed, a newfound ability to carry through and stick to things, insight into yourself, knowing what you feel, knowing who you are, knowing what you are doing, not hating yourself and maybe even loving yourself (another of those paradoxes of alcoholism — you thought all that self-obsessed, self-centeredness that went with drinking was self-love, but it wasn't; it was self-destructive self-hatred), vitality, enthusiasm, an appreciation of life, art, nature, and self you either never knew or haven't known for a long time, and a renewed capacity for joy. Material rewards beyond your wildest dreams may or may not come your way. If you get your priorities straight, all sorts of things become possible. So remember, first things *first,* and your sobriety is first. Without sobriety, you lose it all.

Sobriety is its own reward. AA says it promises nothing but sobriety, and I agree with that. Sobriety, however, is an awful lot. In fact, an enormous amount. It is life and the opportunity to really live it. All the rest are fringe benefits. It may seem that I am contradicting myself, but I am not. Sobriety itself is beyond your wildest dreams, whether or not you also choose to walk through all the doors that sobriety opens up to you. For most recovering alcoholics, there are plenty of fringe benefits, but there is no guarantee. What is guaranteed is sobriety. In any case, *you must first concentrate on maintaining your sobriety.* I want to be very careful here. I don't want to promise too much. I don't think I am. If you are alcoholic, sobriety is pretty wonderful. Of course, it has its down side too. You no longer have an instant painkiller and you lack sober experience so you have all the problems of inexperience to deal with. Sigmund Freud (1895) said that "the purpose of psychoanalytic therapy is to convert neurotic misery into ordinary human unhappiness." I sort of admire that. It doesn't promise too much. It has the virtue of realism, although I guess you could call it kind of pessimistic. It is the opposite of the hype so many of our mental health hucksters are so good at. AA, when it says it only promises sobriety, is in Freud's camp in not promising too much. I don't want to do that, either. So when I say sobriety is beyond your wildest dreams, I mean just that. It really is, whether or not it brings you fame, fortune, health, and love — all of which would sure be nice, but they are not necessities. Sobriety is fantastic stuff in its own right and you have it. All you need to do is to keep it. Time will do the rest. Time is on your side now. It is time to grow. You can help time along in various ways.

THE JOYS AND CHALLENGES OF EARLY SOBRIETY

The newness of being sober, or of living with a sober person, is what gives early sobriety its unique quality. You will never be where you are again. So enjoy it. Early sobriety has an intensity, a freshness, an excitement that you will look back on with nostalgia. You will feel more secure, more in control, more on top of things, and probably happier, but you will never feel the surge of joy that accompanies surviving a fatal disease that you feel now. Joyful it may be, but it is also perilous. You may be hanging on to your sobriety by your fingertips. Getting to that meeting, or to that therapy session may be the difference between slipping and remaining sober. There is a certain enjoyment in the anxiety about remaining sober in early recovery. It has the appeal of any good drama. Each moment you stay sober is an achievement, something you feel good about. Perhaps the enjoyment is greater retrospectively; living through that early doubt is plain scary. But you can stay sober — a day, an hour, a minute at a time.

All kinds of strange things are going to happen to you. Some of them will feel great, some of them will be hard to take. They say that alcoholism is a disease of attitudes. In many ways it is. If you can take the attitude that all this novelty is an adventure, a challenge, you will ride the roller coaster of early sobriety to a state of relative equanimity with relative ease. You know all about the pink cloud and the black depression of early recovery. Enjoy the pink cloud but don't expect it to last; endure the depression and don't expect it to last. Stay close to people and to your support system. Be good to yourself. Eat well. Have fun. Treat yourself.

Rest. Play. Don't put any pressure on yourself. Wait until you are stronger. Treat yourself like a loving parent treats a newborn child. Let your feelings emerge. "Oh! Those tears are my sadness coming out . . . are liquid rage . . . are my joy . . . are my anger . . . are my pain . . . are my sense of loss . . . are my reaction to missing my old life . . . are I don't know what, but awfully powerful."

Very young children aren't sure of what they are feeling. Their feelings are global. It feels good or it feels bad. It is only slowly that we learn to discriminate between our feelings, experience the full range of their gradations; realize the richness of our emotional life. Partly this is maturational, it just happens, partly it is learned. Mother told you, "You are crying because you are angry," and you learned that what you were feeling was anger. You learned to label and hence identify your feelings when somebody labeled and identified them for you. When you drank addictively, you lost your power to discriminate your feelings. They became global again. That vague distress you felt became a drink signal. Psychoanalysts call this *affect regression*. That means that you didn't, and probably still don't, know what you were feeling—it just felt painful and you needed a drink to stop feeling that way. In early sobriety, you have to learn to identify and discriminate between your feelings once again. This can be exciting, albeit frightening, like tasting new foods. You can learn to savor your feelings much like you can savor a good meal. You can become a gourmet of the inner life. You may not wish to do so, and it's quite sufficient if you learn in a reasonably accurate way to tell what's going on inside of you—what you are feeling. The way to do that is to get feedback—to relearn those labels—and the place to get feedback is AA and therapy. Knowledge reduces fear, and knowing what's happening to you, being able to say to yourself, "I'm happy" . . . "I'm a bit sad" . . . "I'm grieving" . . . "I'm ashamed" . . . makes being happy, a bit sad, grief-stricken, or ashamed, things you can process, assimilate, live with, work through, act on, not act on, stay with, or do virtually anything else with except react to by drinking. Knowledge is power; especially knowledge about yourself.

NOT LETTING YOURSELF FEEL YOU DON'T DESERVE IT

In my experience two things more than any others lead to slips — picking up a drink. Anger unfelt and unexpressed, acted out in the form of the screw-you martini; and self-hatred, which is anger turned against the self. You are a lot angrier than you know and at times you are angry without any awareness of it. You may not believe that, but it is true. Nobody drinks like you drank unless they are angry, and so many hurtful things happen to heavy drinkers, let alone alcoholics, that you have to be one angry guy or gal. That's inevitable and that's perfectly okay as long as you know it and don't do anything stupid with it. The trick is to experience but not act on your anger. At least not now — there will be plenty of time to act on it later. Once you accept yourself as an angry son of a bitch, your problems with anger will greatly lessen. Since you don't know when or how deeply you are angry, you *need* someone to tell you — your therapist or your sponsor are in the best positions to do so. Rage is an uncomfortable emotion, but it won't hurt you as long as you don't react to it as a drink signal. As time goes on, you will be less enraged. You will have less to be enraged about and you will not be so vulnerable or easily hurt. You will deal with things as they come up, so you won't have a backlog of anger threatening to get away from you. But for now, just accept that you are angry and make sure that you have somebody who can tell you how angry you are when you don't know that you are.

Not feeling that you deserve sobriety or its fruits will get you drunk for sure. So that's something you have to change fast. Freud (1926) wrote about the various reasons that his patients resisted recovery — wanted to stay sick. He called this *resistance*. The resistance he thought was the most difficult to overcome was what he called resistance from the superego. He thought that his patients stayed sick because they felt that they deserved to be punished and that being ill was a fitting punishment. Freud was right. People including you are like that. Moreover, they make the punishment fit the crime. For instance, if you deserve to be punished for drinking, what better way to punish yourself than to drink some more. Besides, you don't deserve sobriety. After all, you cheated on your mate, swindled your boss, aggravated your parents, didn't pay either your taxes or your bills — not to mention the evil things you didn't actually do but wanted to do. And that's only the guilt you are aware of — most of your guilt is out of your awareness, unconscious. All that unconscious rage makes you feel like a murderer. In fact, you believe that you are a thoroughgoing cad who should die penniless on the Bowery in an alcoholic fit or the DTs. I exaggerate to make a point, but you really do feel guilty, undeserving, and you are filled with self-hate even though you may not know it. All alcoholics are like that. At least while they are actively drinking and for a while — sometimes for quite a while — after they become sober. I am sure that you have many things to feel, more or less realistically, guilty about, and you can work on them with your therapist at your leisure — that part of it is rational guilt, but the kind of guilt that gets you drunk is *irrational guilt,* which you must do something about at once.

What you must do is to change your thinking. You are in error. You believe that you are a bad person trying to be good. The truth is that you are a sick person trying to get well. You have a disease, the disease of alcoholism. Having read this book, you know the scientific evidence for this, but you still don't believe it deep down in your heart. That's another reason to go to AA meetings. They will help you "come to believe" that you are sick, not evil. Sometimes it is easier to see things in other people; hearing the members of the group share their experiences will quickly show you that they were sick and are now getting well. Through identification, you will see that this is the case with you also. Then your self-hatred will drop away and you will be able to fully enjoy your sobriety. The kind of guilt that comes from having wanted to kill your baby brother when you were four, and having wanted to seduce your mother when you were six is best dealt with in therapy. All human beings carry some of that kind of guilt. Further, you have guilt because you have hurt yourself — one of God's creatures, if you are religiously inclined. Guilt for injuring yourself is very real and can easily lead to punishing yourself for having punished yourself. Awareness allows you to break out of that trap. As sobriety advances, you will like yourself better. Again, what is needed is to buy time in which to heal by not drinking, one day at a time. In time, you can make restitution of various sorts, direct or indirect, for the real harm you did while drinking. AA calls this making amends. But this is not for early sobriety. For now just be aware that you don't like yourself and that that is dangerous, and focus on changing your beliefs about yourself. You deserve to recover—everybody does.

DEALING WITH ANXIETY AND DEPRESSION IN SOBRIETY

Since you have been blunting your feelings for a long time, you are not used to feeling intensely. There is a kind of emotional intensity that goes with drinking, but it is chaotic, tempestuous confusion rather than feelings clearly and deeply felt. As I mentioned a moment ago, feelings in early sobriety are rather confused, but they are powerful and quite different than they were when you were drinking. Besides, you no longer have a way of instantly quelling them. Although it sometimes doesn't feel that way, this is a change for the better. You can't selectively stuff or anesthetize feelings, so if you try to stuff or drown the down stuff there is no way not to stuff or drown the up stuff. So you escape some pain, but you miss the freshness of spring days, the vibrance of life itself, and whatever opportunities for joy that life may bring your way. It is not a good trade-off. You are going to be dead long enough, so why rush it and be dead in life? "Okay," you say, "I'll take the whole package, but what do I do when I feel like shit, other than drink?" Talk basically. *Verbalize your feelings. Share them.* That may not seem like much, but it is. It changes the experience. Pain shared is pain transmuted. Tell yourself, "I'll be okay—this is rough because I have very little practice in handling my feelings, no sober experience—I'll learn as I go along." And that's true, you will.

I recall a patient who told me how she had been feeling awful, really awful, and went to a friend's house. Once there she said, "I don't want you to take away my pain. I just want you to be with me so I can share it with you." Then she turned to me and said, "Doctor, when I heard myself saying that I realized that I was getting well." She was. Of course, the idea isn't to stay in pain; it is to experience feelings and move on rather than short-circuit them, running the risk of blowing a fuse. Somebody once said that a neurosis is a failed attempt to cheat. The neurotic tries to escape something and gets paid back in spades. There is a lot of truth in that and all of us are more or less neurotic. Your feelings, all of them, are what make you *feel* alive. I know it often doesn't seem that way, but your feelings are good for you. They are nature's evaluative system telling you what's good and what's bad and warning you of danger within you and danger in the world around you. Without them, you are dangerously undefended. Now that you have accepted that you need some help dealing with your uncomfortable feelings, I'll try to give you some. The feeling states that cause the most trouble are anxiety and depression. Often they go together in a kind of tense depression. That is the feeling that is hardest to deal with in sobriety.

Anxiety is a strange phenomenon. It is partly physical — rapid heartbeat, heavy breathing, sweating palms — and partly emotional — those feelings of dread, fear, and impending doom. Anxiety has many sources. It has some physical causes, which should have been detected and corrected during your physical, but most anxiety is a signal that something is wrong, that you must take some remedial action. The problem is that anxiety isn't a signal for you, but rather an occasion for panic. "I'm going to die this minute," is how you experience anxiety. That's a delusion; it just isn't true. Getting anxious about being anxious leads to panic. Next time you're feeling that way tell yourself, "This too shall pass, nothing awful is going to happen or is happening to me and if I don't panic everything will be okay." Ask yourself, "Am I angry?" For me, being anxious usually means that I am afraid that I will lose control of my repressed rage. My rage and my fear of losing control of it are unconscious. Once I get in contact with my rage, my anxiety goes away. This may work for you too, although anxiety has other mechanisms. However, so many of my early sobriety patients are anxious because they fear losing control of their stuffed rage that I urge you to consider that possibility next time you are super uptight. Many times it will lead to relief.

Another thing you can do is to cut down your time frame. Keep yourself in the day. A great deal of the anxiety of early sobriety comes from guilt and regret. But that guilt and regret are about things past — things you did or did not do while you were drinking. That's over. There is nothing you can do about it. Just do what you can for today. Yet more anxiety comes from your fear of the future, your anticipation of disaster. This is called projection. Again, stay in the day and your anxiety will diminish. Then there is the anxiety of having so many options, the "dizziness of freedom" as the Danish philosopher Soren Kierkegaard called it. The potential for so many things; the fact that so much is now possible frightens you — it makes you anxious. While you were drinking, you were afraid to quit your horrible job, after all, who else would hire you; afraid to go back to school, after all, you couldn't be sure that you would get to class or be able to concentrate if you got there; afraid to take up medieval Sanskrit, after all, you were medieval enough in your preference for wine over water; afraid to climb that mountain, after all, there was no bar at the top; but now all of these actions and so many more are possible for you. You are free and you are terrified by your new freedom. Again, a good tradeoff. Sure all that potentiality makes you anxious, but it's worth it. You can do things, make changes, move ahead once more. But not now; not in your first year of sobriety; you are changing too rapidly and you will continue to change, so wait before making any major decisions or undertaking new projects. You can do all sorts of things a bit later. That's another form of keeping it in the day. AA advises waiting a year before doing anything radical, like getting a divorce. That makes sense to me. So enjoy your new freedom, experience its exhilaration, but don't let it overwhelm you. You don't have to and shouldn't change too much too soon, but being free you can do whatever you wish and that's great stuff.

Your depression is probably mostly neurochemical. Most, if not all, of it should disappear as your sobriety evolves. You may miss John Barleycorn and your old life-style. You probably do — transition is always painful and involves some mourning for the old, for what has been relinquished. Allow yourself to mourn. You have lost something. It was mostly shit, but there were some good times and besides, human beings hold on to everything, even the hurtful, because it is familiar. Try holding a funeral for John Barleycorn and your old life, eulogize him, light a candle for him, say Mass for him, say Kaddish for him, let your tears flow as you say good-bye to a big chunk of your life. It was your life, no matter how ill-advised, disease-ridden, or conflict-ripped. You are sorrowful that it is over.

The rest of your depression is largely anger turned inward and hurt from rebuffs you are not used to handling. You are super-sensitive — narcissistically vulnerable, as the analysts say — right now. Sobriety will toughen you and raise your self-esteem so you will not be so easily hurt. The disasters of your drinking years haunt you. Try not to focus on the injuries and setbacks of your alcohol-drenched past. Don't concentrate on opportunities lost, rather concentrate on the possibilities sobriety has opened for you. After all, you have survived a deadly disease, or at least arrested it, and one day at a time you can reconstruct, or build anew, and realize, or have as good a shot as any of us get at realizing, your as-yet-undreamt dreams. Time is the key. Time and patience. Depression is characterized by feelings of helplessness, hopelessness, and low self-regard. You need no longer feel helpless or hopeless. You are not helpless and there is every reason to hope. Your self-esteem will rise with every day you remain sober. There is something about tolerating discomfort, about not acting out, about staying with your feelings and relationships, including your relationship with yourself, that automatically raises your self-esteem. It is not possible for you to stay sober and not progressively like yourself more and more. Self-esteem comes from dealing with things as they occur and that's exactly what you are doing.

There is another source of anxiety related to that dizziness of freedom and to transition. That is the anxiety that comes from not knowing who you are. From not being sure of your identity. You have lost one identity — your old drink-damp self — in order to create a new one, but you haven't done that yet. You are betwixt and between, and that doesn't feel any too good. Since you're starting out again, it's going to take a while for your new identity to coalesce. In the meantime, you are going to meetings and saying, "My name is _____ and I am an alcoholic." This is what philosophers call a *performative utterance*. That means that your statement, "My name . . ." is not so much a communication, although it is that, as it is an action in its own right. It does something. What it does is affirm your existence — "I am" — and to specify one aspect of that existence — "an alcoholic." That's an identity — of sorts. More precisely, it is a pole around which you will accrue your new identity. In the beginning, being an alcoholic is a negative identity, but as time goes on and you see what you can do and achieve, inwardly and in the world, as a recovering alcoholic, it becomes a positive identity. That probably hasn't happened for you yet. For now, your affirmation of your existence and of your alcoholism in the statement, "My name is . . ." not only breaks down, and/or prevents from reemergence, your denial; it reduces your anxiety about who you are by giving you an identity and by specifying a part, an important part, of who you are.

As you work in therapy and share at your self-help group meetings, your anxiety, depression, and guilt will wane and your sense of well-being will wax. Your inner conflicts, which also cause you discomfort, will move toward resolution, and sobriety will become more and more fun. Speaking of fun, positive feelings like joy can be just as hard to deal with in early sobriety as negative feelings. You aren't used to dealing with them either.

DEALING WITH PLEASURE, JOY, AND SUCCESS IN SOBRIETY

You haven't felt so good in years. You thought that you did, but when you considered it more carefully, you realized that life hasn't been much fun for a long time. How could it be? You have been ill. There are two reasons that handling positive feelings in sobriety is difficult for you. First, their novelty and intensity may overwhelm you. The thing you have been doing for a long time with strong feelings of any sort is anesthetizing them with ethanol. You thought you were celebrating, commemorating a joyful occasion, but you weren't. What you were doing was dampening your feelings. Why would you do that? Because you were afraid of their intensity. The second problem is that old "I don't deserve it" stuff. The better you feel, the worse you feel, because you feel guilty. "How can a bastard like me who did all that awful stuff be so happy? It's not right. There's no justice. Why me?" You used to say "Why me?" meaning why do all those awful things happen to me? Now you say, "Why me?" meaning why should I have recovered while so many do not? Why should I feel so good when so many others suffer? Freud (1923) called this the *negative therapeutic reaction* — the better some of his patients did, the worse they felt. Alcoholics are especially prone to the negative therapeutic reaction.

Tolerating feelings, whether of joy or of sorrow, is a skill. You get better at it with practice. It is like exercising a muscle. At first, even a little effort is difficult and leaves you sore, but with practice the muscle becomes strong and lifts more and more weight without soreness. So it is with "affect tolerance," the ability to sustain, contain, integrate, and enjoy powerful feelings. Pleasure and joy come in many gradations. Some are subtle and quiet, some are flamboyant and spectacular. Many will be new to you. The best advice I can give to you is "let it happen." Go with your good feelings. Don't expect them to last forever any more than a good meal does, but that's no reason not to enjoy the lobster or the happiness while it lasts. Trying too hard to hold on spoils things. Let it happen and let go. You are going to get used to feeling good. Strange as it may seem to you that's going to take some time, and in its own way, it is going to be as difficult as learning to deal with anxiety and depression in sobriety. Again, the trick is to buy time, and all you have to do to accomplish that is not drink. Each and every time a strong feeling wells up in you and you stay with it, your capacity to do so increases. After a while, feeling becomes an okay thing and feeling good no big deal.

What about success, emotional or material? Well, you may not have any, but that's unlikely. Success can wreak you if you feel you don't deserve it. That's why you need to stay close to your group and your therapist once things start to break for you. That old guilt and those old feelings of unworthiness die hard, but die they will. Success can have many unconscious meanings: it may represent a forbidden victory over siblings, perhaps experienced as killing them; it may be experienced as being all alone out there like a point man in combat making you feel vulnerable and engendering separation anxiety; it may elicit guilt over surpassing your parents; it may elicit unconscious fear of retaliation by father for your victory over him and your secret acquisition of mother and her love (or fear of retaliation by mother for your victory over her and secret acquisition of father and his love); and God and your unconscious knows what else. This kind of unconscious stuff can really trip you up, but you have a therapist and a group to help you with it. In early sobriety, what is important is for you to realize that success may make you quite anxious and endanger your sobriety. Unconscious guilt over forbidden childhood wishes has a way of linking up with conscious and unconscious guilt over adult acts of omission and commission while you were drinking to really do a number on you. However, as long as you don't drink, you can work through the unconscious stuff over time in your therapy sessions and reduce your conscious guilt by sharing it at your self-help-group meetings.

THE GIFT SIMPLE

Simple pleasures beyond your wildest dreams are part of sobriety. Some of those simple pleasures come from what you no longer have to do or experience. It was beyond your wildest dreams of only a few months ago for you not to end the evening with your head in the toilet bowl, for your head not to throb in the morning, for your mouth not to taste like a herd of camels passed through it; for your bowels not to ache and explode, for your hands not to shake in the morning, for you to no longer fear yourself or fear others. The absence of those old pains is certainly pleasurable. And there are positive pleasures too above and beyond the absence of the various horrors that were so much a part of your drinking that being rid of them was beyond your wildest dreams. You never dreamt that there could be so much joy in smelling, tasting, touching, hearing, and seeing with a clarity and intensity and vividness and aliveness that you had lost your capacity to even imagine. Beyond your wildest dreams were the absence of nightmares and sweating and terror; beyond your wildest dreams were peace, serenity, simple enjoyment of the moment, aliveness, the possibility of love, connectedness with yourself and with other people, engagement in meaningful activity, development, fulfillment, and productivity. None of them need be beyond your wildest or indeed your most mundane dreams any longer.

FREEDOM FROM CO-DEPENDENCY

Recovery from co-dependency was also beyond your wildest dreams. The essence of what you never envisioned having is your recovery of *yourself*. Once again, or perhaps for the first time, you have a self; you feel entitled to be apart as well as a part; you neither need to control nor be controlled by another human being; you feel free to assert your right to security, to safety, to being treated decently, to being treated as a person in your own right rather than as an appendage of someone else; and you feel worthy of being loved.

All of this is indeed wonderful, but early recovery from co-dependency, like early recovery from alcoholism, is not all peaches and cream. Some of your reactions to your loved one's sobriety may also be beyond your wildest dreams — totally unexpected. You may not like the things you thought you would like and you may thrill to novelties beyond your previous comprehension. There are new joys and new conflicts. One thing is for sure, you will not go back to the status quo ante — there is no turning back. Either you will experience a psychological remarriage, a new relationship (whether or not that relationship is technically a marriage), or you will no longer be with your alcoholic. In either case, what is beyond your wildest dreams is freedom. Freedom to grow, freedom to experiment, freedom to change, freedom to get closer, freedom to leave, freedom to redefine your relationship and yourself.

The task of recovery from co-dependency is the definition of self — it is becoming you. Paradoxically, you can not become yourself by yourself. You can only do that through interaction with other people. Hence, this is a time to stay close to Al-Anon, or your therapy group, or your therapist, or better yet all three. As you have seen, my emphasis is on you, not on your alcoholic, and that is as it should be. As you grow, your alcoholic will grow in his or her sobriety, and the two of you will either grow closer or grow apart and either outcome is fine. Let it happen, or as AA would have it, "Let go and let God." If you are more secular-minded, trust your own drive for health or put your trust in the life-building processes of the universe, however you may understand them. If you do, you will be able to enjoy your loved one's sobriety and enjoy your own recovery from co-dependence. Indeed, your life will, beyond your wildest dreams, be filled with feelings you either never knew or had forgotten.

LOVE, WORK, AND PLAY IN SOBRIETY

"Drink to me only with thine eyes, / And I will pledge with mine; / Or leave a kiss but in the cup, / And I'll not look for wine," as Ben Jonson wrote in "To Celia." Loving sober is different from loving high or hung over. The interplay of mood, dalliance, language, touch, and passion between sober people is qualitatively and quantitatively altered in sobriety. It is richer; it is more intense; it is simultaneously closer and more distant; it is more anxiety-provoking; and it is more rewarding. Every aspect of love, from wanting to be with somebody, to attunement to your lover's moods and feelings, to physical embrace, is different. You really feel the other person's body quivering against yours. You are more aware of his or her "otherness"—he or she is less an extension of you. All this takes some getting used to—it requires readjustment. If you remember those experimental rats who could only run the maze they had learned while drinking—if they were drinking their learning was "state dependent" as the experimental psychologists say—you won't be surprised that some things that you did so easily drunk or high may not be so easy or even possible sober. What is required is new learning—learning to do the things you learned how to do drunk, sober. But you can learn. If you drank to disinhibit, you may be uptight sexually as well as "under schooled." Most of the time performance anxiety simply disappears with sober experience. If it doesn't, you have some sort of conflict about sex that is best worked out in therapy. Remember, don't put any pressure on yourself, or allow anyone else to put pressure on you. You don't have to do anything except not drink one day at a time (and possibly pay taxes and die). There is no requirement that you engage in intercourse your first day sober. Or your twentieth. If you take the pressure off, and regard whatever experience you have as an experiment, as a journey into the unknown, lovemaking in sobriety will be beyond your wildest dreams. The vast majority of folks I have treated over the years have had some initial difficulties with intimacy, emotional and physical, in early sobriety, but have gone on to report that their sober experiences with love were quite different from their drinking experience with love, and quite unexpectedly wonderful.

Working sober is not so optional for most people. They have to work sober fairly soon after the start of their recovery. Nevertheless, I suggest that you give yourself a vacation before returning to work. When you do return, you may feel embarrassed, especially if you have been off to a rehab. I understand your feelings, but it is highly likely that everybody knew you were a drunk and that most of them are delighted that you have done something about it. Prejudice against alcoholics certainly still exists and I would not recommend that you go out of your way to advertise your alcoholism; people, however, are far more accepting than they used to be and you probably won't run into much flack. The heavy hitters may feel threatened by your sobriety and the poker-up-the-ass types may say "naughty, naughty," but most folks at work really don't care what you drink as long as you don't bother them.

Work, like love, will be different sober. You will feel the pressures more, although you will be better able to handle them, and you won't have the anticipation of the five o'clock drink to make your workday more tolerable. Of course, you won't have the torment of trying to hold on till five for that drink either. On most jobs, the main thing is to show up on time. I'm serious; you'll be surprised to see how inefficient most people are — if you're sober and there on time you're ahead of most of the workforce. I exaggerate, but there's a lot of truth in my exaggeration. *Take the pressure off yourself.* Your real job right now is not drinking one day at a time. Some aspects of your work — especially those involving dealing with people — may be more difficult for you now. That's the state-dependent learning thing again. You don't have much experience dealing with people sober. But you will relearn your old tasks and skills, including the interpersonal ones, in sobriety and do them both better and with more pleasure. After all, you are playing with a full deck now and you weren't before. So, put the stresses of work in perspective. Use the AA slogan, "First things first"; career isn't first, sobriety is. Don't expect too much of yourself too soon. Try to accept that you are healing — that you are in the early stages of recovery from an extremely serious disease.

Your goals and values are going to change radically, so I wouldn't recommend making any career changes the first year. Whole new worlds may (or may not) open for you and you will see possibilities for yourself that you never saw before. You are going to take less crap on the job, be more assertive, and more self-confident. But all this takes time. Your work life, like your love life, will be beyond your wildest dreams — unenvisioned, different than you imagined, and most likely not as you tried to program it.

The hurts and slights of the workplace hurt more now, but you increasingly have the inner resources to handle rebuffs and disappointments. Go slowly, keep your eyes open, don't expect too much, and work in sobriety will be possible and even satisfying, although you didn't believe that for a minute during your drinking days.

Drinking alcoholically is grim business. What started out as "fun" ended as a desperate effort devoid of joy, spontaneity, and enthusiasm. Play is playful, it is under the aegis of freedom — alcoholic drinking partakes of the realm of necessity, of the unfree. During your drinking career, you forgot how to play — if you ever knew. Sobriety is playtime — or at least it can and should be. Again, don't put pressure on yourself — you can climb Everest next year. You don't have to "hurry up and relax." But you will find that you have more fun sober — although you couldn't even imagine that while you were drinking. Try new things, new activities, new people, but do so slowly and only when you feel up to it. It is going to take a while for you to relax, but you will. Play in sobriety will be beyond your wildest dreams because it will incorporate activities and experiences that you never envisioned. All you have to do is let yourself enjoy them.

The great American literary critic Edmund Wilson, who was no stranger to the grape, had "Hazak, Hazak, Vitnik Hazak" carved in Hebrew letters on his tombstone. It means "Be strong, be strong, and strengthen one another." It is read at the end of one liturgical year and the beginning of another. They signify an ending and a new beginning. They teach interdependency rather than co-dependency. They imply that you have reservoirs of inner strength, perhaps unknown to you, that you can draw on; and that you both have strength you can lend to others and that others have strength they can lend to you. It is not a bad motto for your recovery, which is an ending and a beginning. In the course of your journey you will become stronger by developing new strengths and by discovering strengths that have been there all along; and in the course of your journey you will discover also that you can strengthen others and be strengthened by them.

Good luck in the adventure that is sobriety. The trip is worth the fare.

References

Cloninger, C. R. (1983). Genetic and environmental factors in the development of alcoholism. *Journal of Psychiatric Treatment and Evaluation* 5:487–496.

Dorland's Illustrated Medical Dictionary (1965). 24th ed. Philadelphia: W. B. Saunders.

Freud, A. (1938). *The Ego and the Mechanisms of Defense,* rev. ed. New York: International Universities Press, 1966.

Freud, S. (1900). The interpretation of dreams. *Standard Edition* 4/5:1–626.

_____ (1920). Beyond the pleasure principle. *Standard Edition* 18:1–64.

_____ (1923). The ego and the id. *Standard Edition* 19:44–50.

_____ (1926). Inhibitions, symptoms, and anxiety. *Standard Edition* 22:1–187.

Freud, S., and Breuer, J. (1895). Studies on hysteria. *Standard Edition* 2:1–318.

Gay, P. (1988). *Freud: A Life for Our Time.* New York: W. W. Norton.

Hegel, G. W. F. (1807). *Phenomenology of Mind,* trans. J. B. Baillie. New York: Macmillan, 1931.

Huxley, A. (1954). *The Doors of Perception.* New York: Harper & Row.

James, W. (1902). *Varieties of Religious Experience.* New York: Longmans.

Jellinek, E. M. (1960). *The Disease Concept of Alcoholism.* New Haven, CT: Yale University Press.

Joyce, J. (1914). *Ulysses.* New York: The Modern Library, 1961. Quoted in Editor's Introduction to *The Portable James Joyce,* p. 7. New York: Viking, 1969.

Jung, C. G. (1973). *C. G. Jung: Letters, vol. 2, 1951–1961,* pp. 623–625. Princeton, NJ: Princeton University Press.

Kohut, H. (1977). Preface to *Psychodynamics of Drug Dependence, National Institute on Drug Abuse Research,* Monograph 12, pp. vii–vix. U.S. Department of Health, Education, and Welfare. Washington, DC: U.S. Government Printing Office.

Masters, W. H., and Johnson, V. E. (1970). *Human Sexual Inadequacy.* Boston: Little, Brown.

Thompson, R. (1975). *Bill W.* New York: Harper & Row.

Tiebout, H. M. (1957). The ego factor in surrender to alcoholism. *Quarterly Journal of Studies on Alcohol* 15:610–621.

Winnicott. D. W. (1958). "The capacity to be alone." In *The Maturational Process and the Facilitating Environment,* pp. 29–36. New York: International Universities Press, 1965.

Index